Teacher Edition

Invitation to Languages

Foreign Language Exploratory Program

Conrad J. Schmitt

Glencoe

New York, New York   Columbus, Ohio   Chicago, Illinois   Peoria, Illinois   Woodland Hills, California

About the Author

Conrad J. Schmitt received his B.A. degree *magna cum laude* from Montclair State College, New Jersey. He received his M.A. from Middlebury College, Vermont. He did additional graduate work at Seton Hall University and New York University.

Mr. Schmitt has taught Spanish and French at all levels from elementary to university graduate courses. He was Coordinator of Foreign Languages for Hackensack, New Jersey Public Schools. He also taught Spanish at Upsala College, New Jersey; Spanish at Montclair State College; and Methods of Teaching a Foreign Language at the Graduate School of Education, Rutgers University. He was Editor-in-Chief of Foreign Languages and Bilingual Education for McGraw-Hill Book Company and Director of English Language Materials for McGraw-Hill International Book Company.

Mr. Schmitt has authored or co-authored more than one hundred books, all published by The McGraw-Hill Companies. He has addressed teacher groups and given workshops throughout the United States. In addition, he has lectured and presented seminars throughout the Far East, Europe, Latin America, and Canada. Mr. Schmitt has traveled extensively throughout the world.

 **Glencoe**

The *McGraw·Hill* Companies

Send all inquiries to:
Glencoe/McGraw-Hill
8787 Orion Place
Columbus, OH 43240-4027

ISBN: 0-07-860578-4 *(Student Edition)*
ISBN: 0-07-860579-2 *(Teacher Edition)*

Printed in the United States of America.

1 2 3 4 5 6 7 8 9 10 027 09 08 07 06 05 04 03

Teacher's Manual

Glencoe/McGraw-Hill's *Invitation to Languages* is your invitation to open the world of foreign language study to your students. The goal of this introductory or exploratory program is to let your students explore and appreciate the richness of some of the world's languages and, thereby begin to understand the rich and diverse cultures associated with them. After they have successfully completed *Invitation to Languages,* your students will be well-prepared to make an informed choice about which language or languages to pursue in secondary school and college.

However, the benefits of foreign language study should not be limited to those students who are going to college. *All* students should be exposed to other languages in order to (1) gain insight into their native language, (2) learn some basic expressions in other languages, and (3) promote understanding of other cultures.

Age Appropriate

Invitation to Languages was planned especially for the middle school/junior high learner. The content was specifically written for this age group. Students are asked to talk about their families, their school subjects, their pets, sports, and so on. The activities are also extremely motivating to these students. Many are gamelike and require active movement. The tasks appeal to students' imagination. For example, students are asked to draw and label the clothing of a student of the next century. Language is used in real situations from the beginning.

Variety of Ancillaries

The number and variety of the ancillary components assist you in tailoring *Invitation to Languages* to the needs of your students. Both the Video and Audio Programs bring the lessons to life. The Workbook contains review, reinforcement, and reteaching activities. The Overhead Transparencies make the vocabulary and the dialogues crystal clear.

Thematic Lessons

Each lesson is built around a theme (colors, numbers, houses, pets, and so on). This concept aids students in learning the dialogues and in conversing from the very beginning. The unifying theme also means that the vocabulary is contextualized and, therefore, much easier to learn.

Focus on Listening and Speaking

The four skills, listening, speaking, reading, and writing, are integrated, but emphasis is placed on listening and speaking. It is suggested that students not be made responsible to learn how to write each language to which they will be introduced. The final decision, however, is up to the discretion of the teacher. Students are provided with the opportunity to copy and supply simple written answers. Middle school students take well to short, interesting lessons in which they have real-life speaking tasks to accomplish. Listening and speaking skills learned in *Invitation to Languages* give them a firm foundation on which to base later, more intensive practice in reading and writing.

Communication

Nothing motivates students more than communication. Communication generates enthusiasm. And enthusiasm is contagious. Communicating real information to a classmate in another language is the goal of every lesson. At this level, complicated grammar explanations are inappropriate. At this introductory level, students are merely made aware that a *hablas* question in Spanish, is answered with *hablo* or that a *du* question in German dictates a response with *ich*.

Culture

Language study inevitably leads to culture because culture is an integral part of all languages. For this reason, brief sections on a culture point related to the lesson theme accompany many lessons. Their purpose is to lead students to an understanding of the similarities and differences between mainstream culture in the United States and the cultures of the languages being studied.

As technology makes the process of international communication faster and easier, it is important for our students to have the tools of international communication readily available to them. Foremost among those tools are the ability to use another language and the ability to see something from the viewpoint of a member of another culture. Both those tools can be acquired by using *Invitation to Languages*.

Invitation to Languages has been developed to permit easy adaptation to the needs of the specific type of introductory or exploratory course offered at your school.

Time allocation for the exploratory course can vary greatly. Some courses meet for an entire year; some meet for a semester, and others meet for a short block of five to eight weeks. Some classes meet daily and in some cases, they meet two or three times weekly or even once a week. Regardless of your time allocation, the flexibility of *Invitation to Languages* enables the text to address your needs.

The philosophy and rationale of the exploratory language course also vary. In some schools, students are given a thorough introduction to just one or two languages at the middle school level. In other school districts, the intent of the exploratory course is to introduce students to all the languages taught in the secondary school foreign language program. This introduction to the various languages helps students in their decision concerning the language they wish to pursue for more in-depth study. Regardless of the philosophy of your program, the flexibility of *Invitation to Languages* once again will allow you to address your specific needs.

The text includes a general introduction by six self-contained chapters. Each of these six chapters explores a different language. Each chapter or language is independent and can be presented as an entity unto itself or it can be omitted. If, for example, a chapter deals with a language that is not offered in your district, you may opt to omit it.

The Introduction has four short lessons. These lessons introduce students to the fascinating concept of language and communication. Students learn why and how languages are related and how different languages function—their similarities and their differences. Throughout the Introduction, students receive insights into what language learning or language acquisition is all about. One exciting activity enables students to make up their own language. This Introduction serves as an interesting "opener" to language study. However, it could be omitted if, for example, time restraints do not enable you to offer this type of introductory material to your class.

The next six chapters each deal with a different language. They are: Spanish, French, Italian, German, Latin, and Japanese. We included these languages since they are the ones most frequently taught in the secondary schools of the United States. Depending upon the time allocation and the philosophy of your program, you can introduce your students to those languages that direct themselves to your needs and omit those that do not. In addition to this selective flexibility, there are other strategies you may wish to follow. If, for example, Italian or Japanese are not offered in your schools, you may opt to omit these language chapters. On the other hand, you may wish to give your students a "smattering" of these languages. In this case, you could present only the short lessons on greetings and farewells and omit the other lessons in these chapters.

Given the fact that Spanish and French are the two most commonly taught languages in the schools of the United States, we have provided a more expansive introduction to these two languages. In addition to learning greetings, farewells, numbers, days of the week, and weather expressions, students also learn to identify themselves, tell where they are from and what languages they speak, identify sports and foods they like, and describe their family and house, etc. Depending upon the time allocation, you can present the entire Spanish and/or French sections or you can stop at an earlier lesson. If the rationale of your program calls for just the introduction of one or both of these languages, the presentation of the complete expanded introduction enables *Invitation to Languages* to meet your needs.

We have also taken into account the background of the teacher in developing the material for *Invitation to Languages*. It would be rare for a teacher to have a background or working knowledge in all six of the languages introduced in the text. In some cases, a middle school teacher without a language background is called upon to teach the exploratory course. More frequently, a foreign language teacher gives the course. Even in the case of the foreign language teacher, he or she usually knows one or two of the languages, but not all of them. The presentation of material in each lesson of the chapters is based on the premise that the teacher does not know the language.

An Audio Program and full-color Overhead Transparencies are provided for the presentation of all new material. In the case of the expanded introductions to Spanish and French, we have also provided a Video for the presentation of new material. The suggestions in the Teacher Edition enable you to use these teaching aids to actually present the material. Once again, the presentation is based on the premise that the teacher does not have a working background in the language. It can be both challenging and fun to learn a language along with your students!

In order to take advantage of the student-centered, "teacher-friendly" curriculum offered by *Invitation to Languages,* you may wish to refer to this section to familiarize yourself with the various resources this program has to offer. *Invitation to Languages* contains the following components:
- Student Edition
- Teacher Edition
- Workbook and Audio Activities
- Workbook, Teacher Edition
- Audio Program (Compact Disc)
- Audio Activities, Teacher Edition
- Video Program, with Script
- Overhead Transparency Binder

The Workbook and Audio Activities

The Workbook and Audio Activities booklet is divided into two parts: all chapters of the Workbook appear in the first half of this ancillary component, followed by all chapters of the Audio Activities.

Workbook The Workbook offers additional practice to reinforce the vocabulary and grammatical structures presented in each lesson of the language chapters in the Student Textbook. The Workbook activities are presented in the same order as the material in the Student Textbook. The activities are contextualized, sometimes centering around illustrations. Workbook activities employ a variety of elicitation techniques, from multiple-choice, true-false, and matching activities to answering personalized questions. The Workbook, Teacher Edition provides the teacher with all the material in the student edition of the Workbook, plus the answers to the activities.

Audio Activities booklet The Audio Activities booklet contains the activity sheets which students will use when listening to the audio recordings. The Teacher Edition of the Audio Activities booklet contains the answers to the recorded activities, plus the complete tapescript of all recorded material.

The Audio Program (Compact Disc)

The recorded material for each chapter of *Invitation to Languages* contains all of the dialogues and active vocabulary in every lesson of the Student Textbook. These dialogues from the Student Edition are presented in dramatized form and there is also a pronunciation section at the beginning of each language. Simple "Listen and choose," "Listen and circle," "Listen and decide," and "Listen and react" activities are designed to further stretch students' receptive listening skills in open-ended situations. Students indicate their understanding of these brief activities by marking the appropriate response on their activity sheets located in the Audio Activities booklet.

The Video Program

The video component for *Invitation to Languages* consists of two 45-minute videos to accompany the Spanish and French chapters. It presents in dramatized form all the dialogues and vocabulary in every lesson of these two language chapters. The additional dialogues are designed to reinforce the grammar presented in the Student Textbook. The Video Program has a complete videoscript of all recorded material.

Overhead Transparencies

These are full-color transparencies reproduced from the dialogues and active vocabulary presented in the Student Textbook. The transparencies can be used for the initial presentation of new phrases and words in each lesson. They can also be used to review or reteach vocabulary during the course of teaching the lesson, or as a tool for giving quick vocabulary quizzes.

SUGGESTIONS FOR TEACHING THE STUDENT TEXT

Focus

These are clear lesson objectives that help you coordinate activities so that definite outcomes are achieved. Both functional (what students should be able to do) and structural (the grammar that students should master) objectives are included.

Teach

The Vocabulary/Dialogue section presents the new material. You can present the new dialogue or vocabulary with the aid of the Video Program, the Audio Program, or the Overhead Transparencies alone.

Video Program

Use the following steps to present a new dialogue with the Video Program.

1. Show the video.
2. Perform the dialogue with one of the more able students.
3. Have two students perform the dialogue.
4. Have pairs of students perform the dialogue.

As you progress through the chapter, you may want to skip the teacher-student step, especially since most of the dialogues are between student-aged peers. Encourage personalizing and varying the dialogues as soon as students are able to handle it. For example, students should address each other by name if appropriate. For example, in Lesson 12 of the Spanish chapter (nationality and geographic origin), students should say where they are really from as soon as they grasp the meaning of *Soy de...*

Use the following steps to present new vocabulary with the Video Program.

1. Show the video.
2. Repeat the names of the items in order.
3. Repeat the names of the items varying the order.

4. Repeat the names of the items, but pause and frown as if you forgot the name of one item. Signal the class to supply the missing word. Smile when they do and proceed.
5. Repeat the pause with another word until the class is responding correctly and consistently.
6. Repeat the pause but signal an individual student to respond.
7. Repeat the pause, signaling individual students to respond until students are responding correctly and consistently.

Audio Program

Use the following steps to present a new dialogue with the Audio Program in connection with the Overhead Transparencies.

1. Play the Audio Program while you point to the speaker on the Overhead Transparency. Repeat this two or three times.
2. Play the Audio Program while you point to the speaker on the Overhead Transparency, and signal the students to repeat after the speaker. Repeat one or two times.
3. Perform the dialogue with one of the more able students.
4. Have two students perform the dialogue.
5. Have pairs of students perform the dialogue.

Use the following steps to present new vocabulary with the Audio Program in connection with the Overhead Transparencies.

1. Play the Audio Program while you point to the items on the Overhead Transparency. Repeat this two or three times.
2. Play the Audio Program while you point to the items on the Overhead Transparency, and signal the students to repeat after the speaker. Repeat one or two times.

3. Repeat the names of the items varying the order.
4. Repeat the names of the items, but pause and frown as if you forgot the name of one item. Signal the class to supply the missing word. Smile when they do and proceed.
5. Repeat the pause with another word until the class is responding correctly and consistently.
6. Repeat the pause but signal an individual student to respond.
7. Repeat the pause, signaling individual students to respond until students are responding correctly and consistently.

Overhead Transparencies

Use the following steps to present a new dialogue with the Overhead Transparencies alone.

1. Say the dialogue while you point to the speaker on the Overhead Transparency. Repeat this two or three times.
2. Say the dialogue while you point to the speaker on the Overhead Transparency, and signal the students to repeat after you. Repeat one or two times.
3. Perform the dialogue with one of the more able students.
4. Have two students perform the dialogue.
5. Have pairs of students perform the dialogue.

Use the following steps to present new vocabulary with the Overhead Transparencies alone.

1. Say the names of the items one by one while you point to them on the Overhead Transparency. Repeat this two or three times.
2. Say the names of the items while you point to them on the Overhead Transparency, and signal the students to repeat after you. Repeat one or two times.
3. Repeat the names of the items varying the order.
4. Repeat the names of the items, but pause and frown as if you forgot the name of one item. Signal the class to supply the missing word. Smile when they do and proceed.
5. Repeat the pause with another word until the class is responding correctly and consistently.

6. Repeat the pause but signal an individual student to respond.
7. Repeat the pause, signaling individual students to respond until students are responding correctly and consistently.

Activities

These activities give students an opportunity to practice the new vocabulary and/or dialogue in realistic situations. The first activity normally is more controlled; subsequent ones are more open-ended. Encourage students to vary the language to the degree they can. If the activity is role-playing, arrange the classroom furniture to fit the situation. Use simple costumes and props if it is feasible. For example, a simple dish towel draped over an arm can suggest a server in a café or restaurant.

Many of the activities lend themselves to cooperative learning. Arrange the seating so that groups can form and re-form easily. When several small groups are working at the same time, it is not necessary to monitor them all. If you use cooperative learning frequently, over a few days you will have ample opportunity to monitor every student. You can also monitor progress by asking one student from each group to present a sample or a summary of the task to the whole class.

Culture

The Culture section integrates cultural information about the countries where the language is spoken with the theme of the lesson. You can use this section in many ways.

1. Have students read it before class, and use the class time to discuss it.
2. Have students read it in class and discuss it in small groups. You can give them a task (some are suggested in the Teacher Edition) to do in their groups. Then have one student from each group report on the task to the class.
3. Have students read it in class and assign a related task for homework. Many of the culture sections lend themselves to further research.

When possible, link the information in the culture sections to what the students are studying in other classes.

Assess

The assessment tasks are the Workbook activities. These activities sometimes include a variation of one of the activities from the textbook lesson. Various kinds of informal and formal assessment are possible. See the Evaluation section for more detailed information.

Close

The closing task enables students to integrate the content of the lesson, to bring together parts of different lessons, and to make explicit some implicit learning. You can assign the close task for the last five minutes of the class, or for homework.

Expansion

The Expansion section includes extra activities and/or information related to the lesson content. It can be used for advanced students, for heritage speakers, or for enrichment for the whole class. The activities can be done by a small group while you are working with the rest of the class. They can also be assigned for homework. The extra vocabulary and grammar information may suggest new activities that you design.

EVALUATION

Evaluation is usually not a major component of exploratory programs, but there are important benefits to keeping students and teachers informed of student progress. Here are some suggestions for assessing student progress with *Invitation to Languages*.

Informal Assessment

After students are accustomed to small group work, you can grade individual students over a few days by discreetly observing small group work and giving them holistic grades for listening and speaking. Be sure students know that you will be grading them on those days, but do not emphasize the grading so as not to raise anxiety levels. The following is a suggested grading scale:

- 3 communicates well, with few errors
- 2 communicates, but a few errors interfere with understanding
- 1 communicates, but many errors interfere with understanding
- 0 tries, but does not manage to communicate

By making this kind of informal assessment a normal part of your classroom, you will do much to relieve student anxiety over assessment.

One way to encourage self-assessment is to ask students to choose their three best tasks over the course of one chapter and to present them to you for inclusion in assessment material.

You may want to let students correct some or all of their tasks and count only the corrected version toward their assessment.

Formal Assessment

If you prefer to give quizzes and chapter tests, you can use the Workbook activities for that purpose. You can also use the Assess and Close activities from the Teacher Edition. Keep the quizzes and tests brief. Use these techniques to give students immediate feedback.

1. Put the answers on an Overhead Transparency. Have students correct their own answers.
2. Ask one or more of your more able students to write their answers on the chalkboard while you involve the rest of the class in another activity. Later on, have students check their own work from the chalkboard.

USEFUL CLASSROOM EXPRESSIONS

Spanish

One Person	Group	
Ven.	Vengan Uds.	Come.
Ve.	Vayan Uds.	Go.
Repite.	Repitan Uds.	Repeat.
Contesta.	Contesten Uds.	Answer.
Escucha.	Escuchen Uds.	Listen.
Lee.	Lean Uds.	Read.
Abre el libro.	Abran Uds. el libro.	Open your books.
Cierra el libro.	Cierren el libro.	Close your books.
Siéntate.	Siéntense (Uds.)	Sit down.
Levántate.	Levántense.	Stand up.
En español.	En español.	In Spanish.
En inglés.	En inglés.	In English.

French

One Person	Group	
Viens!	Venez.	Come.
Va.	Allez.	Go.
Répète.	Répétez.	Repeat.
Réponds.	Répondez.	Answer.
Écoute.	Écoutez.	Listen.
Lis.	Lisez.	Read.
Ouvre le livre.	Ouvrez le livre.	Open your books.
Ferme.	Fermez.	Close.
Assieds-toi.	Asseyez-vous.	Sit down.
Lève-toi.	Levez-vous.	Stand up.
En français.	En français.	In French.
En anglais.	En anglais.	In English.

Italian

One Person	Group	
Vieni.	Venite.	Come.
Va'.	Andate.	Go.
Ripeti.	Ripetete.	Repeat.
Rispondi.	Rispondete.	Answer.
Ascolta.	Ascoltate.	Listen.
Leggi.	Leggete.	Read.
Apri i libri.	Aprite i libri.	Open your books.
Chiudi.	Chiudete.	Close.
Accomodate.	Accomodatevi.	Sit down.
Alzate.	Alzatevi.	Stand up.
In italiano.	In italiano.	In Italian.
In inglese.	In inglese.	In English.

German

Kommen Sie hier, bitte.	Come here, please.
Gehen Sie an die Tafel.	Go to the board.
Wiederholen Sie, bitte.	Repeat.
Bitte, beanworten Sie die Fragen.	Answer the questions.
Hören Sie bitte zu.	Listen.
Lesen Sie, bitte.	Read.
Bitte, machen Sie Ihr Buch auf.	Open your book.
Bitte, machen Sie Ihr Buch zu.	Close your book.
Bitte, setzen Sie sich.	Sit down.
Bitte, stehen Sie auf.	Stand up.
Auf Deutsch, bitte.	In German, please.
Auf Englisch, bitte.	In English, please.

Japanese

Kurikaeshite kudasai.	Please repeat.
Kiite kudasai.	Please listen.
Yomite kudasai.	Please read.
Hon o akete kudasai.	Please open your book.
Hon o tojite kudasai.	Please close your book.
Nihongo de itte kudasai.	Please say it in Japanese.

BIBLIOGRAPHY

Bleiler, Everett F. *Essential Japanese Grammar*. Dover Publications, 1963.

Clark, Fiorenza Consonni and Conrad J. Schmitt. *Schaum's Italian Vocabulary*. McGraw-Hill, 1997.

Crocker, Coffman Mary E. *Schaum's French Vocabulary*, 3rd ed. McGraw-Hill, 1997.

Germano, Joseph E. and Conrad J. Schmitt. *Schaum's Italian Grammar*, 2nd ed. McGraw-Hill, 1997.

Gschossmann-Hendershot, Elke and Lois Feuerle. *Schaum's German Grammar*, 3rd ed. McGraw-Hill, 1997.

Lazzarino, Graziana et al. *Prego*, 5th ed. McGraw-Hill, 2000.

Schmitt, Conrad J. *Schaum's Spanish Grammar*. 3rd ed. McGraw-Hill, 1989.

Schmitt, Conrad J. *Schaum's Spanish Vocabulary*. 2nd ed. McGraw-Hill, 1997.

Schmitt, Conrad J. and Katia Brillié Lutz. *Glencoe French 1: Bon voyage!* Glencoe/McGraw-Hill, 2002.

Schmitt, Conrad J. and Protase E. Woodford. *Glencoe Spanish 1: ¡Buen viaje!* Glencoe/McGraw-Hill, 2003.

Tohsaku, Yaso. *An Invitation to Contemporary Japanese*. McGraw-Hill, 1994.

Ullman, B.L., Charles Henderson, Jr., and Norman E. Henry. *Latin for Americans, First Book*. Glencoe/McGraw-Hill, 2003.

Weiss, Edda and Conrad J. Schmitt. *Schaum's German Vocabulary*. McGraw-Hill, 1997.

Wilson, W. Michael. *Essentials of Latin Grammar*. National Textbook Company, 1995.

Invitation to Languages

Foreign Language Exploratory Program

Conrad J. Schmitt

 **Glencoe**

New York, New York   Columbus, Ohio   Chicago, Illinois   Peoria, Illinois   Woodland Hills, California

Acknowledgements

The author wishes to express his appreciation to those individuals who reviewed the Japanese chapter of the textbook:

Mikako Kohno, Elkhart Community Schools, Elkhart, IN
Cindy Zyniewicz, Elkhart Community Schools, Elkhart, IN

The editor would like to thank the following individuals for their assistance in the development of this program:

Louis Carrillo
Andrea M. Fuchs, Ph.D.
Patricia Ménard
Mary Root Taucher

 **Glencoe**

The *McGraw-Hill* Companies

Send all inquiries to:
Glencoe/McGraw-Hill
8787 Orion Place
Columbus, OH 43240-4027

ISBN: 0-07-860578-4 *(Student Edition)*
ISBN: 0-07-860579-2 *(Teacher Edition)*

Printed in the United States of America.

1 2 3 4 5 6 7 8 9 10 027 09 08 07 06 05 04 03

Invitation to Languages

Introduction to Languages 1

Welcome to Spanish! 28

Contents •   iii

Welcome to French! 94

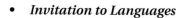

Welcome to Italian! 164

Welcome to Latin! 204

Welcome to German! 228

Welcome to Japanese! 264

Introduction

1

Communication

Activity

A. You may wish to ask the following discussion questions.

1. How do you think life would be different if people could not speak?

2. Why would it be nice to be able to speak to a person from another country in his or her own language?

3. Do you know any people who come from other countries? What countries do they come from? What language(s) do they speak?

Procedure

Go over Activity A on page 6.

¡Hola! ¿Qué tal?

Guten Tag. Wie geht's?

Communication

"Hi there! How are ya?" This is a greeting we probably use a hundred times a day to start a conversation with someone. Just think what life would be like if we couldn't speak to each other. We wouldn't be able to if we didn't have a language. Try to imagine life without language or speech. It certainly would be dull! On the other hand, think how much fun it would be to speak more than one language. It would be great to be able to speak to people from other parts of the world. We can if we study another language.

Learning another language is not difficult. It's actually fun. There are many languages we can choose to study because there are many different languages spoken in the world. Everyone has a language. But, just what is language?

Konnichi wa.

Salut! Ça va?

Ciao. Come va?

2 • *Introduction*

Activities

A. You may wish to ask the following comprehension questions.

1. Can we understand something that has no meaning? Say something that has no meaning. Say something that has meaning.

2. What do humans use to produce speech? What do we use to understand speech?

3. Which form of language do we use most often—spoken or written language?

B. Ask students the following factual recall questions based on the reading.

1. What separates humans from the rest of the animal world?

2. In order to be able to read, what do we need?

3. What does written language represent or depict?

4. What does written language use to represent or depict spoken language?

5. Which form of language existed first—written or spoken language?

Procedure

You may wish to write a word on the chalkboard. Say the word. Explain to students that the letters together form the symbol that represents the spoken word.

Additional Information

Explain to students that in many primitive societies in isolated areas of the world there are still languages that have no written form.

What is Language?

Spoken Language

In its broadest sense, language is the exchange or transfer of meaning. It is a tool of communication. Spoken language or human speech is produced by the human speech organs and received by the ears. Each day we spend hours speaking and listening to friends, relatives, or strangers. Why do we spend so much time talking and listening to each other? We converse to exchange information, to communicate, and to interact. Language lets us exchange ideas, facts, and even emotions. It is a source of knowledge and a source of enjoyment. Language is one of the most fascinating and essential tools possessed by humans. It is our ability to use language that separates us from the rest of the animal world.

Written Language

Spoken language is the most frequently used method of communication. In addition to speaking and listening, however, we obtain much information and enjoyment from reading. To read, we must rely upon written language. Written language uses symbols to represent spoken language. Spoken language, however, existed for thousands, or perhaps millions of years, before the development of written language.

Writing Systems

Pictographs and Ideographs

The writing system for some languages such as ancient Egyptian, as well as modern Chinese, make use of pictographs and ideographs. A pictograph is a symbol or drawing that represents a specific object such as a fish or a chair. In ancient Egypt, the written word for "sun" was a drawing of the sun. It was impossible, however, to draw pictures to represent all words. For this reason,

pictograph
for fish

1 · Communication • 3

Activities

A. You may wish to discuss the following in class.

1. Have a student give in his or her own words a definition of a pictograph.

2. Have a student explain the difference between a pictograph and an ideograph.

B. If there are any students in the class who know an alphabet other than the Roman alphabet, have them write some letters on the chalkboard.

rè = sun

yuè = moon

míng = bright

ideographs were developed. An ideograph is a symbol for "non-picturable" things. An ideograph is used to show actions and to convey ideas. For example, the Chinese put together their pictographs for the "sun" and "moon" to form the ideograph that symbolizes "bright."

Alphabets

Other languages, such as English, use the letters of an alphabet for their written language. The Phoenicians and Hebrews were the first to use an alphabet. An alphabet is a series of symbols. The Phoenicians and Hebrews made up a symbol for each syllable of a word. It is from these people that we have the beginning of a true phonetic alphabet. A phonetic alphabet is one in which each letter represents a sound in the spoken language. Let's take a look at some alphabets:

ABCDEFGHIJKLMNOPQRSTUVWXYZ
Roman alphabet

Hebrew alphabet

ΑΒΓΔΕΖΗΘΙΚΛΜΝΞΟΠΡΣΤΥΦΧΨΩ
Greek alphabet

АБВГДЕЁЖЗИЙКЛМНОПРСТУФХЦЧШЩЪЫЬЭЮЯ
Cyrillic alphabet

Arabic alphabet

Here are some words in each of the above alphabets:

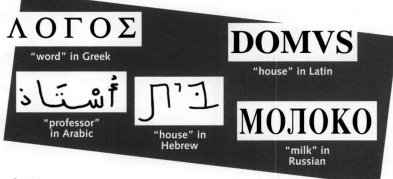

ΛΟΓΟΣ
"word" in Greek

DOMVS
"house" in Latin

"professor" in Arabic

"house" in Hebrew

МОЛОКО
"milk" in Russian

4   •   *Introduction*

4

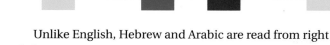

Unlike English, Hebrew and Arabic are read from right to left.

Other Methods of Communication

There are other forms of communication that are neither spoken nor written. Many things that do not involve spoken or written language can convey meaning. For example, a person driving a car stops at a red light. Why does the driver stop? The red light has meaning—it means "stop." On the other hand, a green light indicates "go" and the driver does not stop. The color red stands for "stop" or "danger." The color green stands for "safety" or "go." A transfer of meaning takes place when we see these colors.

Gestures

You are having a conversation with someone. The person you are talking to says nothing, but he uses a gesture. He points his thumb downward. Without a word being said, there is a transfer of meaning. His gesture indicates that he does not agree with you. In a similar conversation, another friend gestures with her thumb up. Without saying a word, she indicates to you that she agrees with what you are saying. She lets you know that you have a good idea.

Sounds

Some non-linguistic forms of communication come close to spoken language. The grunting sound "uh, uh" is an example. It has several meanings depending upon the intonation. Intonation is the melody or pitch that we give to our speech. Have some fun. Say "uh, uh" to convey "yes." Then say the same sound to convey "no." Now, say "uh, uh" with an intonation to convey "maybe."

Procedure
Go over Activities F and G on page 7.

Activity
Have students perform pantomimes to convey meaning. Do not let them say anything. Have them pantomime being happy, sad, funny, big, and small.

Procedure
Go over Activities B and C on page 6.

Procedure
A. Have students say "uh, uh" aloud according to the directions in the paragraph on sounds.

B. Go over Activity D on page 7.

Close
Have students do Activity I on page 7. Students can do this activity independently or work together in small groups.

1 · Communication • 5

5

Procedure

After reading the paragraph on symbols, have students do Activities E and H on page 7.

Answers

A. Answers will vary.

B. To convey "yes," we nod our head up and down. To convey "no," we nod our head from side to side.

C. Answers may vary, but can include the following:

1. Clapping hands, giving "high five's," joyful look on face

2. Shaking head from side to side, frown on face, waving finger from side to side

3. Stroking or rubbing right index finger over left index finger

4. Waving hand from side to side

5. Frown on face, hitting fist to table, waving hand from side to side with palm upward

6. Holding nose pinched shut with one hand, disgusted look on face

D. Answers may vary, but can include the following:

1. Saying "uh, uh" with rising intonation

2. Saying "uh, uh" with falling intonation

3. Saying "yuck!" "ugh!"

4. Whispering "shhh!"

5. Making a clucking noise with the tongue, saying "unh, unh"

6. Making a smacking noise with the lips, sounding out "mm" or "yum"

Symbols

Other non-linguistic forms of communication resemble written language. The dollar sign is an example. When we see "$10," we automatically say "ten dollars." What do the following symbols mean?

Activities

A   Work with a classmate. Say a few words to him or her in English. Then ask what message he or she got from what you said. Was it correct? Did a transfer of meaning take place? Did you communicate with each other?

B   Let's use some gestures to convey meaning. To the ancient Greeks, a downward nod of the head meant "yes." What do we do to convey "yes"? To the ancient Greeks, an upward nod of the head meant "no." What do we do to convey "no"?

C   Use gestures to convey the following meanings.

1. Cool! Right on!
2. You shouldn't do that!
3. Shame!
4. Good-bye.
5. That's it! Enough!
6. Something smells.

D   Make a noise or a sound that is not a word to give the following meanings.

1. Yes.
2. No.
3. That's awful!
4. Be quiet.
5. That's not such a good idea.
6. That tastes good.

6   •   *Introduction*

6

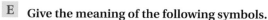

E Give the meaning of the following symbols.

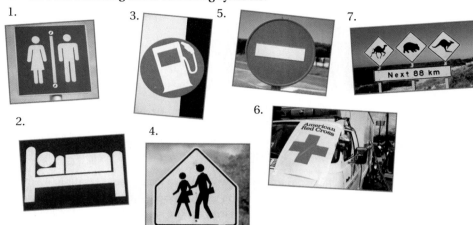

1.
2.
3.
4.
5.
6.
7.

Next 88 km

American Red Cross

F Be creative! Draw some pictographs. See if your classmates can guess what words your pictographs represent. If your pictographs are clear, they should be able to guess at the words.

G Make up ideographs to show the following actions or ideas.

1. to throw
2. to sit
3. to love
4. angry
5. happy
6. interesting

H Convert the following math equation into spoken language. Read it aloud.

$$6 \times 2 = 12 \div 3 = 4 + 4 = 8 - 2 = 6$$

I Have some fun and invent your own language.

1. Make up five sounds. Give each of your sounds a meaning. Then share your sounds with classmates. Say your sounds aloud and tell your classmates what they mean.

2. Invent a symbol for each of your sounds. You can use pictographs, ideographs, or letters from your own alphabet. Read each of your symbols by producing the sound it represents.

Answers

E.

1. restroom (female/male)
2. hotel or motel
3. service station
4. school zone
5. no entry
6. first-aid station
7. animal crossing

F. Answers will vary.

G. Answers will vary.

H. Six times two equals twelve divided by three equals four plus four equals eight minus two equals six.

I.

1. Answers will vary.
2. Answers will vary.

2
Languages of the World

Procedure

Have students locate Nairobi, London, and Tokyo on a map. If necessary, give hints: Nairobi, Africa, Kenya; London, Europe, England; Tokyo, Asia, Japan.

2
Languages of the World

Every person in the world has a language—a tongue. In every city, town, or village of the world people are always talking to one another. They very often express the same ideas, but they all use their own language. People from Nairobi can convey the same message as people from London or Tokyo.

London, England

Activities

A. Call on a student to make a sound. Ask if the sound has meaning. What does it mean?

B. Call on a student to give a word. Ask if the word has meaning. What does it mean?

But in Nairobi, the message is conveyed in Swahili; in London, it's in English; and in Tokyo, it's in Japanese.

Nairobi, Kenya

Activities

A. Have students tell if the following statements are true or false.

1. Linguists study language.   T

2. Linguists are scientists.   T

3. Language has many aspects such as pronunciation, vocabulary, and grammar.   T

4. Humans began to speak two thousand years ago.   F

5. Linguists know when language started.   F

6. Linguists know how people began to speak.   F

B. Have students explain in their own words some theories about the beginning of language.

Each person will use different sounds and words because each language has its own sound system and its own vocabulary. People who share the same language have a great deal in common. Language brings people together.

History of Language

Linguists are scientists who study the many aspects of language. All linguists agree that the origin of human speech is still a mystery. No one knows when or how humans began to speak. No one knows how language started. There are, however, many theories about the origin of language. Some are religious—language was considered a gift from the gods. Others are scientific—language started as an imitation of sounds occurring in nature. For example, humans heard a dog barking. They imitated the sound they heard and said "bow-wow."

2 · Languages of the World • 9

Although linguists have not been able to solve the mystery of the origin of language, they have been able to study and analyze almost all of the world's languages.

Language Families

Almost all of the languages of the world can be assigned to families or groups. Languages are assigned to the same family based upon a definite resemblance to each other.

The Indo-European Family

Indo-European is the name given to the family to which English belongs. The Indo-European family consists of languages now spoken in the Americas, most of Europe, and as far eastward as northern India and some parts of Asia. Almost one-half of the world's population speaks a language that belongs to the Indo-European family.

It is thought that in prehistoric times, long before the introduction of written language, speakers of the original Indo-European language formed a closely knit group. They probably lived in what is now known as central Russia. Because of famine, natural disasters, or wars, there were waves of migration. Some people left their homeland and some people stayed. Those who left did not all go in the same direction. They separated into various groups and went different ways. They, therefore, lost contact with one another and their speech began to change. Over the centuries the changes became so great that the original parent language evolved into many new and different languages.

Germanic
Celtic
Slavic
INDO-EUROPEAN
Latin/Romance
Indo-Iranian
Greek

The modern language which is believed to be the closest to the original Indo-European language is Lithuanian. It is spoken in Lithuania, a small and largely rural country on the Baltic Sea.

In most of the Indo-European languages, there is a striking resemblance in the numerals one to ten. The words for close family relationships are also very similar:

English	seven	brother
German	sieben	Bruder
Latin	septem	frater
Russian	CEMb	БРАТ
Sanskrit	sapta	brata

Within the Indo-European family, there are sub-groups. Examples of some of the larger sub-groups are:

Germanic	Romance	Slavic
German	Latin	Russian
Dutch	Italian	Ukranian
Swedish	Spanish	Polish
Danish	Portuguese	Czech
Norwegian	French	Slovak
Icelandic	Rumanian	Serbo-Croatian
English		Bulgarian

Close Relatives

Some languages are very similar to one another. For example, an Italian speaker and a Spanish speaker could have a conversation together. Each person could speak his or her language and they would be able to understand one another with just a little difficulty. The same would be true for a Portuguese speaker and a Spanish speaker. However, a Spanish, Italian, or Portuguese speaker would not understand a person speaking French or Rumanian. They would have to study French or Rumanian to understand without difficulty.

2 · *Languages of the World* • 11

Additional Information
Explain to students that Lithuanian is a language that has changed little over the centuries. Languages such as Lithuanian that are spoken by only a small number of people in small, isolated, or rural geographical areas change very little. Languages that are spoken by large numbers of people over a vast geographical area change a great deal and at a faster rate.

Ask students if they think English has changed a great deal over the centuries. Ask them to explain their answers.

Procedure
After students have read this material, have them do Activity B on page 13.

Additional Information
Students may be interested to know that many "refined" words came into English from the French language during the Norman conquest. For example, the names of many animals are of Anglo-Saxon origin and existed in Old English prior to the arrival of the Normans: cow, calf, hog. The terms for the flesh of these animals that humans consume come from the French: beef (*bœuf*), veal (*veau*), and pork (*porc*).

Swahili is presently spoken by some 50 million people. In some areas of Africa, it is replacing English and French as the language of commerce and official communications. It is a rich language and the classical plays of Molière, for example, have been translated into Swahili and performed on stage in that language.

Swahili is actually an Arabic word meaning "coasts." Swahili developed on the east coast of Africa. It belongs to the Bantu family of languages. It was originally written in Arabic letters until British missionaries introduced the Roman alphabet in the 1700's. Today, Swahili is written using the Roman alphabet.

Close

Have students do Activity D on page 13.

Swahili sign:
"Stop
Main Road
Turn Left"

A Russian, Pole, and Czech could all have a conversation together. Each one could use his or her own language and achieve a fair degree of understanding without great difficulty. The Slavic tongues are more like each other than the languages of most of the other Indo-European sub-groups.

English

English belongs to the western branch of the Germanic group of the Indo-European family. Anglo-Saxon, an old Teutonic or German language, forms the backbone of English. In 1066, however, a very important event took place. This event brought about many changes in the English language. The Normans invaded England from France bringing their language with them. Because of this Norman invasion and conquest, many French and Latin words and grammatical forms came into the English language.

Other Language Families

Another important language family is the Semito-Hamitic family of North Africa and the Middle East. The two most widespread of the modern Semitic languages are Arabic and Hebrew.

The Ural-Altaic family of languages includes Finnish, Estonian, Hungarian, Turkish, and Mongol. The Sino-Tibetan languages of southeastern Asia are Chinese, Thai, Burmese, and Tibetan. Japanese and Korean, the Dravidian tongues of southern India, and the Polynesian languages of the Pacific are all classified separately.

There are three great language divisions in black Africa. They are the Sudanese-Guinean, Bantu, and Hottentot-Bushman. These three families are further subdivided into 800 tribal languages!

The two most widely-used African languages are Hausa of Nigeria and Swahili of the east coast. There is a possibility that one of these two languages will become the common language for all of Africa's black population. It appears that Swahili is already attaining this status. Hindustani has assumed a similar role on the Indian sub-continent where many languages are also spoken.

Activities

A Explain why it is possible to group many of the world's languages into families.

B It is said that some languages are like first cousins. Others are more like distant cousins. Explain why.

C Does anyone in your family speak a language other than English? If so, find out some information about this language and share it with your classmates. If you can also speak the language, teach a few words and expressions to your classmates.

Answers

A. Many of the world's languages can be grouped into families because they have a definite resemblance to each other.

B. Some languages are like first cousins because they are closely related. Others are more like distant cousins because they are less closely related.

C. Answers will vary depending upon the cultural backgrounds of your students.

3

Words

Words

Words

Activities

A. Have students select which word they would use.

1. I want a bottle of *soda.*/I want a bottle of *pop.*

2. Put it in a *bag,* please./Put it in a *sack,* please.

B. Ask students if they know what the following words mean: roundabout, rotary, traffic circle. Some students may never have used or heard of any of these terms. In the United States, traffic circles are almost exclusively found in the Northeast. The term "traffic circle" is the most commonly used term. The term "rotary" is used in some areas of New England. Traffic circles are also very common in Great Britain where they are called "roundabouts."

C. Ask students if they know any British English. Share the following terms with them: lift (elevator), loo (bathroom), lorry (tractor trailer), push chair (baby stroller).

D. Explain to students that regional differences exist in many of the languages they will study. This is particularly true in Spanish, a language that is spoken throughout a vast geographical area. Some terms for "bus" in Spanish are: *el bus, el autobús, el autocar, el camión, la guagua, el micro.*

Do you think that you could say something if you didn't know any words? Of course, the answer is "no." Without words, we can't speak. Words are an extremely important part of language. The more words we know, the more feelings and ideas we can express. As you study another language, be sure to learn your vocabulary. If you have the words you need, you'll be able to communicate.

Every language provides words for anything its speakers want or need to say. It will be fun for you to learn them. Some words in other languages are similar to English words and others are very different.

BOOK

das Buch (German)

liber (Latin)

el libro (Spanish)

本 **hon** (Japanese)

书 **shū** (Chinese)

kitabu (Swahili)

il libro (Italian)

14 • *Introduction*

What is a Word?

A word is one of the most important parts or components of language. A word is defined as the most elementary unit of meaning. It is the simplest thing or element of a language that conveys meaning. A word can be divided into syllables. However, if you hear a syllable by itself, you will get no meaning. For example, *na* is a syllable. Alone it doesn't mean anything. When we hear several syllables together in a word, we do get meaning— "nana." We get meaning, too, when we hear the word "banana."

Rich Languages

A language is considered a rich language if it has an extensive vocabulary—if it has many words. English, for example, is considered to be a rich language. It is estimated that there are about 500,000 words in the English language! Of course, no one knows or uses all of the words. Estimates vary greatly as to the number of words the average person uses on a daily basis. A recent study estimates that the average person uses about 1,200 words. Many linguists, however, have questioned this figure. Some estimates run as high as 35,000 to 70,000 words! The tremendous difference may be due to the confusion between the number of words a person uses (use vocabulary) and the number of words a person recognizes (recognition vocabulary). For every word we use constantly in everyday speech, there are perhaps ten words that we're able to recognize when we hear them or see them in print.

Rich languages have a large number of words to express almost the same concept. In English, we can say beautiful, comely, exquisite, good-looking, gorgeous, handsome, nice, or pretty. How many of these words do you use frequently? Are there others that you can recognize, but don't often use?

Procedure

A. You may wish to paraphrase: "A word is defined as the most elementary unit of meaning" by saying "A word is the simplest thing we can say that will have meaning for another person. Just one word can have meaning, that is to say, a word all by itself can convey meaning."

B. Pronounce the syllable and words: *na,* nana, banana. Give another example. Say the following three syllables in isolation. Leave a short pause between each one: *po* (pause) *ta* (pause) *to* (pause). The syllables give no meaning. Put them together—potato—and we all know what it is. The syllables together make a word and the word conveys meaning.

Activities

A. Have a student explain in his or her own words the difference between "use vocabulary" and "recognition vocabulary."

B. Have students give another list of words that mean the same thing. Have them identify words they actually use and words that they don't use often but recognize when they see them in print or hear them.

The following are some more examples you may wish to give:

angry, mad, annoyed, irate, infuriated, wrathful, furious, incensed, enraged

happy, glad, pleased, delighted, content, joyous, joyful, blissful, merry, cheerful, blithe, elated, exalted.

A. Another German example you may wish to give is:

German	English
groß	big
Stadt	city
Luft	air
Großstadtluft	big city air (cosmopolitan)

Making Words

It is amazing how languages are able to borrow, adapt, and create new words. The German language makes new words by putting several words together. Let's look at some of them:

German	English
Geburt	birth
Tag	day
Geburtstag	birthday
Geschenk	present
Geburtstagsgeschenk	birthday present
Stadt	town, city
haupt	principal
Hauptstadt	capital (principal city)

All words in the Chinese language have only one syllable. They are monosyllabic. The Chinese put many monosyllabic words together to form new words. Some of the combinations are very interesting and philosophical:

	Chinese	English
有	yǒu	to have
意 思	yìsz	idea
有 意 思	yǒuyìsz	(have an idea) interesting
沒	méi	a part of speech that indicates "not"
沒 有 意 思	méiyǒuyìsz	(not have an idea) boring

Coining New Words

The vocabulary or lexicon of a language constantly changes. For example, as technology advances, the vocabulary must change to enable people to describe and work with the new technology. New words have to be coined to express new ideas and things. Recent additions to the English language are:

CD-ROM

modem

to boot
(a computer)

scanner

Sometimes two or more words already in use are put together to express a new idea:

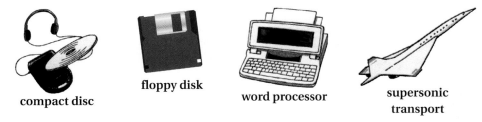

compact disc

floppy disk

word processor

supersonic
transport

Just as new words are invented, other words are often dropped when they identify something that has become obsolete or is no longer used. The expression "to crank a car" is no longer used because cars today are started by turning a key in the ignition.

Activity

Have students give other examples of new or modern terms.

Procedure

After reading this material, have students do Activities A, B, and C on page 19.

3 · Words • 17

Activity

Have students think of other foreign words used in the English language.

Borrowing Words

All languages borrow words from each other. Here are some words that have come into English from other languages:

Spanish	Italian	French	German	Russian
adobe	prima donna	à la carte	dachshund	babushka
rodeo	stucco	resume	kindergarten	tundra

pizza

tacos

delicatessen

borscht

18   •   *Introduction*

Many languages also borrow words from English. As you study other languages, you will notice how many English words you will come across.

Spanish	French	Japanese
el béisbol	le sweat-shirt	asuparagasu
el sándwich	le taxi	fasshon
el tenis	le ticket	konpuutaa
el ticket	le week-end	supu

Activities

A Talk to your grandparents or to an older person. Ask them if they use some words today that did not exist when they were children. Make a list of words they give you. Share your list with classmates. Do your lists contain some of the same words? Why?

B The following are words and expressions that were once in common use in English. Do you know what they mean? Explain why these words are no longer used in everyday speech.

1. horse and buggy
2. water wheel
3. well
4. blacksmith
5. outhouse
6. to stoke the stove
7. to crank the shaft

C Ecology is a new science. It describes all living creatures and their relationships with the environment. What are some ecological words that are new to the English language?

D Make a list of words that you think have come from another language. Tell what language.

Answers

A. Word lists may vary from student to student. Similarities in lists will reflect the influence of technology, etc. upon word usage.

B.

1. The horse and buggy, a popular form of transportation until the early 1900's consisting of a light one-horse carriage with four wheels, was replaced by the automobile.

2. The water wheel, a wheel made to rotate by direct action of water which drove machinery, was replaced by the combustible engine.

3. The well, a pit or hole sunk into the earth to reach a supply of water, was replaced by indoor plumbing.

4. The blacksmith, a worker who forges iron, was replaced by machinery.

5. The outhouse, a toilet within a small shed constructed away from the main house, was replaced by the indoor bathroom.

6. The phrase "to stoke the stove," or to stir up or tend the wood fire inside the stove, is no longer used because the wood stove was replaced by gas and electric heating systems.

7. The phrase "to crank the shaft," or to start up the engine of the early automobiles by turning a crank connected to the engine in front of the automobile, is no longer used because automobiles are now started by turning a key in the ignition.

C. Answers will vary, but some examples of ecological words are: the Gaia principle, biodegradable, green (as in green revolution), recycle, toxic wastes, pollutants, environmental protection, ozone layer.

D. Answers will vary.

4

The Structure of Language

Additional Information

Remind students that a word is the simplest thing in a language that has meaning. When we speak, we put words together to form sentences. A sentence that has several words conveys more meaning than a word in isolation. Give the following example:

> store   John goes to the store every day to buy food.

The sentence conveys more meaning than just the word "store." The sentence gives us a great deal more information. It tells us *who* goes to the store, *when* he goes, and *why* he goes. The way we put words together in a language to form a sentence is referred to as the structure of the language.

Activity

Put this sentence on the chalkboard after reading the text material.

Cornēlius Marcum videt.

Ask students what it means. Have them explain how they know Cornelius is the doer of the action. Ask them how they know Marcus is the receiver of the action.

Procedure

Have students do Activities A, B, and C on pages 25 and 26.

20

4

T*he Structure of Language*

Look at the following phrases in English:

John's book   Mary's pen

In English the *'s* construction is used to indicate possession. "John's book" means that the book belongs to John. "Mary's pen" means that the pen belongs to Mary, it's Mary's. The *'s* construction to express possession or ownership is an example of English structure. All languages can express possession, but they do it in a different way. When speaking English, you could say María's pen, Pierre's book, or Hanada-san's pencil. When speaking Spanish, French, or Japanese, however, you cannot say María's, Pierre's, or Hanada-san's. You would not be understood because the *'s* construction does not exist in these languages.

Let's see how some languages would express "John's book":

English	John*'s* book
French	le livre *de* Jean
Spanish	el libro *de* Juan
German	das Buch *von* Johann
Japanese	Hanada-san *no* hon
Italian	il libro *di* Giovanni
Latin	liber Ioann*i*

Can you tell what languages the books on this page are written in?

Procedure

Pronounce *Petrus Paulum videt* very clearly. Then pronounce the sentence again slurring over *Petrus* and *Paulum* so that they both sound like *Petru* and *Paulu*. This illustrates that one can no longer decide who does and receives the action. If both names sound like they end in *u*, word order becomes important because the necessary ending is no longer heard: *Petru videt Paulu*.

What is Structure?

Structure is another important part or component of language. The structure of a language, sometimes referred to as grammar or syntax, is the way in which words are put together to form phrases or sentences. Each language has its own distinctive structure. Structure can vary greatly from one language to another. This is particularly true among languages that do not belong to the same family.

Inflection

Some languages are inflected languages, particularly the ancient tongues. An inflected language makes use of endings attached to words. Latin, for example, is a highly inflected language. Word order is not important in an inflected language. The ending indicates the function of the word in the sentence. In Latin, you could say:

Petrus videt Paulum.

Petrus Paulum videt.

Videt Petrus Paulum.

Regardless of the word order, we know the sentence always means "Peter sees Paul" because the *-us* ending indicates the doer of the action (subject). The *-um* ending indicates the receiver of the action (direct object).

English is not an inflected language, so word order is very important. The word order can change the meaning of the sentence completely:

Peter sees Paul.

Paul sees Peter.

In English, the following word order must be followed:

doer (subject)	action (verb)	receiver (direct object)
Peter	sees	Paul.

In the case of action words or verbs, inflected languages use endings to indicate who does the action and when the action takes place. Let's look at a Latin verb: *cantābimus.* The one word *cantābimus* actually contains three messages. What are they?

1	2	3
cantā (sing)	**bi** (will)	**mus** (we)

Cantā conveys the meaning of the action word—sing; *bi* indicates when the action takes place, in the future—will; *mus* indicates who will perform the action—we.

Modern English drops the endings and isolates the three meanings into three different words:

3	2	1
We	will	sing.

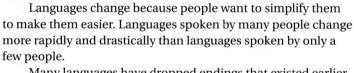

Structural Changes

Languages change because people want to simplify them to make them easier. Languages spoken by many people change more rapidly and drastically than languages spoken by only a few people.

Many languages have dropped endings that existed earlier. Why? When people speak rapidly they tend to drop or eliminate some sounds. When people stopped pronouncing word endings clearly, it became difficult to hear them. If an ending could not be heard in an inflected language, people could not determine the doer and receiver of the action. The meaning of the sentence became unclear. As endings were eliminated, word order became

22   •   *Introduction*

more important. In languages that have very few endings, such as English, word order is crucial.

The Romance languages have kept verb endings, but have dropped the endings for the doer and receiver of the action. However, Russian retains endings in both cases as does German, but in a somewhat different way.

Word Order

Word order in sentences can vary from one language to another. For example, German word order is different from English word order. It is said that German speakers interrupt each other less frequently than do English speakers. The reason for this unproven claim is word order. Key words that convey the important aspects of meaning come at the end of a German sentence. It is difficult to agree or disagree until the listener has heard the entire sentence!

English
I think that you should do your work now.

German
Ich glaube, dass du jetzt deine Arbeit machen sollst.
(I think that you now your work do should.)

Particles

The Japanese language uses many particles. A particle is a small word that indicates how a word functions in a sentence. The particle *no* indicates possession just as the *'s* denotes possession in English:

Hanada-san *no* denwa bangoo   Mr. Hanada's telephone number

The particle *ka* at the end of a Japanese sentence indicates a question:

Hanada-san desu *ka*[?]   Are you Mr. Hanada?

Procedure

Another example you may wish to give is:

English
It pleases me that you don't want to make this trip.

German
Es freut mich, daß du diese Reise nicht machen willst.
(It pleases me that you this trip not make want.)

Procedure

Have students find a Japanese particle *(no)* on page 20.

4 · The Structure of Language • 23

Procedure

Have students do Activity D on page 26.

Close

Have students do Activity E on page 26.

Additional Information

The tone of the particle *bu* changes depending upon the tone of the character.

The Chinese language also uses particles. The particle *ma* indicates a question. The particle *bu* attached to a word means "not."

Nǐ lèi ma[?]	Are you tired?
Wǒ búlèi.	No, I'm not tired.
Wǒ bùhěn lèi.	I'm not very tired.

Stress

Stress is the emphasis or force that we give to a sound or a word. In English, more than in most other languages, the stress put on a word in a sentence can change the meaning of the sentence. Read the following sentences aloud. Put the stress on the word indicated in bold. See how the meaning changes.

Sentence	*Meaning*
He would leave now.	He would certainly leave. Maybe you or the others wouldn't but he would.
He would **leave** now.	He would leave rather than do something else.
He **would** leave now.	I know he would leave even though you may think he wouldn't.
He would leave **now.**	He would leave now rather than later.

Tone

The language spoken by the greatest number of people in the world is Chinese. Chinese relies on word order in a sentence since it does not have inflected endings. It does, however, have tones which are extremely important. In the Beijing dialect, each word has four tones. Some are rising tones and others are falling tones. Each tone changes the meaning of the word. Depending upon the tone, the Chinese word *ma* can have the following meanings: mother, horse, flax, or scold. *Ma* can also be added to the end of a statement to turn it into a question.

24   •   *Introduction*

Beijing, China

A. Yes, these words do retain their Latin endings.

B. The verbs or action words are very similar in the various tenses in both languages.

English: drink, drank, drunk
German: *trinke, trank, getrunken*

English: sing, sang, sung
German: *singe, sang, gesungen*

English: swim, swam, swum
German: *schwimme, schwamm, geschwommen*

Activities

A Look at these Italian and Spanish action words or verbs. Do you think they retain the types of endings they inherited from Latin?

Italian			*Spanish*		
parli	→	parlo	hablas	→	hablo
parlavi	→	parlavo	hablabas	→	hablaba

B Look at the verbs to drink, to sing, and to swim in German. Do they remind you of English in any way? Why?

Ich trinke Wasser.
Ich trank Wasser.
Ich habe Wasser getrunken.

Ich singe mit Hans.
Ich sang mit Hans.
Ich habe mit Hans gesungen.

Ich schwimme im Sommer.
Ich schwamm im Sommer.
Ich bin im Sommer geschwommen.

4 · The Structure of Language • 25

Answers

C.
1. That's between you and *her*.
2. That's between you and *him*.
3. That's between you and *me*.
4. *He* and *I* are good friends.
5. They told *her and me* the same story.
6. *Who* is it?
7. *Whom* did you see?
8. He *sees* you.
9. You *see* him.
10. They *look* good.

D.
1. (Name of another person) didn't.
2. She didn't *throw* the ball.
3. Mary hit the ball, not *the (name of something else)*.

E. Answers will vary.

C As you now know, English has eliminated most endings. There are, however, some words that still change according to their function in a sentence. Choose the correct form in each of the following sentences.
1. That's between you and _____. (her, she)
2. That's between you and _____. (him, he)
3. That's between you and _____. (I, me)
4. _____ and _____ are good friends. (He and I, Him and me)
5. They told _____ the same story. (she and I, her and me)
6. _____ is it? (Who, Whom)
7. _____ did you see? (Who, Whom)
8. He _____ you. (see, sees)
9. You _____ him. (see, sees)
10. They _____ good. (looks, look)

D Read the following sentences aloud putting the stress on the indicated word. Then complete the sentences below.
1. **Mary** hit the ball.
2. Mary **hit** the ball.
3. Mary hit the **ball.**

1. Mary hit the ball. _____ didn't.
2. Mary hit the ball. She didn't _____ the ball.
3. Mary hit the ball, not _____.

E Have some fun. Convert English into an inflected language. Make up a doer ending and a receiver ending. Make up a verb or action ending. Put these endings on English words. Use them to make up your own sentences.

F Read the following short passages. Identify the language.
1. Hwaet! we Gar-dena in geardagem,
   peodcynga brym gefrunon,
   hu pa aepelingas ellen fremedon!

2. Whan that Aprille with his shoures soote
   The droghte of Marche hath perced to the roote,
   And bathed every veyne is swich licour,
   of which vertu engendered is the flour;

The above passages are both in English! The first selection is Old English written down between 500 and 1100 A.D. It is the first three lines of the epic poem *Beowulf*. The second selection is the first four lines of Geoffrey Chaucer's *Canterbury Tales* written in the late 13th century. It is written in Middle English.

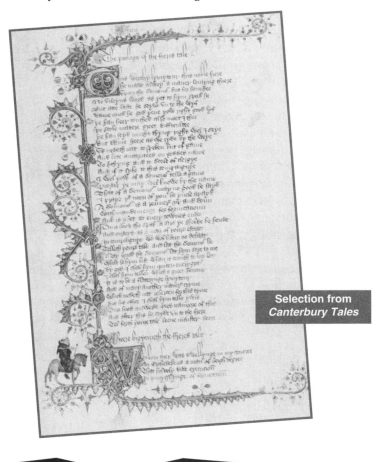

Selection from Canterbury Tales

4 · The Structure of Language • 27

Welcome to

Spanish!

Spanish is the language of more than 350 million people from all over the world. Spanish is sometimes fondly called the "language of Cervantes," the author of the world's most famous novel and character, Don Quijote.

Spanish is one of the five Romance languages. All the Romance languages originally came from Latin, the language of the ancient Romans. Spanish is a beautiful and rich language. It is an extremely useful language and is becoming more and more important in the world of business and commerce.

Spanish is spoken in many parts of the world. It had its origin in Spain. The Spanish *conquistadores* and *exploradores* brought the language with them as they explored the Americas in the fifteenth and sixteenth centuries.

Spanish is the official language of most of the countries of Central and South America. It is also the official language of Mexico and several of the larger islands in the Caribbean. Spanish is also the mother tongue of some 37 million people in the United States.

Caracas, Venezuela

Monte Albán,
Oaxaca, Mexico

28

Ávila, Spain

Spanish to English

You probably already know many Spanish words. If someone said *hola*, *amigo*, or *adiós*, you would know what they mean, *¿no?* Here are some words that have come into English from Spanish:

adobe	llama	rancho
alpaca	mesa	rodeo
canyon	plaza	sombrero
corral	poncho	

La Paz, Bolivia

29

Lesson 1

Video

Audio

Transparencies

Workbook

TEACH

—**¡Hola!** Hi.

—**¡Hola! ¿Qué tal?**
  Hi. How are you?

—**Bien, gracias. ¿Y tú?**
  Fine, thanks. And you?

—**Muy bien.** Fine.

Dialogue

1. Use the video to present the dialogue. Point to the speaker as each line of the dialogue is heard. Or model the dialogue yourself, pointing to the appropriate speaker on the overhead transparency or indicating the appropriate speaker in the audio program. Do not give the English translation.

2. Model the dialogue with one of the more able students.

3. Have two students model the dialogue.

Actividades

A. If your furniture is movable, arrange it so that students can move about easily. Greet several students to get them started.

B. Have students change partners after each conversation so that each has three or four conversations. Encourage the

30

1 Saludos

Greeting People

—¡Hola!
  —¡Hola! ¿Qué tal?
—Bien, gracias. ¿Y tú?
  —Muy bien.

In Spanish-speaking countries, young people usually shake hands when they meet. Pretend that you are in Spain and shake hands with your classmates.

Actividades

A Get up from your desk and walk around the classroom. Say *hola* to each classmate you meet.

B Work in groups of two. Make up a conversation in Spanish. Greet each other and find out how things are going.

Some greetings are more formal than *hola*. When you greet someone, particularly an older person, you can say:

Buenos días, señora. (A.M.)

Buenas tardes, señorita. (P.M.)

Buenas noches, señor. (late P.M.)

When speaking Spanish, the titles *señor, señora,* and *señorita* are most often used without the first or last name of the person:

Buenos días, señor.

Buenas tardes, señora.

Actividades

A Draw five stick figures. Give each one a name. They will represent your friends, family, and teachers. Greet each of your stick figures properly in Spanish.

B Look at these two photographs of Spanish-speaking people greeting each other. Do they do some of the things we do when they greet one another? Do they do some things that are different? Explain.

use of students' names and other variations.

Buenos días, señora.
Good morning, ma'am.

Buenas tardes, señorita.
Good afternoon, miss.

Buenas noches, señor.
Good evening, sir.

Buenos días, señor.
Good morning, sir.

Buenas tardes, señora.
Good afternoon, ma'am.

Explain that the use of the title without a name is common when we don't know the name of the person. We can use the title with a last name when we know the person: *Buenos días, señora Romero.*

Actividades

A. After students greet their stick figures, ask them to move about the room and greet other students' stick figures.

B. Elicit that both young people and adults in Spanish-speaking countries may shake hands and kiss each other on the cheek when meeting.

The numbers are presented in Lesson 4. You may, however, wish to introduce several numbers in each lesson.

Lesson 1: 1–10
Lesson 2: 11–20, 21–29
Lesson 3: 30–100 by tens

Cultura

Assign students to small groups and ask them to identify a Spanish-speaking actor, musician, politician, and athlete. Ask them to identify his or her nationality if they can. Afterward, compile a list on the chalkboard.

ASSESS

Review the lesson and check student progress by using the following:

• Activities Workbook, Lesson 1

CLOSE

Ask students to prepare a brief conversation between two students who meet on the street. Have them illustrate it with pictures cut out from old magazines.

Expansion

Enlist your native speakers to suggest other responses to *¿Qué tal?* Even if you don't have native speakers in your class, you might want to introduce these:

No muy bien.   Not very well.

Así, así.   So-so.

Cultura

Spanish Speakers in the U.S.

There are presently more than 37 million people of Hispanic or Latino origin in the United States. The largest number of Hispanics or Latinos are of Mexican birth or ancestry (12,110,000). Puerto Ricans make up the second largest Hispanic group (2,471,000). Spaniards, Dominicans, Central and South Americans together make up the third group (2,200,000). Cuban Americans number more than one million.

A Mexican American family

Puerto Rican Day parade, New York

Cuban Americans

32   •   *Welcome to Spanish!*

2 Adiós

Saying "Good-bye"

—Adiós, José.
　—Adiós, Maripaz.

—¡Chao, Juanita!
　—Chao. ¡Hasta luego!

2 · Adiós • 33

- Video
- Audio
- Transparencies
- Workbook

FOCUS

Students will

- use and respond to leave-taking expressions

TEACH

—**Adiós, José.** Good-bye, José.

—**Adiós, Maripaz.** Good-bye, Maripaz.

—**¡Chao, Juanita!** Bye, Juanita!

—**Chao. ¡Hasta luego!** Bye. See you later!

Dialogue

1. Use the video or audio program to present the dialogue or model the two brief dialogues yourself, pointing to the appropriate speaker on the overhead transparency. Use appropriate gestures to convey the idea that you are ending an encounter.

2. Model the dialogues with one of the more able students.

3. Have two students model the dialogues.

¡Adiós! Good-bye!

¡Hasta pronto! See you soon!

¡Hasta luego! See you later!

¡Hasta la vista! Until next time!

¡Hasta mañana! See you tomorrow!

¡Chao! Bye!

Actividades

A. If your furniture is movable, arrange it so that students can move about easily.

B. Have students repeat the leave-takings with more than one friend if they can.

C. Repeat this activity just before the end of the class. Have students say *Adiós, señor(a)/señorita (your name)* chorally and *Chao* to another student.

Conversando más

—**¡Hola, José!** Hi, José.

—**¡Hola, Teresa! ¿Qué tal?** Hi, Teresa. How are you?

—**Bien. ¿Y tú?** Fine. And you?

—**Muy bien, gracias.** Fine, thanks.

—**Chao, José.** Bye, José.

—**Chao, Teresa. ¡Hasta luego!** Bye, Teresa. See you later!

1. Use the audio or video programs to model the dialogue.

2. Draw and label José and Teresa on the chalkboard. Model the review dialogue yourself, pointing to the appropriate speaker on the chalkboard.

3. Model the dialogue with one of the more able students, using real names.

4. Have two students model the dialogue, using real names.

The usual expression to use when saying "good-bye" to someone is:

¡Adiós!

If you plan to see the person again soon, you can say:

¡Hasta pronto!   **¡Hasta luego!**   **¡Hasta la vista!**

If you plan to see the person the next day, you can say:

¡Hasta mañana!

An informal expression that you frequently hear, especially in Spain and Argentina, is:

¡Chao!

Chao is an Italian expression *(ciao)* that is used in several other European languages.

Actividades

A Go over to a classmate. Say "so long" to him or her and then return to your seat.

B Work with a friend. Say *chao* to one another and let each other know that you'll be getting together again soon.

C Say "good-bye" to your teacher in Spanish and then say "good-bye" to a friend. Don't forget to use a different expression with each person!

Conversando más

—¡Hola, José!

  —¡Hola, Teresa! ¿Qué tal?

—Bien. ¿Y tú?

  —Muy bien, gracias.

—Chao, José.

  —Chao, Teresa. ¡Hasta luego!

Actividades

A Work with a friend. Speak Spanish together. Have fun saying as much as you can to one another!

B Look at these two photographs of Spanish-speaking people saying "good-bye." Describe what the people are doing.

Cultura

Common First Names

The following are some common names used for boys and girls in Spanish.

Muchachos

Álvaro, Antonio, Alejandro, Daniel, David, Eduardo, Emilio, Enrique, Felipe, Fernando, Francisco, Gerardo, Ignacio, Jaime, José, Juan, Luis, Manuel, Miguel, Pablo, Pedro, Ricardo, Roberto, Tomás, Vicente

Muchachas

Alejandra, Alicia, Ana, Andrea, Beatriz, Catalina, Clara, Débora, Elena, Guadalupe, Isabel, Josefina, Juana, Leonor, Luisa, María, Marta, Patricia, Pilar, Rosa, Teresa

A. Encourage students to use appropriate gestures, such as shaking hands and waving. Have students change partners so that each one has three or four conversations.

B. Discuss which leave-taking behaviors are similar to or different from what we do.

Cultura

Ask students to find the Spanish version of their name on the lists. If there is no Spanish version, ask them to pick a Spanish name for themselves.

ASSESS

Review the lesson and check student progress by using the following:

- Activities Workbook, Lesson 2

CLOSE

Ask students to prepare an ending to the conversation they prepared in the Close section of Lesson 1, by having the students say "good-bye" to each other.

See if you can find some common Spanish first names in this music club ad.

¡VENGA!

The Best Of The Gipsy Kings (Nonesuch) 121•889

POP LATINO

Café Tacuba—Re (WEA Latina) 489•559
Leonardo Favio—20 De Colección 487•405
Ricardo Arjona—Animal Nocturno 481•358
José Luis Perales—Mis Mejores Canciones 481•317
Rocío Jurado—Mis Mejores Canciones 481•283
Ricardo Montaner—Éxitos Y... Algo Más (Rodven) 475•491
Ana Gabriel—Luna (Latin) 472•910

Julio Iglesias—La Carretera 133•835
"My Family"—Orig. Sndtrk. (eastwest) 128•165
Roberto Carlos—Canta Sus Grandes Éxitos 370•585
Ana Gabriel—Joyas De Dos Siglos 142•802
Yuri—Espejos Del Alma 141•994
Plácido Domingo—De Colección (PolyGram Latino) 141•978
Lola Flores—Tributo A La Faraona, Vol.1 (Rodven) 138•859
Boyz II Men—II-Yo Te Voy A Amar (PolyGram Latino) 138•800
Paulina Rubio—El Tiempo Es Oro 122•788
Myriam Hernández—(WEA Latina) 138•305
Los Fantasmas Del Caribe—Marea Azul (Rodven) 138•192
Millie—Sola 122•853
Stars In Spanish—Various Artists (PolyGram Latino) 134•627
Los Fabulosos Cadillacs—Rey Azúcar (SDI) 134•023
Lucero—Siempre Contigo (FonoVisa) 129•181

Jon Secada—(SBK)
Pura Sangre—Various Artists (PolyGram Latino)
Marta Sánchez—Mundo (PolyGram Latino)
Kim Boyce—Pop (Alliance)
Leonardo—Las Más Gr... Éxitos

Ricky Martin—A Medio Vivir 137•760
Gipsy Kings—Love & Liberté 469•817
The Barrio Boyzz—Donde Quiera Que Estés 468•801
Porto Latino (Rodven) 138•909
Leo Dan—Serie De Colección 15 Auténticos Éxitos 416•545

THE GRAMMY AWA...

Luis Miguel—(WEA Latina)
Luis Miguel—(WEA Latina)
Luis Miguel—Desde Siem...
Luis Miguel—Romance (WEA...)
Jerry—Magia
Jerry—Cara

CLUB MÚSICA LATINA

10 CDs / CASETES POR 1¢
¡Y La Oportunidad De Recibir Más Música Gratis!
Vea Detalles Al Dorso.

3 En clase

Identifying Classroom Objects

To find out what something is, you ask:
¿Qué es?

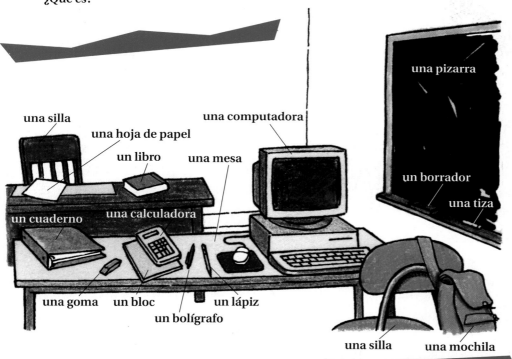

una silla
una hoja de papel
un libro una mesa
una computadora
una pizarra
un cuaderno
una calculadora
un borrador
una tiza
una goma un bloc un lápiz
un bolígrafo
una silla una mochila

To ask for something in a polite way, you say:
Una hoja de papel, por favor.

FOCUS

Students will
- use words for common classroom objects
- request common classroom objects

TEACH

un bolígrafo ball-point pen
un lápiz pencil
un borrador chalk eraser
una goma pencil eraser
un libro book
un cuaderno notebook
un bloc pad
una hoja de papel sheet of paper
una tiza chalk
una calculadora calculator
una computadora computer
una mochila backpack
una silla chair
una mesa table
una pizarra chalkboard

Una hoja de papel, por favor.
(Give me) a sheet of paper, please.

Vocabulary

1. Use the video or audio program to present the vocabulary.
2. Point to each classroom object on the overhead transparency as you say its name. Repeat this step with the actual objects, which you have assembled beforehand.

3. Name each object again, but pause before one as if you forgot its name. Signal the class to say the name chorally. Repeat with a pause before another object three or four times.

4. Name each object again and pause before one, but this time point to a student to respond with the name of the object. Repeat three or four times with different students.

Actividades

A. Answers: 1. Una calculadora, por favor. 2. Una hoja de papel, por favor. 3. Un cuaderno, por favor. 4. Un libro, por favor. 5. Un lápiz, por favor. 6. Una computadora, por favor.

Prepare a box with the smaller classroom objects in it. Have students pass this box around and ask for the objects.

B. Answers: 1. Necesita una tiza. 2. Necesita una mochila. 3. Necesita una calculadora. 4. Necesita una silla.

For students needing special help, you can list the objects needed on a piece of paper and have students match the pictures with the words.

Actividades

A Ask a classmate for the following items in Spanish. Don't forget to ask politely!

1.
2.
3.
4.
5.
6.

B Look at each picture and say in Spanish what each person needs.

Necesita...

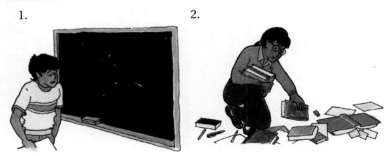

1.
2.

3.

4.

 Point to a classroom object and ask a classmate what it is.

Cultura

Schools in Spain and Latin America

In most schools in Spain and Latin America students must wear uniforms. Do you think it's a good rule to have? Do you wear uniforms at your school?

Students outside school, Madrid, Spain

3 · En clase • **39**

C. Remind students to say *por favor* (please).

Cultura

Bring in pictures of students in school uniform either in the United States, Spain, or Latin America to stimulate discussion.

ASSESS

Review the lesson and check student progress by using the following:

• Activities Workbook, Lesson 3

CLOSE

Ask students to make a list of the items from the lesson vocabulary that they have in their desks or in their backpacks.

Expansion

Ask a small group to locate and cut out pictures of the school supplies from old magazines. Have the group prepare labels for them and attach them to the pictures. Mount the pictures on a poster or bulletin board for reference. With the computer and classroom furniture, have them attach labels to the objects themselves. You may want to add these items to the objects to be labeled:

un escritorio a desk

una bandera a flag

una ventana a window

una puerta a door

un piso a floor

una pared a wall

- Video
- Audio
- Transparencies
- Workbook

FOCUS

Students will

- use and respond to the words for numbers
- ask and respond to a request for the price of something

TEACH

Vocabulary

You might want to teach the numbers in groups (1–30, 31–100, etc.) to make them easier for students to learn.

1. Point to each number in order on the overhead transparency as you say its name.
2. Point to each number in random order on the overhead transparency as you say its name.
3. Point to each number in order, but pause before one as if you forgot its name. Signal the class to say the number chorally. Repeat with a pause before another number three or four times.
4. Point to each number in order and pause before one, but this time point to a student to respond with the number.
5. Or use the audio or video programs to present the vocabulary.

A major reason for being familiar with numbers early in the language learning process is to enable students to understand prices. High numbers are given because the exchange rate for some currencies often exceeds 1,000 to the dollar.

40

4 ◆ **Números**

Counting in Spanish

0	cero	21	veintiuno	50	cincuenta
1	uno		(veinte y uno)	60	sesenta
2	dos	22	veintidós	70	setenta
3	tres	23	veintitrés	80	ochenta
4	cuatro	24	veinticuatro	90	noventa
5	cinco	25	veinticinco		
6	seis	26	veintiséis	100	cien, ciento
7	siete	27	veintisiete	200	doscientos
8	ocho	28	veintiocho	300	trescientos
9	nueve	29	veintinueve	400	cuatrocientos
10	diez	30	treinta	500	quinientos
				600	seiscientos
11	once	31	treinta y uno	700	setecientos
12	doce	32	treinta y dos	800	ochocientos
13	trece	33	treinta y tres	900	novecientos
14	catorce	34	treinta y cuatro	1.000	mil
15	quince	35	treinta y cinco	2.000	dos mil
16	dieciséis	36	treinta y seis		
	(diez y seis)	37	treinta y siete		
17	diecisiete	38	treinta y ocho		
18	dieciocho	39	treinta y nueve		
19	diecinueve	40	cuarenta		
20	veinte				

40 • *Welcome to Spanish!*

Actividades

A Your teacher will write some numbers on the chalkboard. Then he or she will call out the number in Spanish and ask a student to circle the correct number.

B Work with a classmate. One of you will count from 30 to 40. The other will count from 70 to 80.

C Have a contest with a friend. See who can count the fastest from 1 to 100 by tens.

D Have a contest with a friend. See who can count the fastest from 100 to 1000 by hundreds.

Finding Out the Price

To find out how much something costs, you ask:

—¿Cuánto es la calculadora, señora?

—Mil doscientos pesos.

—Gracias, señora.

Actividades

A. You can also have students call out the numbers and ask other students to circle them.

B. Repeat this activity with the numbers 20–30, 40–50, 50–60, 60–70, 80–90, and 90–100.

C. Have students time each other with either a classroom clock or a wristwatch with a second hand.

Finding Out the Price

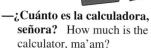

—**¿Cuánto es la calculadora, señora?** How much is the calculator, ma'am?

—**Mil doscientos pesos.** One thousand two hundred pesos.

—**Gracias, señora.** Thank you, ma'am.

1. Model the dialogue yourself, pointing to the appropriate speaker on the overhead transparency. Use props to make the dialogue more realistic.

2. Model the dialogues with one of the more able students.

3. Have two students model the dialogues.

4. Or use the audio or video programs to model the dialogue.

4 · Números • **41**

Bring magazines and newspapers in Spanish for students to locate ads showing numbers. Have them note the different use of the period and comma with numbers.

Cultura

Writing Numbers in Spanish

In some parts of the Spanish-speaking world, the use of the period and the comma with numbers is the reverse of that in English.

inglés	español
24.90	24,90
1,000	1.000

See if you can find the numbers written this way in the Spanish rental car ad below.

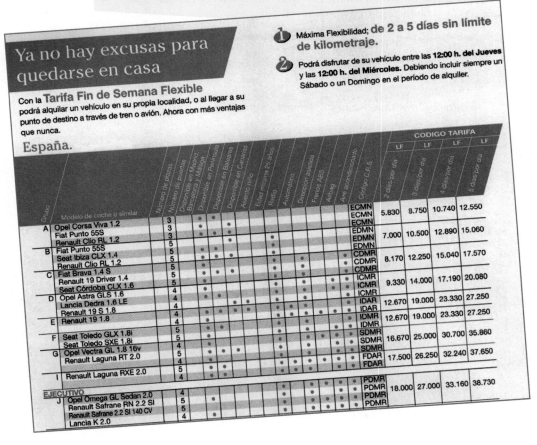

In Spain and some areas of Latin America, the numbers one and seven are written differently. Look at the photograph below to find these numbers. How are they written?

Actividad

A Work with a classmate. One of you will be the customer and the other will be the clerk at a stationery store. Make up a conversation to buy the following things.

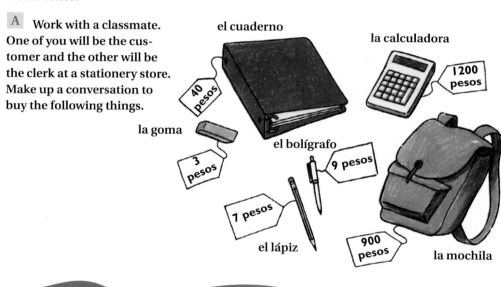

el cuaderno — 40 pesos

la calculadora — 1200 pesos

la goma — 3 pesos

el bolígrafo — 9 pesos

el lápiz — 7 pesos

la mochila — 900 pesos

A. You can extend the exercise by using all the items from Lesson 3.

Sample answer:

—**¿Cuánto es el cuaderno, señor/a/ita?**

—**Cuarenta pesos.**

Prices:

la calculadora: mil doscientos pesos

la goma: tres pesos

El bolígrafo: nueve pesos

el lápiz: siete pesos

la mochila: novecientos pesos

Review the lesson and check student progress by using the following:

- Actividad A, Counting
- Actividad A, Finding Out the Price
- Activities Workbook, Lesson 4

CLOSE

In small groups, ask students to identify the number of:

- numerals 1 on a one-dollar bill
- words "one" on a one-dollar bill

Expansion

In small groups, ask students to do the following calculation in Spanish:

- Take the number of students in the classroom.
- Subtract the number of Mondays in the current month.
- Add the number of students absent that day.
- Subtract the number of legs a spider has. (eight)
- Add the number of players on a baseball team. (nine)
- Subtract the number of digits in their telephone numbers (without the area code). (seven)

Compare the results that the groups got.

Cultura

Money Systems

The monetary unit in Spain is the *euro.*

In many Latin American countries the monetary unit is the *peso.* In Venezuela, the monetary unit is named after the famous Latin American hero Simón Bolívar—*el bolívar.*

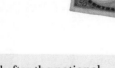

In Guatemala, the currency is named after the national bird—*el quetzal.*

44 • *Welcome to Spanish!*

5 La cortesía

Speaking Politely

—¡Hola!
  —Dos sodas, por favor.

(The server brings the order.)
—Gracias.
  —No hay de qué.

5 · *La cortesía* • 45

 Video

 Audio

 Transparencies

Workbook

FOCUS

Students will

- request common foods and drinks in a restaurant setting
- ask and respond to a request for the cost of common foods and drinks

TEACH

—**¡Hola!** Hi.
—**Dos sodas, por favor.**
  Two sodas, please.

(The server brings the order.)
—**Gracias.** Thank you.
—**No hay de qué.**
  You're welcome.

(A little later.)

—**¿Cuánto es, por favor?** How much is it, please?

—**Ochenta pesos.** Eighty pesos.

Dialogue

1. Use the video or audio programs to present the dialogue. Point to the speaker as each line of the dialogue is heard. Or model the dialogue yourself, pointing to the appropriate speaker on the overhead transparency. Do not translate into English.

2. Model the dialogue with one of the more able students.

3. Have two students model the dialogue.

De nada. You're welcome.
Por nada. You're welcome.

Actividades

A. If your students need more practice with the basic conversation, have them change partners after the first reading so that each student practices the conversation three or four times.

B. Answers: 1. Un sándwich, por favor. 2. Un té, por favor. 3. Una soda, por favor. 4. Una limonada, por favor. 5. Una ensalada, por favor.

Arrange the classroom furniture so that the "customer" is seated at a restaurant "table" or standing at a "counter."

(A little later.)
—¿Cuánto es, por favor?
—Ochenta pesos.

Other ways to express "you're welcome" are:
De nada.   **Por nada.**

Actividades

A With a friend, practice reading the three dialogues on pages 45 and 46 aloud.

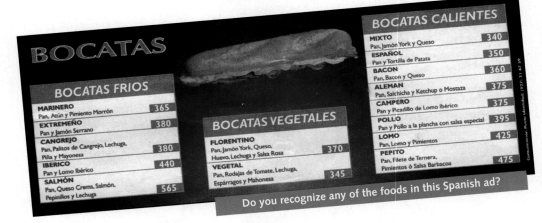

Do you recognize any of the foods in this Spanish ad?

B You are at a café in Playa del Carmen, Mexico. Order the following things. Ask a classmate to be the server.

1. un sándwich   2. un té

C. Answers: 1. Dos tacos, por
favor.   2. Tres enchiladas,
por favor.   3. Una tostada, por
favor.

Encourage students to use the
alternative expressions for
"you're welcome."

3. una soda   4. una limonada

5. una ensalada

C **You would like to order the following foods at a Mexican
restaurant. Be polite when you order them!**

1.

tacos

2.

enchiladas

3.

una tostada

Cultura

Bring in pictures of staple foods of the Spanish-speaking world. Your students may be able to contribute pictures from the library and old magazines at home. Post the pictures around a world map and have students link each picture to the area where the crop is grown with a length of yarn.

Have students check the local supermarket to see if there is a section for Spanish and Latin American foods. Have them make a list of the foods they find.

ASSESS

Review the lesson and check student progress by using the following:

- Give students the basic dialogue with some blanks, and ask them to fill in the blanks.
- Activities Workbook, Lesson 5

CLOSE

Give students the sentences of the basic dialogue in the wrong order. Ask them to arrange them in an order that makes sense. (There is more than one correct order. For example, someone could ask the cost before ordering a cola.)

Expansion

A. Have students design a menu for a Mexican (for example) restaurant. Photocopy the result and have students use it to role-play a group ordering a meal. You may want to teach these expressions:

- **Para mí...** (For me . . .)
- **Para comer...** (To eat . . .)
- **Para beber...** (To drink . . .)

B. If there is an ethnic market near you, plan a field trip to it. Ask students to make a "shopping list" of foods they expect to see. Have them check off those that they see. When you return, have students draw and label the foods they saw.

48

Cultura
Foods of the Hispanic World

It is fascinating to learn what people eat around the world. The products that are available in the area where people live influence what they eat.

The long coast of Chile makes seafood an important part of the Chilean diet. High in the Andes where it is difficult to grow vegetables and raise animals, many dishes are made from potatoes.

Spanish Online

For more information about food in the Spanish-speaking world, go to the Glencoe Web site: glencoe.com

In Argentina, people eat more beef than any other country in the world. There are many cattle ranches on the vast Argentine *pampas*.

Corn and corn products are a staple in the diet of many Mexicans. Many dishes are prepared with corn tortillas. In Cuba, the Dominican Republic, and Puerto Rico people eat a lot of rice, beans, and different types of bananas called *plátanos*.

48 • *Welcome to Spanish!*

6 ◆ La hora

Telling Time

To find out the time, you ask:

Perdón, ¿qué hora es?

To tell the time, you say:

Es la una.

Son las dos.

Son las tres.

Son las cuatro.

Son las cinco.

Son las seis.

Son las siete.

Son las ocho.

Son las nueve.

Son las diez.

Son las once.

Son las doce.

6 · *La hora* • 49

- Video
- Audio
- Transparencies
- Workbook

FOCUS

Students will
- ask and respond to requests for the time
- give the time of events

TEACH

Perdón, ¿qué hora es? Excuse me. What time is it?

Es la una. It's one o'clock.

Son las dos. It's two o'clock.

Son las tres. It's three o'clock.

Son las cuatro. It's four o'clock.

Son las cinco. It's five o'clock.

Son las seis. It's six o'clock.

Son las siete. It's seven o'clock.

Son las ocho. It's eight o'clock.

Son las nueve. It's nine o'clock.

Son las diez. It's ten o'clock.

Son las once. It's eleven o'clock.

Son las doce. It's twelve o'clock.

Because of the popularity of digital clocks, it is becoming more common to tell time based on sixty minutes—*Son las seis cuarenta.* For introductory purposes, we have not presented the other options for telling time. You may, however, wish to teach the alternative—*Son las siete menos veinte.*

Es la una y cinco. It's 1:05 (five minutes after one).

Son las dos y diez. It's 2:10.

Son las cinco cuarenta. It's 5:40.

Son las seis y cuarto (y quince). It's 6:15 (a quarter after six).

Son las siete y media (y treinta). It's 7:30 (half past seven).

La clase es a las ocho y media (a las ocho y treinta). The class is at eight thirty.

El concierto es a las siete y media (a las siete y treinta). The concert is at seven thirty.

Dialogue

1. Ask *Perdón, ¿qué hora es?* with appropriate gestures. Respond, using a clock with movable hands, with the hours from 1 to 12.

2. Using the clock, repeat the hours from 1 to 12. However, pause before one hour and signal the class to respond chorally. Repeat this step with several other hours.

3. Using the clock, repeat the hours from 1 to 12. Pause before one hour and point to a student to respond. Repeat this step with other hours and other students.

Repeat this procedure with the times giving the number of minutes after the hour.

4. You may also present these times with the audio or video programs. Or you may use the overhead transparency.

| Es la una y cinco. | Son las dos y diez. | Son las cinco cuarenta. | Son las seis y cuarto (y quince). | Son las siete y media (y treinta). |

To give the time at which something takes place, you say:

La clase es a las ocho y media (a las ocho y treinta).

El concierto es a las siete y media (a las siete y treinta).

World Youth Orchestra, Girona, Spain

50 • *Welcome to Spanish!*

50

Actividades

A Walk up to a classmate and ask for the time. Your classmate will answer you.

B Tell at what time you have the following classes. Note that these words are cognates. They are very similar in both Spanish and English.

La clase de matemáticas es...

1. matemáticas
2. historia
3. educación física
4. ciencias
5. español
6. inglés

C Draw pictures of some of your daily activities such as getting up in the morning, eating breakfast, walking or riding the bus to school, going to after-school sports, eating dinner, going to bed, etc. Then compare your pictures with those of a classmate. Both of you will tell when you do these activities. Keep track of how many activities you both do at the same time.

Cultura

The 24-Hour Clock

In Spain and in many areas of Latin America, it is common to use the 24-hour clock for formal activities such as reservations, train and airplane departures. Can you tell what time it is below in English?

A las dieciocho horas

A las veinte cuarenta

In most of the Spanish-speaking countries it is not considered rude to arrive a bit late for an appointment. If you have a 10:00 A.M. appointment, you would be expected sometime between 10 and 10:15.

Actividades

A. Answers: Perdón, ¿qué hora es? Es/Son...

   If you don't have a classroom clock, draw one on the chalkboard with the correct time for students to refer to.

B. If your students aren't taking the subjects given, substitute subjects that they are taking.

C. Some students may benefit from adding a clock that shows the time they do the activity to their drawing.

Cultura

A las dieciocho horas At six o'clock (P.M.)

A las veinte cuarenta At eight-forty (P.M.)

Review the lesson and check student progress by using the following:

- Ask students the time at random throughout the class period.

- Activities Workbook, Lesson 6

CLOSE

Using a weekly television guide from a newspaper, have your students make a TV-watching schedule for the weekend. Limit it to a total of five or six hours. Have them list the time and the programs using the 24-hour clock.

Look at the Spanish train schedule below. What do you notice about the times?

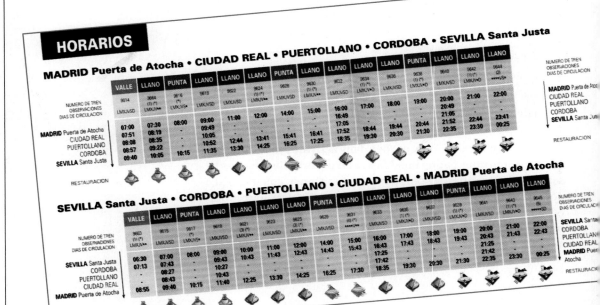

52 • *Welcome to Spanish!*

7 · Los colores

○ Video
▭ Audio
🔦 Transparencies
📄 Workbook

Identifying Colors

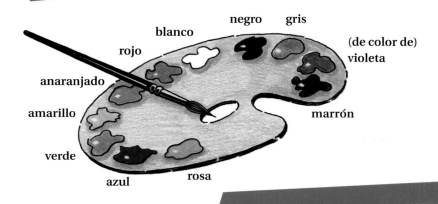

negro gris

blanco

rojo

(de color de) violeta

anaranjado

amarillo

marrón

verde

azul rosa

Actividades

A Give the following information in Spanish.

1. your favorite color
2. your least favorite color
3. the color of your pencil
4. the color of the sky today
5. the colors you like for clothes

Villahermosa, Mexico

7 · *Los colores* • 53

FOCUS

Students will

* use and respond to the names of colors

TEACH

azul blue
verde green
amarillo yellow
anaranjado orange
rojo red
rosa pink
blanco white
negro black
gris gray
(de color de) violeta lavender
marrón brown

Vocabulary

1. Point to each color on the overhead transparency as you name it. Repeat two or three times.
2. Point to each color as you name it, but pause before one as if you forgot it. Signal to the class to respond chorally.
3. Point to each color as you name it, but pause before one and point to a student to respond.
4. You may also use the audio or video programs to present the vocabulary.

Note that no activities with colors are given in this lesson that would necessitate students knowing how to make the adjective agree with the noun.

B **What do you know about color combinations? Complete the following in Spanish.**

1. Los colores rojo y azul combinados hacen el color _____.
2. Los colores azul y amarillo combinados hacen el color _____.
3. Los colores rojo y amarillo combinados hacen el color _____.
4. Los colores negro y blanco combinados hacen el color _____.

C **Draw a classmate. Use crayons to color his or her clothing. Say what colors he or she is wearing in Spanish.**

Cultura

Pablo Picasso

Pablo Picasso is one of the world's most famous modern artists. He was born in Málaga, Spain, in 1881. His mother claimed that Picasso could draw before he could talk. His father was an art teacher at the famous Barcelona Institute of Fine Arts. Pablo wished to enroll in this school. The entrance exam was so difficult that it often took students a month to complete. Picasso took the exam in one day! He was immediately admitted to the advanced classes.

As with many famous artists, Picasso's work went through many different periods or stages. Some of his periods are given the names of colors. The paintings of his "Blue Period" have a deep, dark blue background. They depicted scenes of loneliness, poverty, and suffering.

A "Pink Period" followed his "Blue Period." Picasso was happier during this time. He painted scenes of acrobats and circus performers in warm, rose-colored hues.

54 • *Welcome to Spanish!*

Expansion

For homework, have students copy a famous Picasso painting in other colors. In class have them tell the original colors and the colors they chose to use.

Which painting is from Picasso's "Pink Period"? Which painting is from his "Blue Period"?

The Blind Man's Meal,
Pablo Picasso

Tightrope Walker's Family,
Pablo Picasso

7 · *Los colores* • 55

Lesson 8

 Video

 Audio

 Transparencies

Workbook

FOCUS

Students will

- use the names of the days of the week
- ask and respond to questions about the current day

TEACH

lunes Monday

martes Tuesday

miércoles Wednesday

jueves Thursday

viernes Friday

sábado Saturday

domingo Sunday

—**¿Qué día es hoy?** What day is today?

—**Hoy es lunes.** Today is Monday.

Vocabulary

1. Point to each day of the week on the overhead transparency as you name it. Repeat two or three times.

2. Point to each day as you name it, but pause before one as if you forgot it. Signal to the class to respond chorally. Repeat with other days.

3. Point to each day as you name it, but pause before one and point to a student to respond. Repeat with other days and other students.

4. Use the dialogue expressions to ask the day and to answer.

56

8 Los días de la semana

Telling the Days of the Week

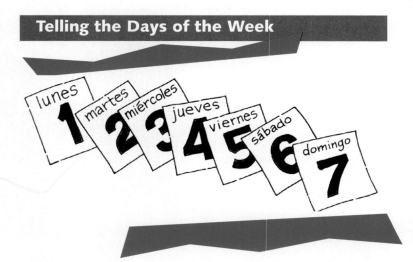

To find out and give the day, you say:

—¿Qué día es hoy?
—Hoy es lunes.

Actividad

A. **Answer the following questions in Spanish.**

1. ¿Qué día es hoy?
2. ¿Y mañana?
3. ¿Cuáles son los días del fin de semana o *weekend*?

Cultura

Weekends and Holidays

In many Spanish-speaking countries the meaning of weekend is different from that in the United States. Many people work on Saturdays and some schools have classes on Saturday mornings. Most people do not work on Sundays. Schools are also closed. Sunday is considered a day of rest.

There are many holidays in the Spanish-speaking world. People do not work on holidays. This makes it easier to go to work on Saturdays. Soon there will be another holiday to enjoy!

Spring fair, Jerez de la Frontera, Seville, Spain

Hispanic family, Austin, Texas

8 · Los días de la semana • 57

Actividad

A. Answers: 1. Answers will vary.
   2. Answers will vary.
   3. sábado, domingo

You may want to have students answer the questions orally in class and prepare the answers for homework.

Cultura

Discuss whether students would rather attend school on Saturday and have more holidays or not.

ASSESS

Review the lesson and check student progress by using the following:

•   Activities Workbook, Lesson 8

CLOSE

Have students draw one activity that they are going to do the next weekend. Have them label it with the day of the week and the time that they are going to be doing it.

Expansion

Choose a Latin American country and have students research its holidays. Good sources of information are the library, online resources, people who have lived in the country, and its embassy or consulate. Have students list the holidays and compare with the holidays we celebrate in the United States.

Lesson 9

Video

Audio

Transparencies

Workbook

FOCUS

Students will
- use the names of the months of the year and the seasons
- ask and respond to requests for the date

TEACH

enero January

febrero February

marzo March

abril April

mayo May

junio June

julio July

agosto August

septiembre September

octubre October

noviembre November

diciembre December

la primavera spring

el verano summer

el otoño fall

el invierno winter

9 Los meses y las estaciones

Telling the Months

ENERO	FEBRERO	MARZO	ABRIL	MAYO	JUNIO
1 2 3 4 5 6	1 2 3	1 2 3 4	1 2 3 4 5 6 7	1 2 3 4	1 2
7 8 9 10 11 12 13	4 5 6 7 8 9 10	5 6 7 8 9 10 11	8 9 10 11 12 13 14	5 6 7 8 9 10 11	3 4 5 6 7 8 9
14 15 16 17 18 19 20	11 12 13 14 15 16 17	12 13 14 15 16 17 18	15 16 17 18 19 20 21	12 13 14 15 16 17 18	10 11 12 13 14 15 16
21 22 23 24 25 26 27	18 19 20 21 22 23 24	19 20 21 22 23 24 25	22 23 24 25 26 27 28	19 20 21 22 23 24 25	17 18 19 20 21 22 23
28 29 30 31	25 26 27 28	26 27 28 29 30 31	29 30	26 27 28 29 30 31	24 25 26 27 28 29 30

JULIO	AGOSTO	SEPTIEMBRE	OCTUBRE	NOVIEMBRE	DICIEMBRE
1 2 3 4 5 6 7	1 2 3 4	1 2	1 2 3 4 5	1 2	1 2 3 4 5 6 7
8 9 10 11 12 13 14	5 6 7 8 9 10 11	3 4 5 6 7 8 9	6 7 8 9 10 11 12	3 4 5 6 7 8 9	8 9 10 11 12 13 14
15 16 17 18 19 20 21	12 13 14 15 16 17 18	10 11 12 13 14 15 16	13 14 15 16 17 18 19	10 11 12 13 14 15 16	15 16 17 18 19 20 21
27 23 24 25 26 27 28	19 20 21 22 23 24 25	17 18 19 20 21 22 23	20 21 22 23 24 25 26	17 18 19 20 21 22 23	22 23 24 25 26 27 28
29 30 31	26 27 28 29 30 31	24 25 26 27 28 29 30	27 28 29 30 31	24 25 26 27 28 29 30	29 30 31

Telling the Seasons

la primavera

el verano

el otoño

el invierno

Finding Out and Giving the Date

Primero is used for the first of the month. For the other days, you use: *dos, tres, cuatro,* etc. For example, *el dos de mayo.*

> —¿Cuál es la fecha de hoy?
> —Hoy es martes, el primero de abril.

Actividades

A Each of you will stand up in class and give the date of your birthday in Spanish. Listen and keep a record of how many of you were born in the same month.

B Based on the information from *Actividad A,* tell in Spanish in which month most of the students in the class were born. Tell in which month the fewest were born.

C Work in groups of two or three. Each group is responsible for drawing a calendar for one month of the year. Include the dates of classmates' birthdays.

D In which season of the year is . . . ?

1. mayo
2. enero
3. julio
4. octubre

9 · *Los meses y las estaciones* • 59

—**¿Cuál es la fecha de hoy?**
   What is today's date?

—**Hoy es martes, el primero de abril.**   Today is Tuesday, the first of April.

Vocabulary

1. Point to each month on the overhead transparency as you name it. Repeat two or three times.

2. Point to each month as you name it, but pause before one as if you forgot it. Signal to the class to respond chorally. Repeat with other months.

3. Point to each month as you name it, but pause before one and point to a student to respond. Repeat with other months and other students.

   Repeat this procedure with the seasons.

4. You may also present the vocabulary with the audio or video programs.

Finding Out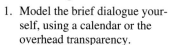
and Giving the Date

1. Model the brief dialogue yourself, using a calendar or the overhead transparency.

2. Model the dialogue with one of the more able students.

3. Have two students model the dialogue.

4. You may also present the dialogue with the audio or video programs.

Actividades

A. To make it easier to tally the birthdays, write the months on the chalkboard and have a student make a mark under each month for each birthday.

B. Review numbers by having students count the number of students who have a birthday each month in Spanish.

C. Post the finished calendar in the classroom.

D. Answers: 1. primavera
   2. invierno 3. verano 4. otoño

Cultura

Have students interview someone they know who is Mexican (or of another nationality) and report to the class on how a Mexican (or other) holiday is celebrated.

ASSESS

Review the lesson and check student progress by using the following:

*   Activities Workbook, Lesson 9

CLOSE

Ask students to write the month in Spanish that these American holidays occur in:

*   Christmas
*   Halloween
*   Presidents' Day
*   Mother's Day
*   Thanksgiving
*   Father's Day

Expansion

A. Some Spanish-language calendars record the name of the saint associated with each day. Try to locate one and have students identify their saint's day based on their name, or the name they chose in Lesson 2.

B. Celebrate the next Hispanic holiday. Have students decorate the classroom. You may want to play music and even serve special food if it is feasible.

Cultura
Hispanic Fiestas

Many fiestas of Hispanic origin are celebrated in the United States.

El Día de los Muertos or All Saints' Day, which is celebrated on *el primero* or *el dos de noviembre,* is the Mexican version of Halloween. Mexican Americans decorate their homes with *esqueletos* that symbolize the spirits of the dead. They often go to the cemetery and take food and flowers to those who have departed from this world.

El Cinco de Mayo is celebrated in Mexico to commemorate a military victory by Mexican troops against the French in the city of Puebla in 1862. *El Cinco de Mayo* is also celebrated in the United States. Many think they are celebrating Mexican Independence Day. But *el Día de la Independencia* is celebrated *el dieciséis de septiembre.*

There are many feasts and parades to celebrate national origins. In New York, the Puerto Rican Day parade and the Dominican Day parade are festive events. Marching bands follow beautifully decorated floats up Fifth Avenue.

10 · *El tiempo*

Describing the Weather

—¿Qué tiempo hace hoy?
—Hace buen tiempo.
 El sol brilla.
 Hay sol. (Hace sol.)

—Hace mal tiempo.
 Está lloviendo.

FOCUS

Students will
- use some common weather expressions

TEACH

—**¿Qué tiempo hace hoy?**
 What's the weather today?

—**Hace buen tiempo.** It's good weather.
 El sol brilla. The sun is shining.
 Hay sol. (Hace sol.) It's sunny.

Hace mal tiempo. It's bad weather.

Está lloviendo. It's raining.

Hace viento. It's windy.

Hace calor. It's hot.

Está nevando. It's snowing.

Hace frío. It's cold.

Vocabulary

1. Look out the window and gesture as you ask *¿Qué tiempo hace hoy?*

2. Point to each picture on the overhead transparency as you give the weather expression associated with it. (Point to the sunny weather for *Hace buen tiempo;* point to the rain, wind, and snow for *Hace mal tiempo.*) Repeat two or three times.

3. Point to each picture as you give the weather expression, but pause before one as if you forgot it. Signal to the class to respond chorally. Repeat with other pictures.

4. Point to each picture as you give the weather expression, but pause before one and point to a student to respond. Repeat with other pictures and other students.

5. You may also present the vocabulary with the audio or video programs.

Actividades

A. Have students work in pairs to ask and give the weather information. Have them change partners so that each has three or four conversations.

B. You may want to have students describe the weather orally in class and write it for homework.

C. Have students describe their pictures in small groups for more efficient individual practice.

Hace viento.

Hace calor.

Está nevando.

Hace frío.

Actividades

A Tell in Spanish what the weather is like today.

B Work in groups of four. Write in Spanish the name of each season on a separate sheet of paper. Put the papers in a pile. Each of you will pull one sheet from the pile. Then describe the weather during the season written on the sheet.

C Draw a picture of your favorite type of weather. Then describe your picture to the class in Spanish.

62   •   *Welcome to Spanish!*

Cultura

Seasons in Latin America

In many Latin-American countries there are only two seasons: *el verano* and *el invierno*. *El verano* is the dry season and *el invierno* is the rainy season.

In South America the seasons are reversed. When it is winter in North America, it is summer in South America. In Chile and Argentina people ski in July and go to the beach in January! Why do you think that the seasons are reversed?

Mar del Plata, Argentina

"La Hoya," ski center in Esquel, Argentina

Cultura

Enlist a science teacher to help you explain how the tilt of the Earth on its axis causes the seasons. Use a beach ball and Ping-Pong ball.

ASSESS

Review the lesson and check student progress by using the following:

- Ask students to pretend that it is yesterday and to give the weather.
- Activities Workbook, Lesson 10

CLOSE

Ask students to predict tomorrow's weather. Have them use the present tense. Have students correct their prediction if necessary the next day. Reward those who predicted correctly.

Expansion

A. Ask students to keep a weather calendar for one week. Use the vocabulary in Lessons 8 and 9 to make a calendar with large boxes for the days. Appoint a different group to observe and write the weather every day in the calendar boxes.

B. Ask a small group of students to prepare and record a world weather report in Spanish. Have them report the weather in cities such as Madrid, Mexico City, San Juan, Santo Domingo, Bogotá, Buenos Aires, and so on. You can get the information from major newspapers, cable television weather channels, and online resources.

Lesson 11

Video
Audio
Transparencies
Workbook

Students will

- ask and respond to requests for one's name
- use the forms *eres* and *soy* appropriately

TEACH

—**¡Hola! ¿Quién eres?** Hi. Who are you?

—**¿Yo? (Yo) soy Juan Gutiérrez. Y tú, ¿quién eres?** Me? I'm Juan Gutiérrez. And you, who are you?

—**(Yo) soy Anita Salas.** I'm Anita Salas.

Dialogue

1. Use the video or audio programs to present the dialogue. Point to the speaker as each line of the dialogue is heard. Or model the dialogue yourself, pointing to the appropriate speaker on the overhead transparency.

2. Have two students model the dialogue, using their real names. Prompt them if necessary.

Explain that in Spanish the subject pronoun (*yo*, in this case) is optional. It can be left out. It is more likely to be used when leaving it out might cause confusion.

Actividades

A. If your furniture is movable, arrange it so that students can move about easily.

11 Yo soy...

Telling Who I Am

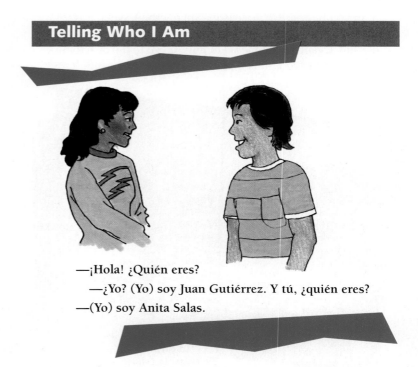

—¡Hola! ¿Quién eres?
   —¿Yo? (Yo) soy Juan Gutiérrez. Y tú, ¿quién eres?
—(Yo) soy Anita Salas.

When you hear a question with *eres* in Spanish, you answer with *soy. Eres* is used to speak to a friend *(tú)* and *soy* is used to speak about yourself *(yo).*

   ¿eres? → soy

Actividades

A Walk around the classroom. Greet each of your classmates. Find out who each one is. Let each one know who you are.

64 • *Welcome to Spanish!*

B Turn to your nearest neighbor. Have a conversation with him or her. Use the following as your guide.

—¡Hola! ¿Quién eres?
   —¿Quién? ¿Yo?
—Sí, tú.
   —Pues, yo soy _____. Y tú, ¿quién eres?
—Soy _____.

*C**ultura*

Names in Spanish

Some Spanish speakers use two last names. A young person, prior to marriage, uses the family name of both his or her father and mother. For example,

María Eugenia Guzmán Morales.

Guzmán is the name of María Eugenia's father's family and Morales is the name of her mother's family.

11 · Yo soy... • **65**

Cultura

An *apodo* is a nickname, often a phrase used after a person's name. It can be taken from a physical characteristic (*el chato,* the one with a flat nose); a job (*el chocolatero,* the one who makes chocolate or comes from a family who does); a place of origin or residence *(el argentino).* Have students share their nicknames with each other. If possible, have them assign each other Spanish nicknames.

ASSESS

Review the lesson and check student progress by using the following:

• Ask students to introduce themselves to each other using the name badges made in Lesson 2.

• Activities Workbook, Lesson 11

CLOSE

Ask students to pretend they are at the airport to meet a Spanish-speaking cousin whom they have never seen. Have them prepare the dialogue that takes place.

Expansion

Ask students to think of the celebrity they would most like to meet. Then have them prepare an imaginary conversation with that celebrity. Use general interest, sports, and celebrity magazines to help students think of someone.

Lesson 12

- ◗◖ Video
- ▭▭ Audio
- Transparencies
- Workbook

FOCUS

Students will

- ask about and respond to requests for geographic origin
- ask for or give a person's nationality

TEACH

—**¿De dónde eres, David?** Where are you from, David?

—**Soy de Dallas.** I'm from Dallas.

—**Ah, eres americano.** Ah, you're American.

—**Sí, soy americano. ¿Y tú? ¿De dónde eres, Anita?** Yes, I'm American. And you? Where are you from, Anita?

—**Soy de Guadalajara. Soy mexicana.** I'm from Guadalajara. I'm Mexican.

Dialogue

1. Use the video to present the dialogue. Or use the overhead transparency and audio program to present it. Point to the speaker as each line of the dialogue is heard. Or model the dialogue yourself, pointing to the appropriate speaker on the overhead transparency.

2. Have two students model the dialogue, using the names David and Anita and their nationalities. Have several other pairs of students model the dialogue.

3. If you have students of other nationalities, have two students model the dialogue using their real names and nationalities.

66

12 ◆ *Soy de...*

Telling Where I Am From

—¿De dónde eres, David?
  —Soy de Dallas.
—Ah, eres americano.
  —Sí, soy americano. ¿Y tú? ¿De dónde eres, Anita?
—Soy de Guadalajara. Soy mexicana.

When you describe a boy in Spanish, you use *-o.* When you describe a girl in Spanish, you use *-a.*

David es americano.   **Anita es mexicana.**
Yo soy americano.   **Yo soy mexicana.**

66 • *Welcome to Spanish!*

Actividades

A Answer the following questions about yourself.

1. ¿Quién eres?
2. ¿De dónde eres?
3. ¿De qué nacionalidad eres?

B Draw a picture of a male friend or relative. Give him a Spanish name. Then tell as much about him as you can.

C Draw a picture of a female friend or relative. Give her a Spanish name. Then tell as much about her as you can.

D Work with a classmate. Find out where he or she is from and his or her nationality. Then give your classmate the same information about yourself.

Conversando más

—¡Hola!
  —¡Hola!
—¿Quién eres?
  —Pues, yo soy David Sanders.
—¿Qué tal, David?
  —Muy bien. ¿Y tú?
—Bien, gracias.
  —Tú eres Anita Salas, ¿no?
—Sí, soy Anita.
  —¿De dónde eres, Anita?
—Soy de México.
  —Ah, eres mexicana.
—Sí. Y tú eres americano, ¿no?
  —Sí, soy de Dallas.

12 · Soy de... • 67

David es americano. David is American.

Yo soy americano. I'm American.

Anita es mexicana. Anita is Mexican.

Yo soy mexicana. I'm Mexican.

Actividades

A. This activity can be enhanced by the use of photos. Have students bring photos of themselves from home, or use photos taken at school activities if available. Have students give the answers orally in class and write the answers for homework.

B., C. Have students write the information under the drawing and post the results.

D. Have Student 1 give the information using *soy*. Have Student 2 write down the information using *es*. Have Student 1 check the paper to verify the information. Then reverse roles.

Conversando más

—¡Hola! Hi.
—¡Hola! Hi.
—¿Quién eres? Who are you?
—Pues, yo soy David Sanders. Well, I'm David Sanders.
—¿Qué tal, David? How are you, David?
—Muy bien. ¿Y tú? Fine. And you?
—Bien, gracias. Fine, thanks.
—Tú eres Anita Salas, ¿no? You're Anita Salas, aren't you?
—Sí, soy Anita. Yes, I'm Anita.
—¿De dónde eres, Anita? Where are you from, Anita?
—Soy de México. I'm from Mexico.
—Ah, eres mexicana. Ah, you're Mexican.
—Sí. Y tú eres americano, ¿no? Yes. And you're American, aren't you?
—Sí, soy de Dallas. Yes, I'm from Dallas.

1. Draw and label David and Anita on the chalkboard or point to the overhead transparency. Model the review dialogue yourself, pointing to the appropriate speaker on the chalkboard. If possible, use puppets for this activity.

2. Have two students model the dialogue, using the names David and Anita and their nationalities. Have several other pairs of students model the dialogue.

3. If you have students of other nationalities, have two students model the dialogue using their real names and nationalities.

4. You may also use the audio or video programs to present the dialogue.

Actividades

A. Have students change partners so that each practices the conversation two or three times.

B. Answers: Dallas, americano, Anita, americana, mexicana

C., D. Post the results of these activities in the classroom.

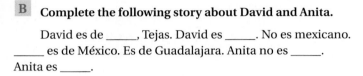

Actividades

A Practice the conversation on page 67 together with a classmate. Use as much expression as you can. One will read the part of David and the other will read the part of Anita.

B Complete the following story about David and Anita.

David es de _____, Tejas. David es _____. No es mexicano. _____ es de México. Es de Guadalajara. Anita no es _____. Anita es _____.

C Look at the photograph of Lynn Smith. She is from New Jersey. Tell all about her in Spanish.

D Look at this photograph of José Garza. He is from Monterrey, Mexico. Tell all about him in Spanish.

Cultura

Nationalities

People from all countries of North America, Central America, and South America are *americanos*. The term *americano* (sometimes *norteamericano*) is more frequently used, however, for citizens of the United States. The term *estadounidense* is not often heard to refer to the nationality of a person. People from other countries of the Americas usually identify themselves more specifically as *colombiano, argentino, mexicano*. Do you know people from these countries?

School celebration, Mexico City

Centennial parade, Pasto, Colombia

High school class, Argentina

12 · Soy de... • 69

Write the following comparison on the chalkboard, and ask what they observe about the capitalization of the words. Elicit that in Spanish we do not capitalize nationalities.

Country	Nationality
México	**mexicano**
Colombia	**colombiano**
Italia	**italiano**
China	**chino**

ASSESS

Review the lesson and check student progress by using the following:

* Activities Workbook, Lesson 12

CLOSE

Ask students to pretend that Anita Salas is going to be an exchange student at their school next year. Have them prepare a brief conversation in which they introduce themselves to her and ask her where she's from.

Expansion

If you have students from these national backgrounds, you may want to introduce these nationalities to the class.

Argentina argentino(a)
Bolivia boliviano(a)
Colombia colombiano(a)
Costa Rica costarricense
Chile chileno(a)
Ecuador ecuatoriano(a)
El Salvador salvadoreño(a)
Guatemala guatemalteco(a)
Honduras hondureño(a)
Nicaragua nicaragüense
Panamá panameño(a)
Perú peruano(a)
Puerto Rico puertorriqueño(a)
República Dominicana
    dominicano(a)
Venezuela venezolano(a)

Video

Audio

Transparencies

Workbook

FOCUS

Students will

- ask and respond to questions about the languages they speak
- use the forms *¿hablas?* and *hablo* appropriately

TEACH

—**¿Hablas inglés, David?** Do you speak English, David?

—**Sí, hablo inglés. ¿Hablas español, Anita?** Yes, I speak English. Do you speak Spanish, Anita?

—**Sí, hablo español.** Yes, I speak Spanish.

—**¿Hablas inglés, también?** Do you speak English, too?

—**Sí, hablo inglés también.** Yes, I speak English, too.

Dialogue

1. Use the video to present the dialogue. Or use the overhead transparency and audio program to present it. Point to the speaker as each line of the dialogue is heard. Or model the dialogue yourself, pointing to the appropriate speaker on the overhead transparency.

2. Have two students model the dialogue as David and Anita. Have several other pairs of students model the dialogue.

3. If you have students who speak other languages, have two students model the dialogue using their real names and the languages that they speak.

70

---

13 ◆ Hablo español

Telling What I Speak

—¿Hablas inglés, David?
  —Sí, hablo inglés. ¿Hablas español, Anita?
—Sí, hablo español.
  —¿Hablas inglés también?
—Sí, hablo inglés también.

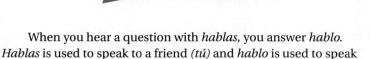

When you hear a question with *hablas,* you answer *hablo.*
Hablas is used to speak to a friend *(tú)* and *hablo* is used to speak about yourself *(yo).*

   ¿hablas? → **hablo**

70   •   *Welcome to Spanish!*

Look at the Spanish names of these languages. You can probably guess at the meaning as all of these words are cognates.

italiano	ruso
francés	polaco
portugués	árabe
chino	griego
japonés	latín

What languages are taught at this school in Colombia?

Actividades

A Walk around the room and greet a classmate. Find out what language(s) he or she speaks. Then tell your classmate what language(s) you speak.

B Get a beach ball. One person throws the ball to another as he or she asks, *¿Hablas español?* The person who catches the ball answers, *Sí, hablo...* or *No, no hablo...*

C If you speak a language other than English at home, tell the class what language you speak.

Cultura

Spanish in the World

Spanish is the official language of more countries in the world than any other language. It is the language of more than twenty countries. However, it is not the language with the most speakers. Do you know which language is spoken by the largest number of people in the world? The answer is Chinese. Chinese is spoken by more than one billion people!

italiano Italian
francés French
portugués Portuguese
chino Chinese
japonés Japanese
ruso Russian
polaco Polish
árabe Arabic
griego Greek
latín Latin

In the photograph, *Alemán* on the sign of the Academia de Idiomas means "German."

Actividades

A. If your furniture is movable, arrange it so that students can move about easily.

B. If you don't have a beach ball, use another kind of soft ball or a beanbag.

C. Be sensitive to the fact that some students may speak non-standard dialects of another language at home. In addition, some students may speak other languages even if they speak English at home.

Cultura

Some U.S. cities rank among the largest Spanish-speaking cities in the world. Los Angeles, for example, has more Spanish speakers than Guadalajara, Mexico and Caracas, Venezuela.

Have students name a city near you where there are many Spanish-speakers.

Review the lesson and check student progress by using the following:

- Activities Workbook, Lesson 13

CLOSE

Ask students to pretend that they are lost in Madrid, Paris, or Rome. Have them prepare a brief dialogue with a stranger their own age to find out what language they have in common.

Expansion

Ask students to use a map or globe to plan an imaginary trip around the world. Have them prepare an itinerary and list the three languages that would be the most useful for them to know on the trip.

One of the largest cities in the world is also a Spanish-speaking city. Mexico City has a population of approximately 8.5 million inhabitants. Mexico City, along with Shanghai and Tokyo, rates among the largest cities in the world.

Mexico City, Mexico

Tokyo, Japan

Shanghai, China

72 • *Welcome to Spanish!*

14 Estudio...

Telling What I Study

—David, ¿estudias español en la escuela?

—Sí, estudio español. Y tú, ¿qué lengua estudias en la escuela?

—Estudio inglés.

Actividades

A Get a beach ball. One person throws the ball to another as he or she asks, *¿Estudias español?* The person who catches the ball answers, *Sí, estudio...* or *No, no estudio...*

FOCUS

Students will

* ask and respond to questions about what subjects they are taking

* use the forms *¿estudias?* and *estudio* appropriately

TEACH

—**David, ¿estudias español en la escuela?** David, do you study Spanish in school?

—**Sí, estudio español. Y tú, ¿qué lengua estudias en la escuela?** Yes, I study Spanish. And you, what language do you study in school?

—**Estudio inglés.** I study English.

Dialogue

1. Use the video to present the dialogue. Or use the overhead transparency and audio program to present it. Point to the speaker as each line of the dialogue is heard. Or model the dialogue yourself, pointing to the appropriate speaker on the overhead transparency. Do not translate the conversation into English.

2. Have two students model the dialogue as David and Anita. Have several other pairs of students model the dialogue.

3. Write the other school subjects on the chalkboard. Ask another pair of students to model the dialogue, but point to another school subject before each one asks *¿Estudias... ?*

4. Finally, ask a pair of students to model the dialogue, but let them choose the subjects to ask about.

Actividades

A. If your furniture is movable, arrange it so that students can throw the ball easily.

B. Have students change partners after each conversation so that each has three or four conversations. Encourage the use of students' names and other variations.

C. Have students use the names of actual school subjects and teachers.

David habla inglés pero estudia español en la escuela. David speaks English but he studies Spanish in school.

Anita habla español pero estudia inglés en la escuela. Anita speaks Spanish but she studies English in school.

Remind students that they know to use *es* to talk about someone:

David *es* americano. Él *habla* inglés pero *estudia* español en la escuela.

B **Work with a classmate. Find out what you each study in school. You can easily guess at the meaning of the words you'll need.**

español	ciencias	arte
inglés	historia	música
matemáticas	geografía	educación física

C **Tell a classmate about one of your classes—math, for example. Use the following questions as a guide.**

1. ¿Estudias matemáticas?
2. ¿Cómo es el curso de matemáticas? ¿Es interesante?
3. ¿Quién es el profesor o la profesora de matemáticas?
4. ¿A qué hora es la clase de matemáticas?

When you talk about someone, you say *estudia* or *habla*.

David habla inglés pero estudia español en la escuela.

Anita habla español y estudia inglés en la escuela.

Actividades

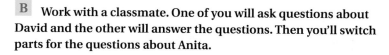

A **Read the following story about David and Anita.**

David es americano. Es de Dallas. David habla inglés. En la escuela él estudia español. Toma un curso de español.

Anita es mexicana. Es de Guadalajara. Anita habla español. En la escuela ella estudia inglés. Toma un curso de inglés en la escuela.

B **Work with a classmate. One of you will ask questions about David and the other will answer the questions. Then you'll switch parts for the questions about Anita.**

Estudiante A

1. ¿De qué nacionalidad es David?
2. ¿Qué lengua habla?
3. ¿Qué estudia?
4. ¿Dónde toma un curso de español?

Estudiante B

1. ¿De qué nacionalidad es Anita?
2. ¿Qué lengua habla?
3. ¿Qué estudia?
4. ¿Dónde toma un curso de inglés?

C **Answer the following questions about yourself.**

1. ¿Quién eres?
2. ¿De dónde eres?
3. ¿Qué lengua hablas?
4. ¿Qué lengua estudias en la escuela?

Actividades

A. Have students read silently. If students need help, have them form small groups and read aloud, each student taking one sentence.

B. Answers: 1. David es americano. 2. (Él) habla inglés. 3. (Él) estudia español. 4. Toma un curso de español en la escuela.

   1. Anita es mexicana. 2. (Ella) habla español. 3. (Ella) estudia inglés. 4. Toma un curso de inglés en la escuela.

C. Have students answer the questions orally in small groups. You may wish to have them write the answers for homework.

Cultura

Discuss whether students would like to take more classes and meet fewer times a week or not.

ASSESS

Review the lesson and check student progress by using the following:

- Ask students to write about three friends or family members using this sentence starter:

  (Name) **estudia...**

- Activities Workbook, Lesson 14

CLOSE

Ask students to prepare three sentences about someone they know using *es*, *habla*, and *estudia*.

Expansion

You might want to expand on some of the words used in this lesson.

Toma (to take) can also mean "to drink."

Toma una limonada.
Toma un café.

*C*ultura
Education in Spain and Latin America

In many schools of Spain and Latin America classes do not meet every day. The students' schedules vary from day-to-day. Many subjects meet three times a week, for example. For this reason students take more subjects per semester than do American students.

Chemistry class, Colombia

15 ◆ Mi casa

Describing My House

el cuarto de baño

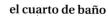

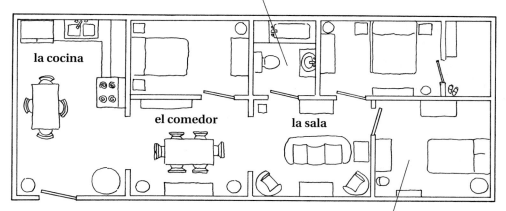

la cocina

el comedor

la sala

el apartamento

el cuarto de dormir
(el dormitorio, la recámara)

el garaje

el jardín   la casa   el carro

una casa pequeña

Hay means "there is" or "there are"
in Spanish:

Hay un jardín alrededor de la casa.

Hay un carro en el garaje.

**Hay seis cuartos en la casa. Es una
casa grande.**

15 · Mi casa •   77

FOCUS

Students will

- use the names of the rooms of
  a house
- use the form *hay* appropriately

TEACH

la casa house

el apartamento apartment

el jardín yard, garden

el garaje garage

el carro car

la sala living room

el comedor dining room

la cocina kitchen

**el cuarto de dormir (el dormito-
rio, la recámara)** bedroom

el cuarto de baño bathroom

una casa pequeña a small house

**Hay un jardín alrededor de la
casa.** There is a garden around
the house.

Hay un carro en el garaje. There
is a car in the garage.

Hay seis cuartos en la casa. There
are six rooms in the house.

Es una casa grande. It's a big
house.

Vocabulary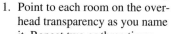

1. Point to each room on the overhead transparency as you name
   it. Repeat two or three times.

2. Point to each room as you name it, but pause before one as if you forgot its name. Signal to the class to respond chorally. Repeat with other rooms.

3. Point to each room as you name it, but pause before one and point to a student to respond. Repeat with other rooms and other students.

4. Point to the *jardín,* the *carro,* and the *cuartos* as you say the sentences with *hay.*

5. Point to the *jardín,* the *carro,* and the *cuartos,* and ask students to say the sentences with *hay.*

6. You may also use the audio or video programs to present the vocabulary.

Actividades

A. If students would be uncomfortable describing their houses or apartments, distribute pictures of houses or apartments cut from old magazines for them to describe.

B. Answers: 1. la sala 2. el cuarto de dormir (el dormitorio, la recámara) 3. el comedor 4. el cuarto de baño 5. la cocina

Actividades

A Draw a picture of your house. Write the title *Mi casa* at the top of your drawing. Then answer the following questions.

1. ¿Es grande o pequeña tu casa?
2. ¿Cuántos cuartos hay en tu casa?
3. ¿Hay un jardín alrededor de tu casa?

B Look at these photographs of the interiors of houses in Spanish-speaking countries. Give the name in Spanish for each room.

C Describe your dream house to a classmate. Say as much as you can about it in Spanish.

Actividades

A Look at the address book below and give the following information.

1. la dirección de la señorita Gómez
2. el número de teléfono de la señorita Gómez

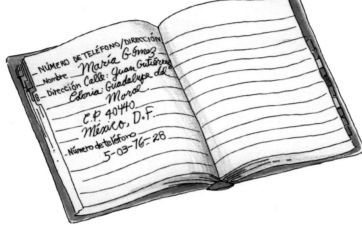

B Provide the following information about yourself.

1. mi dirección
2. mi número de teléfono

C. Distribute pictures of large houses, mansions, and castles to inspire students.

Actividades

A. Answers:

1. Calle: Juan Gutiérrez
   Colonia: Guadalupe de Moral
   C.P. 40440
   México, D.F.

2. cinco-cero tres-setenta y seis-veintiocho

   Have students illustrate an address book similar to the one in the textbook and provide the information.

ASSESS

Review the lesson and check student progress by using the following:

- Ask students to list the rooms of their house or apartment in order of where they spend the most time to where they spend the least time.

- Activities Workbook, Lesson 15

CLOSE

Ask students to design and draw a doll house or a tree house and to label the rooms in Spanish.

Expansion

You might want to teach these terms to help students talk about their houses or apartments:

la planta baja the first floor

el primer piso the second floor

Note that the first floor in Spanish is referred to as the "ground floor." The "first floor" is called the second floor in English.

FOCUS

Students will

• use common terms for members of a family

• use the form *¿tienes?* and *tengo* appropriately

TEACH

mi madre   my mother

mi padre   my father

mi abuela   my grandmother

mi abuelo   my grandfather

yo   I (me)

mi hermano   my brother

mi hermana   my sister

mi tío   my uncle

mi tía   my aunt

Mi tío Carlos es el hermano de mi padre.   My uncle Carlos is my father's brother.

Mi tía Antonia es la hermana de mi madre.   My aunt Antonia is my mother's sister.

mi prima   my cousin (girl)

mi primo   my cousin (boy)

Mi prima Lupita es la hija de mi tío Carlos.   My cousin Lupita is the daughter of my uncle Carlos.

Mi primo Luis es el hijo de mi tío Juan.   My cousin Luis is the son of my uncle Juan.

16 Mi *familia*

Describing My Family

mi abuela   mi abuelo

mi tío   mi tía

mi madre   mi padre

mi prima   mi primo

mi hermano   yo   mi hermana

Mi tío Carlos es el hermano de mi padre.

Mi tía Antonia es la hermana de mi madre.

Mi prima Lupita es la hija de mi tío Carlos.

Mi primo Luis es el hijo de mi tío Juan.

80   •   *Welcome to Spanish!*

—¿Tienes un hermano?

—Sí, tengo un hermano. (o) No, no tengo un hermano.

—¿Tienes una familia grande o pequeña?

—Yo tengo una familia _____. Hay _____ personas en mi familia.

When you hear a question with *tienes* in Spanish, you answer with *tengo. (Tú) tienes* is used to speak to a friend. *Tengo* is used to speak about yourself *(yo).*

¿tienes?   →   tengo

Actividades

A **Answer the following questions about your family.**

1. ¿Tienes una familia grande o pequeña?
2. ¿Tienes hermanos?
3. ¿Cuántos hermanos tienes?
4. ¿Cuántas personas hay en tu familia?
5. ¿Cuántos cuartos hay en tu casa?

B **Work with a classmate. Ask each other questions about your families in Spanish.**

C **Who is it? Answer in Spanish.**

1. la hija de mi padre
2. el hijo de mi madre
3. el hermano de mi madre
4. la madre de mi padre
5. el padre de mi madre
6. la hija de mi tío

When you talk about someone, you use *tiene.*
Mi amigo José tiene una familia grande.
Él tiene seis hermanos.

Con profundo amor
para mi *Madre*
EN SU CUMPLEAÑOS

AGC, Inc. Reprinted with Permission.

16 · Mi familia • **81**

—¿Tienes un hermano? Do you have a brother?

—Sí, tengo un hermano. (o) No, no tengo un hermano. Yes, I have a brother. (or) No, I don't have a brother.

—Tienes una familia grande o pequeña? Do you have a large family or a small one?

—Yo tengo una familia _____. Hay _____ personas en mi familia. I have a _____ family. There are _____ people in my family.

Vocabulary

1. Starting with *yo,* point to each person on the overhead transparency as you give the relationship. Repeat two or three times.

2. Point to each person as you name the relationship, but pause before one as if you forgot it. Signal to the class to respond chorally. Repeat with the other people.

3. Point to each person as you name the relationship, but pause before one and point to a student to respond. Repeat with the other people and other students.

Dialogue

1. Draw two stick figure families on the chalkboard. Point to one of the children from each family as you read the dialogue. Have the stick figure child respond with information about his or her family as you have drawn it.

2. Make the families larger or smaller. Repeat Step 1.

3. Have two students model the dialogue using their real names and family information. Prompt them the first time if necessary. Have several other pairs of students model the dialogue using real information.

4. You may also use the audio or video programs to present the vocabulary and the dialogue.

Actividad

A **Look at the photograph of *la familia González*. Say as much as you can about the family in Spanish.**

Telling Age

To tell how old you or someone else is, you say:

Yo tengo doce años.

Mi hermana tiene quince años.

To ask how old someone is, you say:

¿Cuántos años tienes?

Actividades

A Ask each of your classmates his or her age. Tell each one your age.

B Give the ages of some of your friends and relatives.

Especialmente Para Ti
EN TU CUMPLEAÑOS

AGC, Inc. Reprinted with Permission.

Cultura

The Family in Hispanic Culture

La familia is an extremely important unit in all Spanish-speaking cultures. The family gets together to celebrate the major holidays, as well as all personal events such as birthdays, baptisms, anniversaries, etc. In addition to the parents and children, the extended Hispanic family often includes grandparents, uncles, aunts, distant cousins, and godparents.

16 · Mi familia • **83**

Actividades

A. Since many students in a class are likely to be the same age, have them roleplay teachers, doctors, and police officers asking them and their siblings their age. Remind students that it isn't polite to ask adults their age.

B. After students give the ages of their friends and relatives, use pictures of people in books and magazines for further practice.

Cultura

Introduce the terms "nuclear family" (parents and children) and "extended family." The term "extended family" means anyone, besides the parents and children, who is considered a member of a family.

ASSESS

Review the lesson and check student progress by using the following:

*   Ask students to write the relationship terms of this lesson in two columns labeled "Nuclear Family" and "Extended Family."

*   Activities Workbook, Lesson 16

CLOSE

Ask students to figure out the ages of these celebrities.

Name	Born
Enrique Iglesias	1976
Lou Diamond Phillips	1963
Jennifer Lopez	1970
Geraldo Rivera	1943

Expansion

A. Ask students to draw and label a family tree of their family or a relative's family.

B. As in English, when we give the age of babies, we use the word for months, *meses:*

El bebé tiene un mes.

Tiene dos / tres / etc. / meses.

Lesson 17

- Video
- Audio
- Transparencies
- Workbook

FOCUS

Students will

- use the names of common pets
- ask and respond to questions about likes and dislikes
- use the forms *¿te interesan?, me interesan, me gustan, me encantan,* and *me fascinan* appropriately

TEACH

un perro dog

un gato cat

un hámster hamster

un gerbo gerbil

los pájaros birds

un papagayo parrot

un perico parakeet

un canario canary

una jaula de (para) pájaros birdcage

un pececillo tropical fish

un pez dorado goldfish

un pecero, un acuario aquarium

Vocabulary

1. Point to each pet and item on the overhead transparency as you give the name. Repeat two or three times.
2. Point to each pet and item as you name it, but pause before one as if you forgot it. Signal to the class to respond chorally. Repeat with other items.

84

17 Mi mascota

Talking About My Pet

un perro

los pájaros

un canario

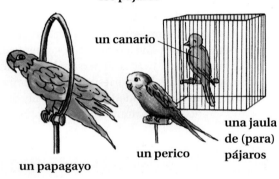

una jaula de (para) pájaros

un perico

un papagayo

un gato

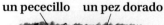
un pececillo   un pez dorado

un hámster

un gerbo

un pecero, un acuario

84   •   *Welcome to Spanish!*

Telling What I Like

—¿Te interesan los animales?

—Sí, los animales me interesan mucho.
Me encantan los animales.
Me fascinan.
Me gustan mucho.

—¿Te gusta tu perro?
—Sí, me gusta mucho.

Actividades

A Answer the following personal questions in Spanish.

1. ¿Te encantan los animales? ¿Te gustan mucho?

2. ¿Tienes un perro o un gato? ¿Te gusta tu perro o tu gato?

3. ¿Te encantan los pájaros? ¿Te gustan mucho? ¿Tienes un pájaro? ¿Qué tipo de pájaro tienes?

4. ¿Te encantan los peces? ¿Te gustan mucho? ¿Tienes peces? ¿Qué tipo de pez tienes?

B Ask a classmate all about his or her pet. Use the following questions as a guide.

1. ¿Tienes una mascota?

2. ¿Qué tienes?

3. ¿Tiene nombre?

4. ¿Cuántos años (meses) tiene?

5. ¿Es adorable?

Boy with pet llama, Cuzco, Peru

17 · Mi mascota • 85

3. You may also use the audio or video programs to present the vocabulary.

Telling What I Like

—**¿Te interesan los animales?**
Are you interested in animals?

—**Sí, los animales me interesan mucho.** Yes, I'm very interested in animals.

Me encantan los animales. I love animals.

Me fascinan. They fascinate me.

Me gustan mucho. I like them very much.

—**¿Te gusta tu perro?** Do you like your dog?

—**Sí, me gusta mucho.** Yes, I like (him, her) very much.

1. Use the video or audio programs to present the dialogue. Point to the speaker as each line of the dialogue is heard. Or model the dialogue yourself, pointing to the appropriate speaker on the overhead transparency. Use gestures and facial expressions to convey the meaning of *me fascinan, me encantan,* and *me gustan.* Do not give English equivalents.

2. Have two students model the dialogue. Let the second speaker choose any appropriate response. Repeat with other pairs of students.

Actividades

A. Prepare several sets of cards with the names of the pets. Have students work in small groups. Assign one student in each group to deal the cards, face down, to the others. Students should ask another student a question about the pet they drew. Deal the cards three or four times.

B. Have Student 1 ask Student 2 questions. Student 1 will write down the information. Student 2 will check the paper to verify the information. Students will then

Telling What My Pet Does

El perro ladra. Ladra y salta. Juega mucho.   The dog barks. He barks and jumps. He plays a lot.

El gato maúlla. El gato salta y juega mucho también.   The cat meows. The cat jumps and plays a lot, too.

El papagayo habla.   The parrot talks.

El pececillo nada en el pecero (acuario).   The tropical fish swims in the aquarium.

El canario canta en su jaula. The canary sings in its cage.

1. Point to each picture on the overhead transparency as you say what the animal is doing. Repeat two or three times.

2. Point to each picture as you say what the animal is doing, but pause before saying one verb, as if you forgot it. Signal to the class to respond chorally. Repeat with other verbs.

3. Point to each picture as you say what the animal is doing, but pause before one verb and point to a student to respond. Repeat with other pictures and other students.

4. You may also use the audio or video programs to present the vocabulary.

Actividades

A. Answers: 1. El pez dorado no juega.   2. El perro juega.   3. El papagayo no juega.   4. El hámster juega.   5. El gato juega.

B. Answers: 1. c   2. b, e, f   3. b, e, g   4. d   5. e   6. c   7. e   8. a

---

Telling What My Pet Does

El perro ladra. Ladra y salta. Juega mucho.

El gato maúlla. El gato salta y juega mucho también.

El papagayo habla.

El pececillo nada en el pecero (acuario).

El canario canta en su jaula.

Actividades

A Tell if the following animals or pets play.

1. el pez dorado
2. el perro
3. el papagayo
4. el hámster
5. el gato

B Match the name of the animal with what it does.

1. un pájaro
2. un perro
3. un gato
4. un pez
5. un gerbo
6. un canario
7. un hámster
8. un papagayo

a. habla
b. salta
c. canta
d. nada
e. juega
f. ladra
g. maúlla

86   •   *Welcome to Spanish!*

C If you have a pet, bring a photograph of your pet to class or draw a picture. Tell your classmates about your pet in Spanish.

Cultura

Pets

Until recently, families living in the cities of Spain and Latin America tended not to have pets. Animals were considered better off on a farm. Today, however, many families are acquiring pets, particularly in the more wealthy metropolitan areas. *El perrito* is usually the preferred pet.

Every language has its imitations for animal sounds. In English, we say a dog goes "woof, woof" and a cat goes "meow." Let's see what the Spanish animals say:

el perro: "jau, jau"   el gallo: "quiquiriquí"

el gato: "miau, miau"   la oveja: "be, be"

la vaca: "mu, mu"

17 · Mi mascota • 87

C. Encourage students who don't have pets to talk about the pets of friends or relatives.

Cultura

Explain that keeping pets is just one example of the way North American culture influences the cultures of many people in Spain and Latin America.

el perro: "jau, jau"
   the dog: "bow-wow"

el gato: "miau, miau"
   the cat: "meow-meow"

la vaca: "mu, mu"
   the cow: "moo-moo"

el gallo: "quiquiriquí"
   the rooster: "cock-a-doodle-doo"

la oveja: "be, be"
   the sheep: "baa-baa"

ASSESS

Review the lesson and check student progress by using the following:

• 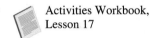 Activities Workbook, Lesson 17

CLOSE

Ask students to predict which pets are the most popular in class. Have students rank the pets from highest number to lowest number on a piece of paper and turn it over. Then write the names of the pets on the chalkboard and ask each student how many of each pet he or she has (for example, *dos gatos y un perro*). Have a student tally the results on the chalkboard. Finally, have students compare the ranking obtained with their predictions.

Expansion

Use a bilingual dictionary to teach the names of other animals to the class. You can also use a simple story in Spanish to reinforce the animal sounds in the lesson and those that other animals make.

Lesson 18

 Video

 Audio

 Transparencies

Workbook

FOCUS

Students will
- use the names of popular sports
- use the forms *juegas* and *juego* appropriately

TEACH

el fútbol soccer

el vólibol volleyball

el balón (inflated) ball

el béisbol baseball

el básquetbol (el baloncesto) basketball

el tenis tennis

la pelota ball

el jugador player

el equipo team

el campo field

la cancha field or court

—**Antonio, ¿juegas fútbol?** Antonio, do you play soccer?

—**Sí, juego fútbol.** Yes, I play soccer.

—**¿Juegas con el equipo de la escuela?** Do you play on the school team?

—**Sí, es un equipo muy bueno.** Yes, it's a very good team.

Vocabulary

Be sure students understand the difference between *el fútbol* (soccer) and *el fútbol americano* (football).

1. Point to each item on the overhead transparency as you name it. Repeat two or three times.

88

---

18 ◆ Los deportes

Sports

el campo

el equipo

el béisbol

el balón

el vólibol

el fútbol

la pelota

la cancha

el tenis

88 • *Welcome to Spanish!*

el jugador

la jugadora

el básquetbol, el baloncesto

—Antonio, ¿juegas fútbol?

—Sí, juego fútbol.

—¿Juegas con el equipo de la escuela?

—Sí, es un equipo muy bueno.

Actividades

A Write a list of the sports that you enjoy playing.

Juego...

Me gusta...

B Get a beach ball. One student throws the ball to another. The one who throws the ball asks a question with *¿Juegas...?* The one who catches the ball answers with *Sí, juego...* or *No, no juego...*

18 · Los deportes • 89

2. Point to each item as you name it, but pause before one as if you forgot its name. Signal to the class to respond chorally. Repeat with other items.

3. Point to each item as you name it, but pause before one and point to a student to respond. Repeat with other items and other students.

4. You may also use the audio or video programs to present the vocabulary.

Dialogue

1. Use the video or audio programs to present the dialogue. Point to the speaker as each line of the dialogue is heard. Or model the dialogue yourself, pointing to the appropriate speaker on the overhead transparency.

2. Model the dialogue with one of the more able students.

3. Have two students model the dialogue.

Actividades

A. Have students work in pairs and check each other's work.

B. If you don't have a beach ball, use another kind of soft ball or a bean bag.

   Note that *juego* can be used with or without *a. Juego fútbol* and *Juego al fútbol* are both acceptable.

C. Answers: 1. Sí, me interesan los deportes. (or) Sí, los deportes me interesan. Note that students can also answer in the negative with *no*.   2. Sí, me gustan mucho. (or) No, no me gustan mucho.   3. Me gusta más el ____. El ____ es mi deporte favorito.   4. Sí, juego con el equipo de la escuela. (or) No, no juego con el equipo.   5. Sí, el equipo es bueno.

D. Answers: 1. Mi deporte favorito es ____.   2. Sí, es un deporte de equipo. (or) No, no es un deporte de equipo.   3. Hay ____ jugadores en el equipo.   4. Sí, juego ____. (or) No, no juego ____.   5. Juego con ____.

E. To help students talk about the photo, ask them to ask a question about *el deporte, el jugador, el equipo,* and *los colores.*

Espanyol is the Catalan spelling for *Español.*

C **Answer the following personal questions.**

1. ¿Te interesan los deportes?
2. ¿Te gustan mucho?
3. ¿Qué deporte te gusta más? ¿Cuál es tu deporte favorito?
4. ¿Juegas con el equipo de la escuela?
5. ¿Es bueno el equipo?

D **Give the following information about your favorite sport.**

1. ¿Cuál es tu deporte favorito?
2. ¿Es un deporte de equipo?
3. ¿Cuántos jugadores hay en el equipo?
4. ¿Juegas ____?
5. ¿Juegas ____ con un balón o con una pelota?

E **Here's a photograph of a German team, "VFE Stuttgart" playing a Spanish team, "Espanyol" in Barcelona, Spain. Say as much about the photograph as you can.**

90   •   *Welcome to Spanish!*

Cultura

Sports in the Spanish-Speaking World

Sports are very popular in Spain and Latin America, particularly *fútbol*. However, it is not very common for schools to have organized sports teams. Competition between schools (intermural sports) is almost unheard of. Intramural sports are more popular. There are many local sports clubs which compete, mainly in *fútbol*. The *fútbol* played in Spain and Latin America is soccer, not American football.

Marathon, Mexico City

Field hockey team, Argentina

18 · *Los deportes* • 91

FOCUS

Students will

• use the names of common clothing items

TEACH

la camisa shirt
la camiseta T-shirt
el pantalón pants
un pantalón corto shorts
un pantalón largo long pants
el blue jean blue jeans
la sudadera sweatshirt
la chaqueta (el saco) jacket
la falda skirt
la blusa blouse
los zapatos shoes
los tenis tennis shoes
el gorro cap

Vocabulary

1. Point to each clothing item on the overhead transparency as you name it. Repeat two or three times.

2. Point to each clothing item as you name it, but pause before one as if you forgot its name. Signal to the class to respond chorally. Repeat with other clothing items.

3. Point to each clothing item as you name it, but pause before one and point to a student to respond. Repeat with other clothing items and other students.

4. You may also use the audio or video programs to present the vocabulary.

92

---

19 La ropa

Clothing

la camisa

**el pantalón,
un pantalón largo**

el gorro

la falda

los zapatos

la camiseta

la blusa

la sudadera

**la chaqueta,
el saco**

**un pantalón
corto**

los tenis

el blue jean

92   •   *Welcome to Spanish!*

Actividades

A **In Spanish, tell what you are wearing today.**

Llevo...

B **Talk about the dress code in your school. Use the following questions as a guide.**

1. ¿Llevan uniforme a la escuela los alumnos?
2. ¿Llevan blue jeans los muchachos y las muchachas?
3. ¿Llevan los alumnos una sudadera en la clase de educación física?
4. ¿Llevan los alumnos tenis a la escuela?

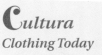

Lavandería
Laundry

HOTEL COLON
INTERNACIONAL

Cultura

Clothing Today

The clothing usually worn by young people today in many parts of Spain and Latin America is the same as the clothing you wear. But there are also many interesting and different local clothing styles worn for *fiestas*.

Mexico City, Mexico

Santiago, Chile

19 · La ropa • 93

Actividades

A. Tell students to use the indefinite articles (*un, una*) with the clothing items. For example, *Llevo una blusa y una falda.*

B. You can extend this activity by talking about another school that the students know about.

Cultura

Bring some pictures of both contemporary and traditional Latin American clothing to class. Stress that it is much more common to see clothing like the kind we wear both in the country and in the city. Ask students to supply examples of U.S. traditional clothing (cowboy outfits, American Indian regalia, Quaker clothing, Pilgrim clothing).

ASSESS

Review the lesson and check student progress by using the following:

• Ask students to tell what a person in a magazine or clothing catalogue is wearing.

• Activities Workbook, Lesson 19

CLOSE

Ask students to draw a boy or girl of the next century and to label the clothing and its color in Spanish.

Expansion

You might want to introduce these words to help your students describe clothing:

el abrigo overcoat
la bolsa purse
las botas boots
la bufanda scarf
los calcetines socks
los guantes gloves
las medias stockings
el traje suit
el vestido dress

Welcome to

French!

Nice, France

French, like Spanish, is a Romance language. It also comes from Latin. French is a beautiful language spoken on many continents of the world. It is also the second language of many people. To speak French is considered the sign of an educated person in many parts of the world.

French is spoken by some 125 million people. It is, of course, the official language of France. It is also the language of parts of Belgium and Switzerland, as well as the principality of Monaco. It is widely spoken in Algeria, Morocco, and Tunisia in North Africa. It is also the language used in many other parts of Africa: the Ivory Coast, Mali, Togo, the Democratic Republic of Congo, Senegal, Niger, and Mauritania. French is also spoken in Southeast Asia: Vietnam, Cambodia, Laos, as well as some of the Polynesian islands of the Pacific.

Closer to home, French is the language of Martinique, Guadeloupe, and Haiti in the Caribbean. It is also the language of Quebec, Canada. Because New England is so close to Quebec, there are many families of French Canadian background living in New England. The state of Louisiana received its name from the famous French king, Louis XIV. There is still much French influence in Louisiana.

Provence, France

Toulouse

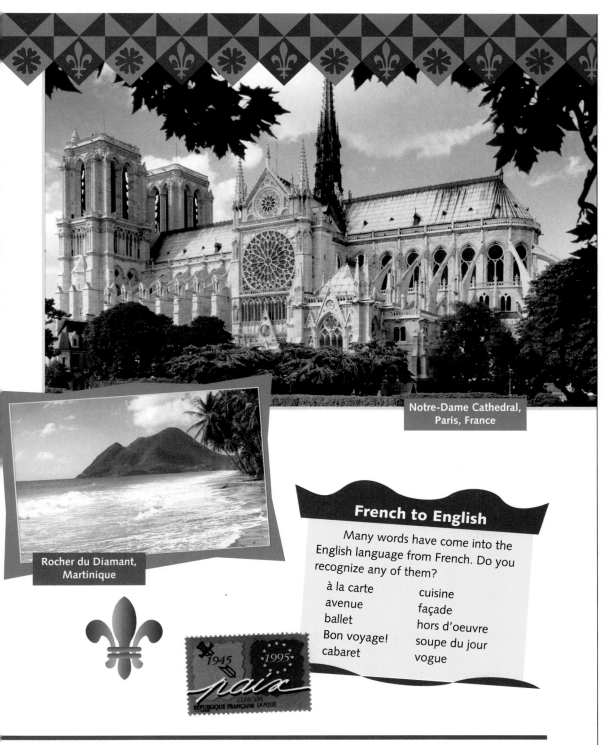

Notre-Dame Cathedral,
Paris, France

Rocher du Diamant,
Martinique

French to English

Many words have come into the English language from French. Do you recognize any of them?

à la carte	cuisine
avenue	façade
ballet	hors d'oeuvre
Bon voyage!	soupe du jour
cabaret	vogue

95

Lesson 1

- ◗◖ Video
- ▭ Audio
- ♟ Transparencies
- ▤ Workbook

FOCUS

Students will

- use and respond to greetings with peers
- use and respond to greetings with older people

TEACH

—Salut, Philippe. Hi, Philippe.

—Salut, Émilie. Ça va?
Hi, Émilie. How's it going?

—Ça va. Et toi? Okay. And you?

—Ça va bien, merci. It's going fine, thanks.

Dialogue

1. Use the video to present the dialogue. You may also use the audio program and overhead transparency to present it. Do not give the English translation.

2. Model the dialogue with one of the more able students.

3. Have two students model the dialogue.

4. Explain that French people often kiss each other on each cheek when greeting each other. This occurs most often between two females or between a male and a female. Males just shake hands. In some regions of France, a third kiss on the first cheek is common.

5. Refer to page 102 for a list of French names. Allow each student to choose one to use in class.

1 ◆ L*es salutations*

Greeting People

—Salut, Philippe.
—Salut, Émilie. Ça va?
—Ça va. Et toi?
—Ça va bien, merci.

In French-speaking countries, young people usually shake hands when they meet. Pretend that you are in France and shake hands with your classmates as you greet them.

96 • *Welcome to French!*

96

Activités

A Get up from your desk and walk around the classroom. Say "hi" in French to each classmate you meet. Don't forget to shake hands.

B Work in groups of two. Make up a little conversation in French. Greet each other and find out how things are going.

Bonjour is a more formal greeting than *salut*. You would say *bonjour* when greeting adults, for example. You would also use the person's title with *bonjour*:

> **Bonjour, Monsieur.**
> **Bonjour, Madame.**
> **Bonjour, Mademoiselle.**

In French, people say *Bonjour, Monsieur* or *Bonjour, Madame*. They do not use the person's name with the title. What do we say in English?

When you want to find out how things are going, you ask:

> **Ça va?**

There are many different responses to *Ça va?* Some common ones are:

> **Ça va, merci.**
> **Oui, ça va.**
> **Ça va bien, merci.**
> **Bien, merci.**
> **Pas mal. Et toi?**

Pont Alexandre, Paris, France

Do you know what this candy wrapper says?

1 · Les salutations • 97

A. If your furniture is movable, arrange it so that students can move about easily. Greet several students to get them started.

B. Have students change partners after each conversation so that each one has three or four conversations. Encourage the use of students' names and other variations.

Bonjour, Monsieur. Hello, Sir.

Bonjour, Madame. Hello, Ma'am.

Bonjour, Mademoiselle. Hello, Miss.

Ça va? How's it going?

Ça va, merci. Fine, thanks.

Oui, ça va. Fine.

Ça va bien, merci. It's going well, thanks.

Bien, merci. Quite well, thanks.

Pas mal. Et toi? Not bad. And you?

The numbers are presented in Lesson 4. You may, however, wish to introduce several numbers in each lesson.

> Lesson 1: 1–10
> Lesson 2: 11–20, 21–29
> Lesson 3: 30–100 by tens

Activités

A. After students greet their stick figures, ask them to move about the room and greet other students' stick figures. Remind them to use names and shake hands.

B. Have students count how many times people may kiss each others' cheek. Explain that this kiss is called *une bise* or *un bisou.*

ASSESS

Review the lesson and check student progress by using the following:

- Activities Workbook, Lesson 1

CLOSE

Ask students to prepare a brief conversation between two people who meet on the street. Have them illustrate it with pictures cut out from magazines.

Expansion

If you have students who speak French at home, ask them for additional responses to *Ça va?* Even if you don't have native speakers, you might want to introduce these:

Très bien, merci.   Very well, thanks.

Comme ci, comme ça.   So-so.

Ça boume!   It's going fine.

Activités

A   Draw and cut out five stick figures. Give each one a name. They will represent your friends, family, and teachers. Greet each of your stick figures properly in French.

B   Work with a classmate. Make up a conversation in French. Greet each other and find out how things are going. Then pretend one of you is a teacher and make the necessary changes.

C   Look at these photographs of people greeting each other in Lyon, France. Do they do some of the things we do when they greet each other? Do they do some things that are different? Explain.

2 *Au revoir*

Saying "Good-bye"

—Au revoir, Didier.
—Au revoir, Nathalie.

—Ciao, Christian.
—Ciao, Catherine.
À tout à l'heure!

FOCUS

Students will

• use and respond to leave-taking expressions

TEACH

—**Au revoir, Didier.** Good-bye, Didier.

—**Au revoir, Nathalie.** Good-bye, Nathalie.

—**Ciao, Christian.** Bye, Christian.

—**Ciao, Catherine. À tout à l'heure!** Bye, Catherine. See you soon!

Au revoir.   Good-bye.

À bientot. À tout à l'heure.
   See you later.

À demain.   Until tomorrow.

Ciao! Bye!

Dialogue

1. Use the video or audio programs to present the dialogue. Or model the two brief dialogues yourself, pointing to the appropriate speaker on the overhead transparency. Use appropriate gestures to indicate that you are ending an encounter.
2. Model the dialogues with one of the more able students.
3. Have two students model the dialogues.
4. *À tout à l'heure* is used only if you are going to see the person again the same day.

Activités

A. If your furniture is movable, arrange it so that students can move about easily.

B. Have students repeat the leave-takings with more than one friend if they can. Remind them that one person can say *Au revoir* and the other person can say *Ciao.*

C. Repeat this activity just before the end of class. Have students say *Au revoir, Monsieur/Madame/Mademoiselle* chorally and *Ciao* to another student.

Récapitulons!

—**Salut, Pierre.**   Hello, Pierre.

—**Salut, Martine. Ça va?** Hello, Martine. Are things going OK?

—**Oui, ça va. Et toi?**   Yes, all's well. And you?

—**Pas mal, merci.**   Not bad, thanks.

—**Ciao, Pierre.** Bye, Pierre.

—**Au revoir, Martine. À demain.**
   Good-bye, Martine. Until tomorrow.

100

The usual expression to use when saying "good-bye" to someone is:

Au revoir.

If you plan to see the person again quite soon, you can say:
À bientôt.
À tout à l'heure.

If you plan to see the person the next day, you can say:
À demain.
An informal way to say "good-bye" that you frequently hear is:
Ciao!

Ciao is an Italian expression that is used in several other European languages.

Activités

A Go over to a classmate. Say "so long" to him or her and then return to your seat. Don't forget to use his or her French name.

B Work with a friend in class. Say *ciao* to one another and let each other know that you'll be getting together again soon.

C Say "good-bye" to your teacher in French and then say "good-bye" to a friend. Use a different term with each person!

Récapitulons!

—Salut, Pierre.
   —Salut, Martine. Ça va?
—Oui, ça va. Et toi?
   —Pas mal, merci.
—Ciao, Pierre.
   —Au revoir, Martine. À demain.

Activités

A **Work with a friend. Speak French together. Have fun saying as much as you can to each other!**

B **Look at these photographs of people saying "good-bye" in Guadeloupe and France. Describe what the people are doing.**

1. Use the audio or video programs to model the dialogue.

2. Draw and label *Pierre* and *Martine* on the chalkboard. Model the review dialogue yourself, pointing to the appropriate speaker on the board.

3. Model the dialogues with one of the more able students, using his or her French name.

4. Have two students model the dialogues, using their French names.

Activités

A. Encourage students to use appropriate gestures, such as shaking hands, giving a *bise/bisou,* and waving. Have students change partners so that each one has three or four conversations.

B. Discuss leave-taking behaviors that are similar or different from ours.

Culture

On an ongoing basis, ask students to look through newspapers or weekly magazines to find articles relating to events and people in France or the French-speaking world.

ASSESS

Review the lesson and check student progress by using the following:

- Activities Workbook, Lesson 2

CLOSE

Ask students to add an ending to the conversation they prepared in the Close section, Lesson 1, by having the students say "good-bye" to each other.

Expansion

If you have collected many names of famous French people on the chalkboard, students may want to assume the identity of one of them for a brief period and engage in a conversation with another famous personality. Prepare name tags for each. Some names you may want to add to the list include:

Marie-Antoinette, Jeanne d'Arc, Brigitte Bardot, Simone de Beauvoir, Surya Bonaly, Coco Chanel, Marie Curie, Catherine Deneuve, Berthe Morisot, Empress Joséphine, Marie-José Perec, George Sand, Marguerite Yourcenar

Napoléon Bonaparte, Albert Camus, Philippe Candeloro, Pierre Cardin, Frédéric Chopin, Jacques-Yves Cousteau, Pierre Curie, Gérard Depardieu, Général de Gaulle, Victor Hugo, Jean-Claude Killy, François Mitterand, Claude Monet

Culture

Common First Names

The following are some common names for boys and girls in French.

Garçons

Alain, Albert, Bruno, Bernard, Charles, Christian, Denis, Éric, Eugène, François, Georges, Guy, Henri, Jean, Joseph, Louis, Marcel, Nicolas, Patrice, Paul, René, Richard, Sébastien, Serge, Thierry, Thomas, Victor, Xavier, Yves

Jeunes filles

Adèle, Anne, Bernadette, Brigitte, Catherine, Chantal, Danielle, Dominique, Émilie, Ève, Françoise, Gabrielle, Germaine, Hélène, Isabelle, Jacqueline, Jeanne, Lise, Louise, Marie, Nathalie, Pauline, Sara, Thérèse, Valérie

3 *En classe*

Identifying Classroom Objects

To find out what something is, you ask:
Qu'est-ce que c'est?

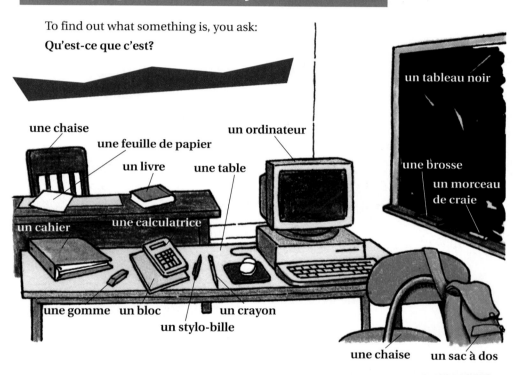

un tableau noir

une chaise
une feuille de papier
un livre
un ordinateur
une table
une brosse
un morceau de craie
un cahier
une calculatrice
une gomme   un bloc
un crayon
un stylo-bille
une chaise   un sac à dos

To ask for something in a polite way, you say:
Une feuille de papier, s'il vous plaît.

When speaking to a friend, however, you would say:
Une feuille de papier, s'il te plaît.

3 · En classe • 103

FOCUS

Students will
- use words for classroom objects
- request common classroom objects

TEACH

un stylo-bille ball-point pen
un crayon pencil
une brosse chalk eraser
une gomme pencil eraser
un cahier notebook
un bloc pad
un livre book
un morceau de craie piece of chalk
une feuille de papier sheet of paper
une calculatrice calculator
un ordinateur computer
un sac à dos backpack
une chaise chair
une table table
un tableau noir chalkboard

Une feuille de papier, s'il vous plaît. (Give me) a sheet of paper, please. (formal)
Une feuille de papier, s'il te plaît. (Give me) a sheet of paper, please. (informal)

Vocabulary

1. Use the video or audio programs to present the vocabulary.

103

2. Point to each classroom object on the overhead transparency as you say its name. Repeat this step with the actual objects which you have assembled beforehand.

3. Name each object again, but pause before one as if you forgot its name. Signal the class to say the name chorally. Repeat with another object.

4. Name each object again and pause before one, but this time point to a student to respond with the name of the object. Repeat three or four times with different students.

Activités

A. Answers: 1. Une calculatrice, s'il te plaît.   2. Une feuille de papier, s'il te plaît.   3. Un cahier, s'il te plaît.   4. Un livre, s'il te plaît.   5. Un crayon, s'il te plaît.   6. Un ordinateur, s'il te plaît.

B. Answers: Une calculatrice, s'il vous plaît.   2. Une feuille de papier, s'il vous plaît. 3. Un cahier, s'il vous plaît. 4. Un livre, s'il vous plaît. 5. Un crayon, s'il vous plaît. 6. Un ordinateur, s'il vous plaît.

Have students act out this *Activité*. Student 1 can say *Une feuille de papier, s'il te plaît.* Student 2 supplies the paper and says *Voilà* as he/she hands it to Student 1. Student 1 replies *merci.*

C. Answers: 1. un morceau de craie 2. un sac à dos   3. une calculatrice   4. une chaise

Activités

A Ask a classmate for the following items in French. Don't forget to ask politely!

1.
2.
3.
4.
5.
6.

B Look again at the drawings in Activité A. Pretend you are the student and ask your teacher for what you need. Be polite!

C Look at each picture below and say in French what each person needs.

1.
2.

3.

4.

D Point out a classroom object and ask a classmate what it is.

*C*ulture

Schools in France

In France, a middle school is called *un collège*. Students attend *un collège* for four years. They then go on to high school, *un lycée*. The last year of high school is called *la terminale*. At the end of *la terminale*, students take a very difficult exam called *le baccalauréat*. Students call it *le bac*. A student who passes *le bac* can enter any university in France.

Lycée Mignet,
Aix-en-Provence, France

3 · En classe • 105

Explain that French students have a much longer school day than we do in the U.S., often from 8:00 until 5:00 in the afternoon (sometimes 5:30 in high schools). French students also have school Saturday mornings, but schools are generally closed on Wednesday afternoons. There are many fewer extra curricular activities in a French school than in a U.S. school.

ASSESS

Review the lesson and check student progress by using the following:

- Activities Workbook, Lesson 3

CLOSE

Ask students for a list of the items from the lesson vocabulary that they have in their desks or in their backpacks.

Expansion

Ask a small group to locate and cut out pictures of classroom objects from old magazines. Prepare labels for them and attach them to the pictures. Mount the pictures on a poster or bulletin board for reference. With the computer and larger classroom furniture, you may want to attach the labels directly to the objects. You may want to add these items to the objects to be labeled:

un bureau a teacher's desk
un drapeau a flag
une fenêtre a window
une porte a door
un mur a wall
une carte a map

Lesson 4

- Video
- Audio
- Transparencies
- Workbook

FOCUS

Students will
- use and respond to the words for numbers 1 to 1,000
- ask and respond to a request for the price of something

TEACH

Vocabulary

You might want to teach these numbers in smaller groups. Logical places to break are 1–20, 21–69, 70–100, 101–1,000.

Note that the French for "zero" is *zéro*.

(See Note in Lesson 1.) It is recommended that you teach the numbers in smaller groups presenting one or two groupings as you do each lesson.

You might also have students figure out how to arrive at the French numbers for 71–99 (using addition and multiplication).

1. Point to each number on the overhead transparency as you say its name.

2. Point to each number in random order on the overhead transparency as you say its name.

3. Point to each number in order, but pause before one as if you forgot its name. Signal the class to say the number chorally. Repeat with a pause before another number.

 4 **L***es nombres*

Counting in French

1	un	21	vingt et un	40	quarante
2	deux	22	vingt-deux	50	cinquante
3	trois	23	vingt-trois	60	soixante
4	quatre	24	vingt-quatre	70	soixante-dix
5	cinq	25	vingt-cinq	80	quatre-vingts
6	six	26	vingt-six	90	quatre-vingt-dix
7	sept	27	vingt-sept		
8	huit	28	vingt-huit	100	cent
9	neuf	29	vingt-neuf	200	deux cents
10	dix	30	trente	300	trois cents
				400	quatre cents
11	onze	31	trente et un	500	cinq cents
12	douze	32	trente-deux	600	six cents
13	treize	33	trente-trois	700	sept cents
14	quatorze	34	trente-quatre	800	huit cents
15	quinze	35	trente-cinq	900	neuf cents
16	seize	36	trente-six	1.000	mille
17	dix-sept	37	trente-sept		
18	dix-huit	38	trente-huit		
19	dix-neuf	39	trente-neuf		
20	vingt				

Activités

A Your teacher will write some numbers on the chalkboard. Then he or she will call out the number in French and ask a student to circle the correct number.

B Work with a classmate. One of you will count from 30 to 40. The other will count from 70 to 80.

C Have a contest with a friend. See who can count the fastest from 1 to 100 by tens.

D Have a contest with a friend. See who can count the fastest from 100 to 1000 by hundreds.

Finding Out the Price

To find out how much something costs, you ask:

—S'il vous plaît, Madame.
C'est combien le stylo-bille?

—Huit euros.

—Merci, Madame.

Note the following differences when writing numbers in English and French:

anglais	français
24.90	24,90
1,000	1.000
2:40	2^h40

---

4. Point to each number in random order and pause before one, but this time call on a student to respond with the number. Repeat three or four times with different students.

5. Or use the audio or video programs to present the vocabulary.

It is recommended that you not make students write out the numbers since this is seldom necessary in real-life situations. The spelling of French numbers also presents unnecessary problems for the introductory student. *Cent* and *vingt* do take an -*s* when no number follows: *deux cents, quatre-vingts.* When followed by another number, the -*s* is dropped:

**deux cents   deux cent un
quatre-vingts quatre-vingt-dix**

Mille never takes an -*s:*

mille   deux mille

Activités

A. You can also have students call out the numbers and ask the rest of the students to circle them.

B. Repeat this activity with the numbers 20–30, 40–50, 50–60, 60–70, 80–90, and 90–100.

C. Have students time each other with either a classroom clock or a wristwatch with a second hand.

D. Have students time each other with a classroom clock or a wristwatch with a second hand.

Finding Out the Price

—**S'il vous plaît, Madame. C'est combien le stylo-bille?** Please, Ma'am. How much is the ballpoint pen?

—**Huit euros.** Eight euros.

—**Merci, Madame.** Thank you, Ma'am.

1. Model the dialogue yourself, pointing to the appropriate speaker on the overhead transparency. Use props to make the dialogue more realistic.

2. Model the dialogue with one of the more able students.

3. Have two students model the dialogue.

4. Or use the audio or video programs to model the dialogue.

Activité

A. Extend the exercise by putting price tags on all the classroom objects from Lesson 3.

Sample answer:

—**S'il vous plaît, Madame/ Monsieur/Mademoiselle. C'est combien le cahier?**

—**Cinq euros.**

—**Merci, Madame/Monsieur/ Mademoiselle.**

Prices

la calculatrice: quatre euros
la gomme: un euro
le stylo-bille: deux euros
le crayon: un euro
le sac à dos: vingt-cinq euros

Activité

A Work with a classmate. One of you will be the customer and the other will be the clerk at a stationery store. Make up a conversation to buy the following things.

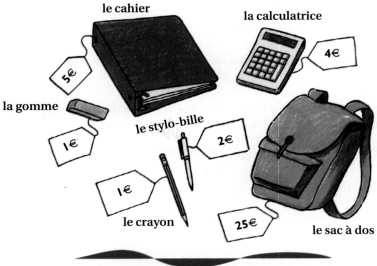

le cahier
la calculatrice
la gomme
le stylo-bille
le crayon
le sac à dos

Culture

French Money

The monetary unit in France is the euro.

108 • *Welcome to French!*

Activité

A Give the price of each item from the clothing store ad.

REVUE DE DETAILS
NEWS MODE Repéré aux quatre coins de la mode, tout ce qui nous plaît. De la tête aux pieds.

Coloris: noir, beige.
Tailles: du 36 au 40 pour la femme; du 40 au 45 pour l'homme.

modèle femme du 36 au 40	76,00 €
modèle homme du 40 au 45	76,00 €

l'une 15,00 €

Chemise 77% viscose, 23% polyester. Coloris assortis. Du 37/38 au 43/44.

l'une 15,00 €

Cravate 100% soie. Coloris assortis.

(1) Robe en velours (150 €, 5 tailles, 8 coloris).
(2) Veste sur jupe en taffetas de soie (75 €, 3 tailles, 5 coloris (veste) et 150 €, du 36 au 42, en noir ou bronze (jupe)).

1. une chemise
2. une cravate
3. les sandales

4. deux robes
5. trois cravates

Activité

A. Answers: 1. 15,00€ 2. 15,00€
   3. 76,00€ 4. 300,00€
   5. 45,00€

ASSESS

Review the lesson and check student progress by using the following:

- Activité A, Counting
- Activité A, Finding Out the Price
- Activities Workbook, Lesson 4

CLOSE

In small groups, ask students to identify the number of:

- numerals 1 on a one-dollar bill
- words "one" on a one-dollar bill

Expansion

In small groups, have students do the following calculation in French:

- Take the number of students in the classroom.
- Subtract the number of Mondays in the current month.
- Add the number of students absent that day.
- Subtract the number of legs a spider has. (eight)
- Add the number of players on a baseball team. (nine)
- Subtract the number of digits in their telephone numbers (without the area code). (seven)

Compare the results that the groups got.

Lesson 5

 Video

 Audio

 Transparencies

 Workbook

FOCUS

Students will

• request common foods and drinks in a restaurant setting

• ask and respond to a request for the cost of common foods and drinks

TEACH

—**Bonjour. Deux cocas, s'il vous plaît.** Hello. (I would like) two sodas, please.

(The server brings the order.)
—**Merci.** Thank-you.
—**Je vous en prie.** You're welcome.

5 La politesse

Speaking Politely

—Bonjour. Deux cocas, s'il vous plaît.

(The server brings the order.)
—Merci.
 —Je vous en prie.

110 • *Welcome to French!*

110

(*A little later.*)
　　—C'est combien, s'il vous plaît?
—Trois euros.

In addition to *je vous en prie,* other ways to express "you're welcome" are:

De rien.

Il n'y a pas de quoi.

In French there is a difference between formal and informal speech. When you are speaking with someone you know well or someone your own age, you would say:

S'il te plaît.

Je t'en prie.

(*A little later.*)
—**C'est combien, s'il vous plaît?**
　How much is it, please?
—**Trois euros.** Three euros.

De rien. You're welcome.

Il n'y a pas de quoi. You're welcome.

S'il te plaît. Please.

Je t'en prie. You're welcome.

Dialogue

1. Use the video or audio programs to present the dialogue. Point to the speaker as each line of the dialogue is heard. Or model the dialogue yourself, pointing to the appropriate speaker on the overhead transparency.

2. Model the dialogue with one of the more able students.

3. Have two students model the dialogue.

With an adult or someone that you have just met, however, you would say:

S'il vous plaît.

Je vous en prie.

Activités

A With a friend, practice reading the conversation on pages 110–111 aloud.

B You are at a café in the village of St. Rémy de Provence, France. Order the following things. Ask a classmate to be the server.

1. un sandwich

2. un thé

3. un coca

4. une limonade

5. une salade

C You would like to order the following foods at a French restaurant. Be polite when you order them!

C. Answers: 1. Un steak, s'il vous plaît.   2. Trois crêpes, s'il vous plaît.   3. Une tarte aux fruits, s'il vous plaît.   4. Une soupe à l'oignon, s'il vous plaît. 5. Une omelette, s'il vous plaît.

Encourage students to use the alternative expressions for "thank you" and "you're welcome."

un steak

trois crêpes

une tarte aux fruits

une soupe à l'oignon

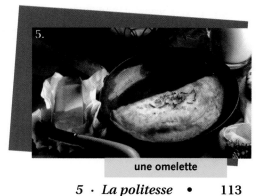

une omelette

5 · La politesse • 113

113

D. Note the popularity of soft drinks in French culture.

Culture

Bring in pictures of staple foods from all over the French-speaking world. Students may also be able to contribute pictures from the library and old magazines from home. Post the pictures around a world map and have students link each picture to the part of the world where the crop is grown or the food dish is typically eaten.

ASSESS

Review the lesson and check student progress by using the following:

• Give students the basic dialogue with some words omitted and ask them to fill in the blanks.

•   Activities Workbook, Lesson 5

CLOSE

Give students the sentences of the basic dialogue in the wrong order. Ask them to put them or copy them in an order that makes sense. There is more than one correct order. For example, someone could ask the cost before ordering a soda.

D Look at this photograph of French-speaking teenagers from Canada enjoying a snack together. Describe what you see.

*C*ulture

"Fast Food" in Paris

In Paris there are many restaurants that cater to students. These restaurants serve good food at reasonable prices. Many are ethnic restaurants serving Greek, Italian, North African, or Middle Eastern food.

If you are really in a hurry, there are little sandwich and pastry shops where you can get a quick snack and eat on the run. There are also little carts on the street where you can buy a packaged sandwich or salad.

114 • *Welcome to French!*

114

Le temps des semailles

RESTAURANT

15, rue Brueys
AIX EN PROVENCE
TEL.
FAX. 42.38.38.62

RESTAURANT
VIÊT-NAM
Spécialités
Vietnamiennes et Chinoises
98, Avenue De Lattre de Tassigny
(Ex. Avenue de la Gare)
04100 MANOSQUE

5 · *La politesse* • 115

Lesson 6

- Video
- Audio
- Transparencies
- Workbook

FOCUS

Students will
- ask and respond to requests for the time
- give the time of events

TEACH

Il est quelle heure? What time is it?

Pardon, vous avez l'heure? Excuse me, do you have the time?

Il est une heure. It is one o'clock.

Il est deux heures. It is two o'clock.

Il est trois heures. It is three o'clock.

Il est quatre heures. It is four o'clock.

Il est cinq heures. It is five o'clock.

Il est six heures. It is six o'clock.

Il est sept heures. It is seven o'clock.

Il est huit heures. It is eight o'clock.

Il est neuf heures. It is nine o'clock.

Il est dix heures. It is ten o'clock.

Il est onze heures. It is eleven o'clock.

Il est douze heures. It is twelve o'clock.

116

6 ◆ L'heure

Telling Time

To find out the time, you ask:

Il est quelle heure?

Pardon, vous avez l'heure?

To tell the time, you say:

Il est une heure.	Il est deux heures.	Il est trois heures.	Il est quatre heures.

Il est cinq heures.	Il est six heures.	Il est sept heures.	Il est huit heures.

Il est neuf heures.	Il est dix heures.	Il est onze heures.	Il est douze heures.

Il est une heure cinq.

Il est deux heures dix.

Il est cinq heures quarante.

Il est six heures quinze.

Il est sept heures et demie. Il est sept heures trente.

Activités

A Give the following times.

6 · *L'heure* • 117

Il est une heure cinq. It is 1:05.

Il est deux heures dix. It is 2:10.

Il est cinq heures quarante.
It is 5:40.

Il est six heures quinze. It is 6:15.

Il est sept heures et demie.
It is 7:30.

Because of the popularity of digital clocks, it is becoming more common to tell time based on sixty minutes—*Il est six heures quarante.* For introductory purposes, we have not presented the other options for telling time. You may, however, wish to teach the alternative—*Il est sept heures moins vingt.*

Il est cinq heures quinze.

Il est cinq heures et quart.

Il est cinq heures quarante-cinq.

Il est six heures moins quinze.

Il est six heures moins le quart.

Dialogue/ Vocabulary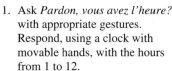

1. Ask *Pardon, vous avez l'heure?* with appropriate gestures. Respond, using a clock with movable hands, with the hours from 1 to 12.

2. Using the clock, repeat the hours from 1 to 12. However, pause before one hour and signal the class to respond chorally. Repeat this step with several other hours.

3. Using the clock, repeat the hours from 1 to 12. Pause before one hour and point to a student to respond. Repeat this step with other hours and other students. Repeat this procedure to practice giving the minutes after the hour.

4. You may also present these times with the audio or video programs. Or you may use the overhead transparency.

Activités

A. Answers: 1. Il est dix heures quinze. 2. Il est cinq heures dix. 3. Il est huit heures douze. 4. Il est deux heures quinze. 5. Il est neuf heures.

117

B. Students can use homemade clocks to ask and answer questions about the time, or draw them on the chalkboard. Have students use *Il est quelle heure?*

Telling At What Time

La classe est *à* neuf heures et demie. The class begins *at 9:30.*

La classe est *à* quelle heure? At what time is the class?

À dix-huit heures At 18:00 (6:00 P.M.)

À vingt heures quarante At 20:40 (8:40)

Teach students that in France (and much of Europe), the 24-hour clock is used in schedules and most official capacities. To convert from the 12-hour to the 24-hour clock, add 12 for each hour after noon. Thus, 1:00 P.M. is 13.00.

B Walk up to a classmate and ask for the time. Your classmate will answer you.

Telling at What Time

To ask and tell at what time something takes place, you say:

La classe est *à* quelle heure?

La classe est *à* neuf heures et demie.

In France, it is common to use the 24-hour clock for formal activities such as reservations, train and plane departures.

À dix-huit heures (18h00)

À vingt heures quarante (20h40)

118 • *Welcome to French!*

118

Activités

A Tell at what time you have the following classes. You will note that these words are cognates. They are similar in both French and English.

1. le cours de maths
2. le cours d'histoire
3. le cours de gymnastique
4. le cours de sciences
5. le cours d'anglais

B Draw pictures of some of your daily activities such as getting up in the morning, eating breakfast, walking or riding the bus to school, going to afternoon sports, eating dinner, going to bed, etc. Then compare your pictures with those of a classmate. Tell at what time each of you does the particular activity. Keep track of how many activities both of you do at the same time.

Culture

Time Zones

It's not the same time in all the countries of the French-speaking world. French is the official or second language in countries that stretch over many different time zones.

Quebec, Canada

Activités

A. If your students aren't taking the subjects given, substitute subjects they are taking.

B. Some students may benefit from adding a clock that shows the time they do the activities in the drawing. You may want to teach the following expressions:

du matin in the morning

de l'après-midi in the afternoon

du soir in the evening

Culture

Use a world map to point out the far-reaching influence of French culture. In Europe, French is an official language in France (including Corsica), Belgium, Luxembourg, Monaco, and Switzerland. In Africa, French is the first or second language in Senegal, Mali, Niger, French Guinea, Burkina-Faso, Ivory Coast, Togo, Benin, Cameroon, Congo, Democratic Republic of Congo, Central African Republic, Mauritania, Chad, Djibouti, and the islands Madagascar, Reunion, Mayotte, Comores, and Seychelles. In the South Pacific are Tahiti, Wallis-and-Futuna, Vanuatu, and New Caledonia. Southeast Asia still retains much French influence in Vietnam, Laos, and Cambodia. In the Americas, French is spoken in Quebec province, Haiti, Guadeloupe, Martinique, French Guyana, and has considerable cultural influence in Maine, Vermont, and Louisiana.

Review the lesson and check student progress by using the following:

- Asking students the time at random throughout the class period.

- 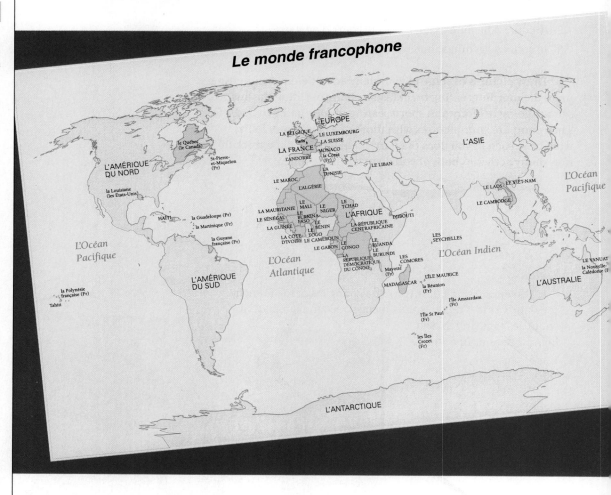 Activities Workbook, Lesson 6

CLOSE

Using a weekly television guide from a newspaper, have your students make a TV-watching schedule for the weekend. Limit it to a total of five or six hours. Have them list the time and the programs using the 24-hour clock.

Expansion

You may want to teach your students another way to say the number of minutes after the hour.

- 9:40 **Il est dix heures moins vingt.**

- 9:45 **Il est dix heures moins le quart** (minus a quarter).

- 9:50 **Il est dix heures moins dix.**

During the 19th century, French colonies extended from Asia to the Americas. The French language is still widely spoken in many of these ex-colonies of France.

Le monde francophone

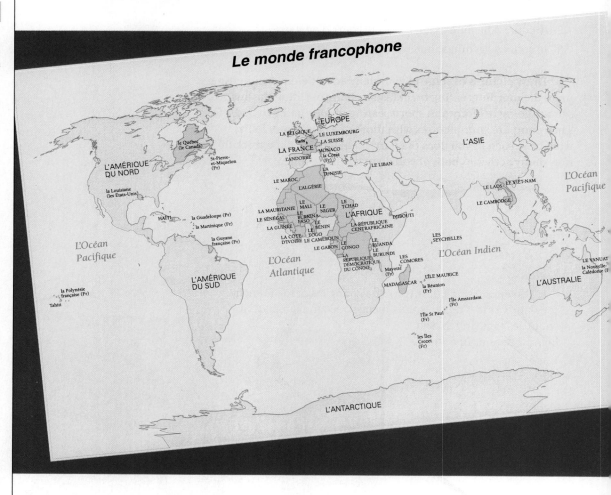

120 • *Welcome to French!*

7 **L** *es couleurs*

Identifying Colors

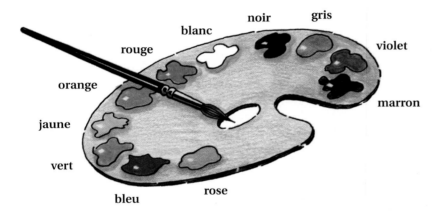

noir gris
blanc
rouge violet
orange
marron
jaune
vert
rose
bleu

Activités

A **Give the following information in French.**

1. your favorite color
2. your least favorite color
3. the colors you like for clothes
4. the color of an apple

Les îles de la Madeleine, Canada

7 · *Les couleurs* • 121

 Video

 Audio

Transparencies

Workbook

FOCUS

Students will

- use and respond to the names of colors

TEACH

bleu blue
vert green
jaune yellow
orange orange
rouge red
rose pink
blanc white
noir black
gris gray
violet purple
marron brown

Vocabulary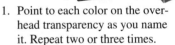

1. Point to each color on the overhead transparency as you name it. Repeat two or three times.
2. Point to each color as you name it, but pause before one as if you forgot it. Signal to the class to respond chorally.
3. Point to each color as you name it, but pause before one and point to a student to respond.
4. You may also use the audio or video programs to present the vocabulary.

Note that no activities with colors are given in this lesson that would necessitate students knowing how to make the adjective agree with the noun.

121

Activités

A. As each student announces his or her favorite color, have one student keep track of all the preferences on a chart. Using French numbers, announce how many students like each color. Do the same for the least favorite colors. To say the colors you like or don't like, say *J'aime le noir.* (I like black) or *Je déteste le vert.* (I hate green).

B. Have students use markers or colored pencils if crayons are unavailable.

Culture

1. Explain that a former Paris train station, the gare d'Orsay, has been transformed into a museum featuring the impressionists. It includes not only paintings but sculptures as well.

2. Bring in pictures of other famous impressionists: Edgar Degas, Edouard Manet, Paul Gauguin, Camille Pissarro, Paul Cézanne, Gustave Caillebotte, Albert Sisley, Eugène Boudin. You can often find calendars that are dedicated to their works.

ASSESS

Review the lesson and check student progress by using the following:

• Point to the various colors on the flag and on posters and ask, *C'est quelle couleur?*

• Activities Workbook, Lesson 7

CLOSE

Have students design a school uniform for a girl or for a boy. Have them draw a girl or boy in the uniform and label the colors in French. You may prefer to have students design a band uniform or an athletic team uniform.

B **Draw a classmate. Use crayons to color his or her clothing. Say what colors he or she is wearing in French.**

Culture

French Impressionism

Impressionism is a style of painting that started in France during the 1860s. Two leaders of this famous movement were Claude Monet and Pierre Renoir.

The impressionists took their easels, brushes, and paints outdoors to paint rather than work in a studio. They stressed the effects of sunlight on the subject they were painting. They used quick, short brushstrokes and bright colors. This gave the effect of small dabs or dots of paint on the canvas. When you look at an impressionist painting from a distance, these dabs of color blend together and create a beautiful effect.

Look at these paintings by Claude Monet and Berthe Morisot, another French impressionist painter. Tell the colors they use in French.

"The Sisters," 1869
Berthe Morisot

"Banks of the Seine,
Vétheuil," 1880
Claude Monet

122 • *Welcome to French!*

122

Les jours de la semaine

Telling the Days of the Week

To find out the day, you ask:
—C'est quel jour (aujourd'hui)?
(ou) Quel jour est-ce?

To answer, you say:
—C'est lundi.
(ou) Aujourd'hui c'est lundi.
—Et demain?
—Demain, c'est mardi.

8 · *Les jours de la semaine* • 123

Lesson 8

	Video
	Audio
	Transparencies
	Workbook

FOCUS

Students will

- use the names of the days of the week
- ask and respond to questions about the current day

TEACH

lundi Monday
mardi Tuesday
mercredi Wednesday
jeudi Thursday
vendredi Friday
samedi Saturday
dimanche Sunday

—**C'est quel jour (aujourd'hui)?**
What day is today?

Quel jour est-ce? What day is it?

—**C'est lundi.** It's Monday.

Aujourd'hui c'est lundi. Today is Monday.

—**Et demain?** Tomorrow?

—**Demain, c'est mardi.**
Tomorrow is Tuesday.

Vocabulary/
Dialogue

1. Point to each day of the week on the overhead transparency as you name it. Repeat two or three times.

2. Point to each day as you name it, but pause before one as if you forgot it. Signal to the class to respond chorally. Repeat with other days.

3. Point to each day as you name it, but pause before one and call on a student by name to name the day.

123

Activités

A. Answers: 1. Aujourd'hui c'est
_____. 2. Demain c'est
_____. 3. samedi, dimanche

B. Ask students if they know on
what day of the week they
were born.

Culture

Discuss whether students would
rather attend school on Saturday
and have more holidays or not.

Expansion

Choose a French-speaking country
and have students research its holidays. Good sources of information
are the library, on-line resources,
people who have lived in the country, and its embassy or consulate.
Have students list the holidays and
compare them with the holidays we
celebrate in the United States.

Activités

A **Answer the following questions in French.**

1. C'est quel jour aujourd'hui?
2. Et demain? C'est quel jour?
3. Quels sont les jours de la fin de semaine (du weekend)?

B **Work with a partner. One person says a day of the week, the other responds with the next day. Then do just the opposite. One person says the name of the day and the other partner gives the day before it.**

Lycée Mignet
Aix-en-Provence, France

Culture

The French Calendar

The first day of the week on a French calendar is *lundi* and the last day of the week is *dimanche*. How does this compare with American calendars? In France, schools are in session on Saturday mornings. Most schools, how-ever, do not have classes on Wednesday afternoon.

  LE MENU DE LA SEMAINE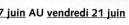

DU <u>lundi 17 juin</u> AU <u>vendredi 21 juin</u>

LUNDI 17
Maquereux à la moutarde
Cordon bleu
Petits pois à la française
Fromage
Pêche

MARDI 18
Pamplemousse / Sucre
Sauté de bœuf
Pâtes au gruyère
Compote

MERCREDI 19
Tomates mayonnaise
Vol au vent aux fruits
  de mer
Riz au gruyère
Fraises chantilly

JEUDI 20
Salade verte
Jambon
Raviolis
Glace

VENDREDI 21
Salade Niçoise
Poulet rôti aux herbes
Haricots verts au beur
Fromage
Fruit

124 • *Welcome to French!*

Les mois et les saisons

Video

Audio

Transparencies

Workbook

Telling the Months

JANVIER	FÉVRIER	MARS	AVRIL	MAI	JUIN
1 2 3 4 5 6 7 8 9 10 11 12 13 14 15 16 17 18 19 20 21 22 23 24 25 26 27 28 29 30 31	1 2 3 4 5 6 7 8 9 10 11 12 13 14 15 16 17 18 19 20 21 22 23 24 25 26 27 28	1 2 3 4 5 6 7 8 9 10 11 12 13 14 15 16 17 18 19 20 21 22 23 24 25 26 27 28 29 30 31	1 2 3 4 5 6 7 8 9 10 11 12 13 14 15 16 17 18 19 20 21 22 23 24 25 26 27 28 29 30	1 2 3 4 5 6 7 8 9 10 11 12 13 14 15 16 17 18 19 20 21 22 23 24 25 26 27 28 29 30 31	1 2 3 4 5 6 7 8 9 10 11 12 13 14 15 16 17 18 19 20 21 22 23 24 25 26 27 28 29 30
JUILLET	AOÛT	SEPTEMBRE	OCTOBRE	NOVEMBRE	DÉCEMBRE
1 2 3 4 5 6 7 8 9 10 11 12 13 14 15 16 17 18 19 20 21 22 23 24 25 26 27 28 29 30 31	1 2 3 4 5 6 7 8 9 10 11 12 13 14 15 16 17 18 19 20 21 22 23 24 25 26 27 28 29 30 31	1 2 3 4 5 6 7 8 9 10 11 12 13 14 15 16 17 18 19 20 21 22 23 24 25 26 27 28 29 30	1 2 3 4 5 6 7 8 9 10 11 12 13 14 15 16 17 18 19 20 21 22 23 24 25 26 27 28 29 30 31	1 2 3 4 5 6 7 8 9 10 11 12 13 14 15 16 17 18 19 20 21 22 23 24 25 26 27 28 29 30	1 2 3 4 5 6 7 8 9 10 11 12 13 14 15 16 17 18 19 20 21 22 23 24 25 26 27 28 29 30 31

Telling the Seasons

au printemps

en été

FOCUS

Students will

- use the names of the months of the year and the seasons
- ask and respond to requests for the date

TEACH

janvier January

février February

mars March

avril April

mai May

juin June

juillet July

août August

septembre September

octobre October

novembre November

décembre December

au printemps in the spring

en été in the summer

en automne in the fall/autumn

en hiver in the winter

Vocabulary

1. Point to each month on the overhead transparency as you name it. Repeat two or three times.

2. Point to each month as you name it, but pause before one as if you forgot it. Signal to the class to respond chorally. Repeat with other months. Repeat two or three times.

3. Point to each month as you name it, but pause before one and call on a student by name to name the month. Repeat two or three times. Repeat this procedure with the seasons.

4. You may also present the vocabulary with the audio or video programs.

Finding Out and Giving the Date

—Quelle est la date aujourd'hui? What is today's date?

—Le premier avril. April 1st.

1. Model the brief dialogue yourself, using a calendar.

2. Model the dialogue with one of your more able students.

3. Have two students model the dialogue.

Activités

A. Students may want to work in small groups to produce a calendar. Post the finished calendars in the classroom.

B. To make it easier to tally the birthdays, write the months on the chalkboard and assign a student to make a mark as each birthday is announced. If you want, another student can tally the dates for each birthday.

en automne

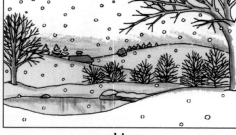

en hiver

Finding Out and Giving the Date

—Quelle est la date aujourd'hui?
—Le premier avril.

Premier is used for the first of the month. For the other days, *deux, trois, quatre* are used. For example, *le trois juin.*

Activités

A Draw your own French calendar. Label correctly all the months and days of the week. Do it in the French style.

B Each of you will stand up in class and give your birthday. Listen and keep a record of how many of you were born in each month.

C Based on the information from *Activité B*, tell in French in which month most of the students in the class were born. Tell in which month the fewest were born.

D In which season of the year is ... ?

1. janvier
2. mai
3. août
4. novembre

Bon anniversaire!

Culture

Vacation Time in France

The month of August is vacation month in France—*les grandes vacances*. Almost all businesses close for the entire month and people leave the cities for the beaches and mountains. Paris and the other major French cities are deserted in August.

Study the photograph on the left. You will see that the beautiful beach at Nice is not sandy. It has stones which are called *galets*.

9 · *Les mois et les saisons* • 127

C. For the reporting, you may want to teach this sentence: *Il y a (cinq) anniversaires en (janvier)*.

D. Answers: 1. en hiver
2. au printemps 3. en été
4. en automne

Culture

Have students interview someone they know who is French or has lived in a French-speaking country for some time and report to the class on how a French holiday is celebrated.

ASSESS

Review the lesson and check student progress by using the following:

• Activities Workbook, Lesson 9

CLOSE

Ask students to write the month in French that these American holidays occur in:

• Christmas/Hanukah
• Halloween
• Presidents' Day
• Mother's Day
• Thanksgiving
• Father's Day

Expansion

Celebrate the next French holiday. Have students decorate the classroom. You may want to play music and even serve special food if it is feasible.

Lesson 10

- Video
- Audio
- Transparencies
- Workbook

FOCUS

Students will

- use some common weather expressions

TEACH

Quel temps fait-il aujourd'hui?
What's the weather like today?

Il fait très beau. It's beautiful.
Il y a du soleil. It's sunny.

Il fait mauvais. It's bad weather.
Il pleut. It's raining.

10 Le temps

Describing the Weather

—Quel temps fait-il aujourd'hui?
—Il fait très beau.
  Il y a du soleil.

—Il fait mauvais.
  Il pleut.

128 • *Welcome to French!*

128

Il y a du vent.

Il fait chaud.

Il neige.

Il fait froid.

Activités

A **Tell in French what the weather is like today.**

B **Work in groups of four. Write in French the name of each season on a separate sheet of paper. Put the papers in a pile. Each of you will pull one sheet from the pile and describe the weather of the season written on the sheet.**

C **Draw a picture of your favorite type of weather. Then describe your picture to the class in French.**

METEO LOISIRS
WEEK-END • VACANCES • SPORTS • RANDONNÉE
Par téléphone
Composez le code minéralogique du département désiré
36 68 02
Par minitel
3615
METEO
METEO FRANCE

Do you know what information this card provides?

Il y a du vent. It's windy.

Il neige. It's snowing.

Il fait chaud. It's hot.

Il fait froid. It's cold.

Vocabulary

1. Look out the window and gesture as you ask *Quel temps fait-il aujourd'hui?*
2. Point to each picture on the overhead transparency as you give the weather expression associated with it. (Point to the sunny weather for *Il fait très beau;* point to the rain, wind, snow for *Il fait mauvais.*) Repeat two or three times.
3. Point to each picture as you say the weather expression, but pause before one as if you forgot it. Signal to the class to respond chorally. Repeat with other pictures.
4. Point to each picture as you say the weather expression, but pause before one and point to a student to describe the weather. Repeat two or three times.
5. You may also present the vocabulary with the audio or video programs.

Activités

A. Have students work in pairs to ask and give information about the weather.

B. You may want to have students describe the weather orally in class and write it for homework.

C. Have students describe their picture in small groups for more efficient individual practice.

Culture

Ask students what they think about *les classes de neige.* Could this type of experience happen in the United States? Why or why not?

ASSESS

Review the lesson and check student progress by using the following:

- Ask students to pretend that it is yesterday to give the weather.
- Activities Workbook, Lesson 10

CLOSE

Give students a few cities and months or seasons and ask them to describe the weather there:

- Orlando, *en été*
- Chicago, *en automne*
- Buffalo, *en hiver*
- Seattle, *en avril*
- Los Angeles, *en juillet*
- Boston, *en mai*

Expansion

A. Ask students to keep a weather calendar for one week. Use the vocabulary in Lessons 8 and 9 to make the calendar with large boxes for days. Appoint a different group each day to make weather observations and write them on the calendar.

B. Look in the newspaper to find out the weather in certain French-speaking cities. Then let the students work in small groups to put together a short weather report for several cities.

   You can also get weather information from cable television weather channels and on-line resources.

*C*ulture

A Special Winter Class

During the winter, French elementary schools offer *classes de neige.* Elementary school students are taken to a winter resort where they learn to ski. In the morning they take their regular school subjects. In the afternoon they have skiing lessons. The *classes de neige* last for about one week.

Isola deux mille, France

130 • *Welcome to French!*

11 Je suis...

Telling Who I Am

—Salut! Tu es un ami de Jean-Luc, n'est-ce pas?

—Oui, je suis David Sanders. Et tu es Nathalie, n'est-ce pas?

—Oui, je suis Nathalie Gaudin. Je suis une amie de Jean-Luc.

When you hear the question *tu es?* in French, you answer with *je suis. Tu es* is used to speak to a friend and *je suis* is used to speak about yourself.

tu es? → **je suis**

Video

Audio

Transparencies

Workbook

FOCUS

Students will
- ask and respond to requests for one's name
- use the forms *tu es?* and *je suis* appropriately

TEACH

—**Salut! Tu es un ami de Jean-Luc, n'est-ce pas?** Hi! You are a friend of Jean-Luc, aren't you?

—**Oui, je suis David Sanders. Et tu es Nathalie, n'est-ce pas?** Yes, I am David Sanders. And you are Nathalie, right?

—**Oui, je suis Nathalie Gaudin. Je suis une amie de Jean-Luc.** Yes, I am Nathalie Gaudin. I am a friend of Jean-Luc.

tu es? are you?

je suis I am

Tu t'appelles comment? What's your name?

Je m'appelle... My name is . . .

Dialogue

1. Use the video or audio programs to present the dialogue. Point to the speaker as each line of the dialogue is heard. Or model the dialogue yourself, pointing to the appropriate speaker on the overhead transparency.

2. Have two students model the dialogue, using their real names. Prompt them if necessary.

131

Activités

A. If your furniture is movable, arrange it so that students can move about easily.

B. Have students change partners after each conversation so that each has three or four conversations.

—**Tu t'appelles comment?**
What's your name?

—**Je m'appelle <your name>.**
My name is <your name>.

Culture

You may want to point out that it is fairly common to add an *e* to make a "boy's" name into a girl's name (sometimes the last consonant is doubled): Martin—Martine, Michel—Michèle/Michelle, Daniel—Danièle/Danielle, Jean—Jeanne, Pascal—Pascale.

Nathalie est une amie de Jean-Luc. Nathalie is a friend of Jean-Luc.

Et David est un ami de Jean-Luc. And David is a friend of Jean-Luc.

ASSESS

Review the lesson and check student progress by using the following:

• Asking students to introduce themselves using the name badges they made in Lesson 2.

• Activities Workbook, Lesson 11

CLOSE

Ask students to pretend they are at the airport to meet a French-speaking cousin they have never met. Prepare the dialogue that takes place.

Expansion

Ask students to think of a famous French-speaking person they would like to meet. Write out an imaginary conversation with that person. You might want to suggest some of the people listed in Lesson 2.

132

If you want to find out the name of a person the same age as you, you can ask:

Tu t'appelles comment?

The response would be:

Je m'appelle (your name).

Activités

A Walk around the classroom. Greet each of your classmates. Find out who each one is. Let each one know who you are.

B With a friend, walk up to a classmate. Pretending you don't know him or her, tell the classmate who your friend is. Then find out if he or she is a friend of the same person.

*C*ulture

French Spelling

Many American students think spelling is a difficult subject. English words are not easy to spell because many different sounds are spelled or written the same way. French students also find spelling difficult. You will note that many French words sound the same but are spelled differently:

Nathalie est une *amie* de Jean-Luc.
Et David est un *ami* de Jean-Luc.

- Video
- Audio
- Transparencies
- Workbook

12 *J*e suis de...

Telling Where I Am From

—Tu es d'où, David?
 —Moi, je suis de Dallas.
—Ah, tu es américain.
 —Oui, je suis américain.
 Et toi, Nathalie, tu es
 d'où?
—Je suis de Lyon. Je suis
 française.

Note the difference in sound and spelling when describing a boy and a girl:

Je suis *américaine*.
Je suis *française*.
Nathalie est *française*.

Je suis *américain*.
Je suis *français*.
David est *américain*.

12 · Je suis de... • 133

FOCUS

Students will
- ask about and respond to questions about geographic origin
- ask for or give a person's nationality

TEACH

—**Tu es d'où, David?** Where are you from, David?

—**Moi, je suis de Dallas.** I am from Dallas.

—**Ah, tu es américain.** Ah, you are American.

—**Oui, je suis américain. Et toi, Nathalie, tu es d'où?** Yes, I am American. And you, Nathalie, you're from where?

—**Je suis de Lyon. Je suis française.** I am from Lyon. I am French.

Je suis américaine. I am American (female).

Je suis française. I am French (female).

Nathalie est française. Nathalie is French.

Je suis américain. I am American (male).

Je suis français. I am French (male).

David est américain. David is American.

Dialogue

1. Use the video to present the dialogue. Or use the overhead transparency and the audio program to present it. Point

133

to the speaker as each line is heard. Or model the dialogue yourself, pointing to the appropriate speaker on the overhead transparency.

2. Have two students model the dialogue, using the names David and Nathalie and their nationalities. Have several other pairs of students model the dialogue.

3. If you have students in your class of other nationalities, have two students model the dialogue using their real names and nationalities.

Activités

A. Answers: 1. Je m'appelle
_____. 2. Je suis de _____.
3. Je suis _____.

B., C. Have students write the information under the drawing and post the results.

D. Have Student 1 give the information using *je suis*. Have Student 2 give the information using *tu es*. Then reverse roles.

Récapitulons!

—**Salut!** Hello!

—**Salut!** Hello!

—**Tu es un ami de Jean-Luc, n'est-ce pas?** You are a friend of Jean-Luc, right?

—**Oui, je suis David Sanders.** Yes, I am David Sanders.

—**Ça va, David?** How's it going, David?

—**Oui, ça va bien. Et toi?** It's going well. And you?

—**Pas mal.** Not bad.

—**Tu es Nathalie Gaudin, n'est-ce pas?** You are Nathalie Gaudin, right?

—**Oui, je suis Nathalie.** Yes, I am Nathalie.

—**Tu es d'où, Nathalie?** Where are you from, Nathalie?

Activités

A **Answer the following questions about yourself.**

1. Tu t'appelles comment?

2. Et tu es d'où?

3. Tu es de quelle nationalité?

B **Draw a picture of a female friend or relative. Give her a French name. Then tell as much about her as you can.**

C **Draw a picture of a male friend or relative. Give him a French name. Then tell as much about him as you can.**

D **Work with a classmate. Find out where he or she is from and his or her nationality. Then give the same information about yourself.**

Récapitulons!

—Salut!

   —Salut!

—Tu es un ami de Jean-Luc, n'est-ce pas?

   —Oui, je suis David Sanders.

—Ça va, David?

   —Oui, ça va bien. Et toi?

—Pas mal.

   —Tu es Nathalie Gaudin, n'est-ce pas?

—Oui, je suis Nathalie.

   —Tu es d'où, Nathalie?

—Je suis de Lyon.

   —Ah, tu es française.

—Oui. Et toi, tu es américain, n'est-ce pas?

   —Oui, je suis de Dallas.

134 • *Welcome to French!*

Activités

A Practice the conversation on page 134 with a classmate. Use as much expression as you can.

B Complete the following story about David and Nathalie.

David est de _____ au Texas. David est _____. _____ est de Lyon. Elle est _____. Nathalie est une _____ de Jean-Luc.

C Look at the photograph of Julie Carter. She is from Cleveland. Tell all about her.

D Look at this photograph of Patrick Benoît. He is from Rennes, France. Tell all about him.

—**Je suis de Lyon.** I am from Lyon.

—**Ah, tu es française.** Ah, you are French.

—**Oui. Et toi, tu es américain, n'est-ce pas?** Yes. And you, you are American, aren't you?

—**Oui, je suis de Dallas.** Yes, I am from Dallas.

1. Draw and label David and Nathalie on the chalkboard. Model the review dialogue yourself, pointing to the appropriate speaker on the chalkboard.

2. Have two students model the dialogue, using the names David and Nathalie and their nationalities. Have several other pairs of students model the dialogue.

3. If you have students of other nationalities, have two students model the dialogue using their real names and nationalities.

Activités

A. Have students change partners so that each practices the conversation two or three times.

B. Answers: Dallas, américain, Nathalie, française, amie

C., D. Post the results of these activites in the classroom.

Culture

Have students research French-speaking parts of Canada. One group can write to the Ministry of Culture in Quebec or Montreal or another Canadian city to obtain information. Other students can visit a travel agent for tourist information. Another group can do library research. Some students may have old magazines with pictures of cities in Quebec province.

ASSESS

Review the lesson and check student progress by using the following:

- Activities Workbook, Lesson 12

CLOSE

Ask students to pretend that Nathalie Gaudin is going to be an exchange student at their school next year. Have them prepare a brief conversation in which they introduce themselves to her and ask where she is from.

Expansion

Other nationalities you might want to introduce are the following (the masculine form is on the left and the feminine form is on the right):

canadien	canadienne
italien	italienne
vietnamien	vietnamienne
polonais	polonaise
irlandais	irlandaise
espagnol	espagnole
japonais	japonaise
chinois	chinoise
mexicain	mexicaine

Culture

French-Speaking Cities

Montreal is a beautiful city in the Canadian province of Quebec. It was founded in 1642. Montreal, with some three million people, is the second largest French-speaking city in the world. The largest, of course, is Paris.

Paris, France

Montreal, Canada

French Online

For more information about Paris, Montreal, and other French-speaking cities, go to the Glencoe Web site: glencoe.com

136 • *Welcome to French!*

13 ◆ *Je parle français*

Telling What I Speak

—Tu parles anglais, David?

—Oui, je parle anglais. Tu parles français, Nathalie?

—Oui, je parle français.

—Tu parles anglais aussi?

—Oui, un petit peu.

As you can see, French words are often pronounced the same even though they are spelled differently:

—Tu *parles?*

—Oui, je *parle.*

—Et Jean-Luc *parle* aussi?

—Il *parle* français.

—Et Nathalie?

—Elle *parle* français aussi.

Remember that you use *tu* to speak to a friend, *je* to speak about yourself, and *il* or *elle* to speak about someone else.

13 · Je parle français • 137

FOCUS

Students will
* ask and respond to questions about the languages they speak
* use the forms *tu parles?* and *je parle* appropriately

TEACH

—Tu parles anglais, David? Do you speak English, David?

—Oui, je parle anglais. Tu parles français, Nathalie? Yes, I speak English. Do you speak French, Nathalie?

—Oui, je parle français. Yes, I speak French.

—Tu parles anglais aussi? Do you speak English, too?

—Oui, un petit peu. Yes, a little bit.

—Tu *parles?* Do you speak?

—Oui, je *parle.* Yes, I speak (am speaking, do speak).

—Et Jean-Luc *parle* aussi? And Jean-Luc also speaks?

—Il *parle* français. He speaks French.

—Et Nathalie? And Nathalie?

—Elle *parle* français aussi. She also speaks French.

Dialogue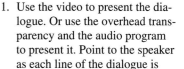

1. Use the video to present the dialogue. Or use the overhead transparency and the audio program to present it. Point to the speaker as each line of the dialogue is heard. Or model the dialogue

yourself, pointing to the appropriate speaker on the overhead transparency. You may also wish to use a puppet.

2. Have two students model the dialogue as David and Nathalie. Have several other pairs of students model the dialogue.

3. If you have students in your class who speak other languages, have two students model the dialogue using their real names and the languages they speak.

4. Point out that languages are not capitalized in French.

Activités

A. If your furniture is movable, arrange it so that students can move about easily.

B. If you don't have a beach ball, use another kind of soft ball or a beanbag.

Activités

A Walk around the room and greet a classmate. Find out what language(s) he or she speaks. Then tell your classmate what language(s) you speak.

B Get a beach ball. One person throws the ball to another as he or she asks, *Tu parles français?* The person who catches the ball answers, *Je parle...*

C If you speak a language other than English at home, tell the class what language you speak.

Look at the French names of these languages. Since they are cognates, you can probably guess at their meaning:

italien	polonais
espagnol	arabe
portugais	grec
chinois	hébreu
japonais	swahili
vietnamien	

Did you know that Japanese is studied in France?

138   •   *Welcome to French!*

Culture

The French-Speaking World

Here are two friends from different areas of the world. They both have something very important in common. They both speak French.

Bonjour. Je m'appelle Ahmed.
Je suis d'Algiers en Algérie.
Je parle français et arabe.

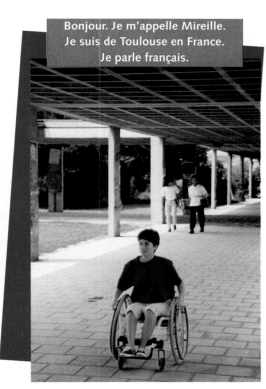

Bonjour. Je m'appelle Mireille.
Je suis de Toulouse en France.
Je parle français.

13 · Je parle français • 139

Culture

Some U.S. cities have large French- or Creole-speaking populations. Students might want to learn more about the Acadians and their influence on the Cajun culture in Louisiana. Explain that the word "Cajun" has evolved from the pronunciation of "acadien."

Bonjour. Je m'appelle Ahmed. Je suis d'Algiers en Algérie. Je parle français et arabe. Hello. My name is Ahmed. I am from Algiers, Algeria. I speak French and Arabic.

Bonjour. Je m'appelle Mireille. Je suis de Toulouse en France. Je parle français. Hello. My name is Mireille. I am from Toulouse, France. I speak French.

ASSESS

Review the lesson and check student progress by using the following:

- Ask students to make French sentences using *parle* and these lists:

Boris Yeltsin	**anglais**
Bill Clinton	**russe**
Charles de Gaulle	**chinois**
Mao Tse-tung	**français**

- Activities Workbook, Lesson 13

CLOSE

Ask students to pretend they are lost in Paris. Have them prepare a brief dialogue with someone of their own age to find out what language they have in common.

Expansion

Ask students to use a map or a globe to plan an imaginary trip around the world. Have them prepare an itinerary and list three languages that would be the most useful for them to know on the trip.

139

Lesson 14

 Video

 Audio

 Transparencies

 Workbook

FOCUS

Students will

- ask and respond to questions about what subjects they are taking
- use the forms *tu aimes?* and *j'aime* correctly
- make sentences negative

TEACH

—Carole, tu aimes les maths?
Carole, do you like math?

—Moi, oui. J'aime bien les maths.
Me? Yes. I really like math.

—Et Henri, tu aimes les maths?
And Henri, do you like math?

—Pas du tout. Je n'aime pas les maths. Not at all. I don't like math.

Dialogue

1. Use the video to present the dialogue. Or use the overhead transparency and the audio program to present it. Point to the speaker as each line of the dialogue is heard. Or model the dialogue yourself, pointing to the appropriate speaker on the overhead transparency.

2. Have two students model the dialogue as Carole and Henri. Have several other pairs of students model the dialogue.

3. Write the other school subjects on the chalkboard. Ask another pair of students to model the dialogue, but point to another school subject before the partner asks about it.

140

---

14 ◆ J'aime...

Telling What I Like

—Carole, tu aimes les maths?

  —Moi, oui. J'aime bien les maths.

—Et Henri, tu aimes les maths?

  —Pas du tout. Je n'aime pas les maths.

Note once again that French words are very often pronounced the same even though they are spelled differently:

—Tu *aimes* les maths?

  —Oui, j'*aime* les maths.

—Carole *aime* les maths aussi.

  —Mais Henri n'*aime* pas les maths.

140 • *Welcome to French!*

Saying "No"

Here's how you say "no" to someone:

Non, je *ne* suis *pas* français.

Non, je *ne* parle *pas* espagnol.

Non, je *n'*aime *pas* les maths.

Activités

A **Work with a classmate. Find out what subjects each of you likes or dislikes. You can guess at the words you'll need to use since they are cognates.**

le français	l'histoire
l'anglais	l'art
les maths	la musique
les sciences	la gymnastique

B **Get a beach ball. One person throws the ball to another as he or she asks,** *Tu aimes _____?* **naming a particular subject. The person who catches the ball answers,** *J'aime...* **or** *Je n'aime pas...*

Music class,
Montreal, Canada

14 · J'aime... • 141

---

4. Finally, ask a pair of students to model the dialogue, but let them choose the subjects to talk about.

5. Point out that students often use the shortened form *les maths.*

—**Tu** *aimes* **les maths?** Do you like math?

—**Oui, j'***aime* **les maths.** Yes, I like math.

—**Carole** *aime* **les maths aussi.** Carole likes math, too.

—**Mais Henri n'***aime* **pas les maths.** But Henri doesn't like math.

Saying "No"

Non, je *ne* suis *pas* français. No, I am not French.

Non, je *ne* parle *pas* espagnol. No, I don't speak Spanish.

Non, je *n'*aime *pas* les maths. No, I don't like math.

Explain to students that *ne... pas* makes a "sandwich." *Ne... pas* is the "bread" and the verb or action word is the "filler." *Ne* is *n'* before a vowel.

Activités

A. Have students change partners after each conversation so that each has three or four conversations.

B. If your furniture is movable, arrange it so that students can throw the ball easily.

C. Suggested answers:

1. Oui, j'aime le français.
2. M. (Mme, Mlle)_____ est le(la) prof de français.
3. Oui, le cours de français est intéressant.   4. Le cours de français est à _____ heures.
5. Oui, je parle français en classe. Have the student who is doing the listening retell his or her partner's story to a third person. Remind students to use *Il aime (Il n'aime pas)* or *Elle aime (Elle n'aime pas)*.

D. Have students read the story silently. If they need help, have them form small groups and read aloud, each student taking one sentence.

E. Answers: 1. Paul est américain. 2. Il parle anglais.   3. Il aime le français.   4. Il ne déteste pas le français.

1. Nathalie est française.   2. Elle est de Lyon.   3. Elle parle français.   4. Elle aime l'anglais.
5. Elle n'aime pas la biologie.

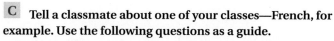

C **Tell a classmate about one of your classes—French, for example. Use the following questions as a guide.**

1. Tu aimes le français?
2. Qui est le prof de français?
3. Le cours de français est intéressant?
4. Le cours de français est à quelle heure?
5. Tu parles français en classe?

D **Read the following story about Paul and Nathalie.**

Paul est américain. Il est de Dallas. Paul parle anglais. Et il parle français aussi. Il parle un peu. Il aime le français. Le cours de français est très intéressant. Mais Paul n'aime pas les maths. Il déteste les maths.

Nathalie n'est pas américaine. Elle est française. Elle est de Lyon. Nathalie parle français. Et elle parle anglais. Elle parle un petit peu. Elle aime l'anglais. Le cours d'anglais est très intéressant. Mais Nathalie n'aime pas la biologie. Elle déteste les sciences.

E **Work with a classmate. One of you will ask the questions about Paul and the other will answer the questions. Then you'll switch parts for the questions about Nathalie.**

Élève A

1. Paul est de quelle nationalité?
2. Il parle quelle langue?
3. Il aime le français?
4. Il déteste le français?

Élève B

1. Nathalie est de quelle nationalité?
2. Elle est d'où?
3. Elle parle quelle langue?
4. Elle aime l'anglais?
5. Elle n'aime pas quel cours?

142   •   *Welcome to French!*

Culture

School Schedule

In French schools, classes for all subjects do not meet every day. Some meet twice a week and others may meet four times a week. For this reason, French students take more courses each semester than American students do.

Culture

Discuss whether students would prefer to take more classes and meet fewer times a week or not.

ASSESS

Review the lesson and check student progress by using the following:

- Have students tell about a friend saying what he or she likes and doesn't like to study in school.

- Activities Workbook, Lesson 14

CLOSE

Ask students to write three sentences about someone they know using *est, parle,* and *aime.*

Lycée Janson, Paris, France

Lycée Henri IV, Paris, France

14 · J'aime... •   **143**

143

Lesson 15

- **Video**
- **Audio**
- **Transparencies**
- **Workbook**

FOCUS

Students will
- use the names of the rooms of a house
- use the form *il y a* appropriately

TEACH

la maison house
l'appartement apartment
le jardin garden
le garage garage
la voiture car

les pièces rooms
le salon living room
la salle à manger dining room
la cuisine kitchen
la chambre bedroom
la salle de bains bathroom

Il y a un jardin autour de la maison. There is a garden around the house.

Il y a une voiture dans le garage. There is a car in the garage.

Il y a dix pièces dans la maison. C'est une grande maison. There are ten rooms in the house. It's a large house.

Vocabulary

1. Point to each room on the overhead transparency as you name it. Repeat two or three times.

---

15 *Ma maison*

Describing My House

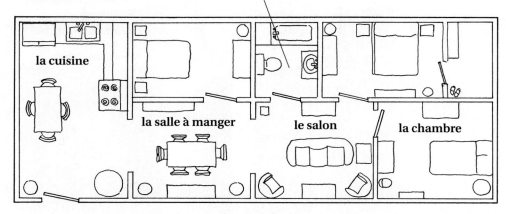

la salle de bains

la cuisine

la salle à manger   le salon   la chambre

l'appartement

Il y a means "there is" or "there are" in French:

Il y a un jardin autour de
la maison.

Il y a une voiture dans le garage.

Il y a dix pièces dans la maison.
C'est une grande maison.

le garage

le jardin   la maison   la voiture

une petite maison

144   •   *Welcome to French!*

144

Activités

A Draw a picture of your house. Write the title *Ma maison* at the top of your drawing. Then answer the following questions.

1. Ta maison est grande ou petite?
2. Il y a combien de pièces dans ta maison?
3. Il y a un jardin autour de la maison?

B Look at the photographs of the interior of a house in Strasbourg, France. Give the name in French for each room.

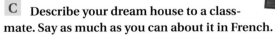

C Describe your dream house to a classmate. Say as much as you can about it in French.

15 · Ma maison • 145

2. Point to each room as you name it, but pause before one as if you forgot its name. Signal to the class to respond chorally. Repeat with other rooms.

3. Point to each room as you name it, but pause before one and point to a student to respond. Repeat with other rooms and other students.

4. Point to *le jardin, la voiture,* and *les pièces* as you say sentences with *il y a.*

5. Point to *le jardin, la voiture,* and *les pièces* and ask students to say sentences with *il y a.*

6. You may also use the audio or video programs to present the vocabulary.

Activités

A. If students would be uncomfortable describing their houses or apartments, distribute pictures of houses or apartments cut from old magazines for them to describe.

B. Answers: 1. la salle de bains 2. la salle à manger 3. la chambre 4. la cuisine 5. le salon

C. Distribute pictures of castles, mansions, and large houses to inspire students.

Activités

A. Answers: 1. 3, rue de la Paix, 75002 Paris   2. quarante-sept, soixante-huit, cinquante-neuf, trente-deux

B. Answers will vary.

ASSESS

Review the lesson and check student progress by using the following:

- Ask students to list the rooms of their house or apartment in order of where they spend the most time and the least time.

-  Activities Workbook, Lesson 15

CLOSE

Ask students to design and draw a tree house or a doll house and label the rooms in French.

Expansion

You might want to teach the following terms to help students talk about their houses or apartments:

au rez-de-chaussée   on the first floor/ground floor

au premier étage   on the first floor (on the second floor in the U.S.)

au deuxième étage   on the second floor (on the third floor in the U.S.)

la salle de séjour   the family room

Note that the "first floor" in French is referred to as the "ground floor." The "first floor" is what is called the second floor in the United States.

146

Activités

A   **Look at the address book below and give the following information.**

1. l'adresse de Madame Boileau
2. le numéro de téléphone de Madame Boileau

B   **Give the following information about yourself.**

1. mon adresse
2. mon numéro de téléphone

A French telephone card

16 **M**a *famille*

Describing My Family

ma grand-mère   mon grand-père

mon oncle   ma tante

ma mère   mon père

ma cousine   mon cousin

mon frère   moi   ma sœur

Oncle Maurice est le frère de ma mère.

Et tante Geneviève est la sœur de ma mère.

Le fils de tante Geneviève est mon cousin.

Et la fille de tante Geneviève est ma cousine.

16 · Ma famille •   147

FOCUS

Students will

- use common terms for family members

- use the forms *tu as?* and *j'ai* appropriately

TEACH

ma mère my mother

mon père my father

ma grand-mère my grandmother

mon grand-père my grandfather

moi me

ma sœur my sister

mon frère my brother

mon oncle my uncle

ma tante my aunt

Oncle Maurice est le frère de ma mère. Uncle Maurice is the brother of my mother.

Et tante Geneviève est la sœur de ma mère. And aunt Geneviève is the sister of my mother.

ma cousine my cousin (girl)

mon cousin my cousin (boy)

Le fils de tante Geneviève est mon cousin. The son of aunt Geneviève is my cousin.

Et la fille de tante Geneviève est ma cousine. And the daughter of aunt Geneviève is my cousin.

Vocabulary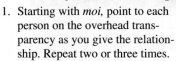

1. Starting with *moi*, point to each person on the overhead transparency as you give the relationship. Repeat two or three times.

2. Point to each person as you name the relationship, but pause before one as if you forgot it. Signal to the class to respond chorally. Repeat with the other people.

3. Point to each person as you name the relationship, but pause before one and point to a student to respond. Repeat with other people and other students.

4. You may also use the audio or video programs to present the vocabulary and the dialogue.

Talking About My Family

—**Tu as un frère?** Do you have a brother?

—**Oui, j'ai un frère. (ou) Non, je n'ai pas de frère.** Yes, I have a brother. (or) No, I don't have a brother.

—**Tu as combien de frères?** How many brothers do you have?

—**J'ai deux frères.** I have two brothers.

—**Tu as une grande famille ou une petite famille?** Do you have a big family or a small family?

—**J'ai une ____ famille. Il y a ____ personnes dans ma famille.** I have a ____ family. There are ____ people in my family.

Dialogue

1. Have two students model the dialogue using their real names and family information. Prompt them the first time if necessary. Have several other pairs of students model using real information.

2. You may also use the audio program to present the dialogue.

tu as? Do you have?

j'ai I have

148

Activité

A Draw your family tree and identify your relatives in French.

Talking About My Family

—Tu as un frère?

 —Oui, j'ai un frère. (ou) Non, je n'ai pas de frère.

—Tu as combien de frères?

 —J'ai deux frères.

—Tu as une grande famille ou une petite famille?

 —J'ai une _____ famille. Il y a _____ personnes dans ma famille.

When you hear a question with *tu as* in French, you answer with *j'ai. Tu as* is used to speak to a friend and *j'ai* is used to speak about yourself.

tu as? → **j'ai**

To answer "yes" or "no" to a question, you say:

Tu as *un* frère?

Oui, j'ai *un* frère.

Non, je n'ai pas *de* frère.

Tu as *une* sœur?

Oui, j'ai *une* sœur.

Non, je n'ai pas *de* sœur.

Tu as *des* cousins?

Oui, j'ai *des* cousins.

Non, je n'ai pas *de* cousins.

Activités

A **Answer the following questions about your family.**

1. Tu as une grande famille ou une petite famille?
2. Tu as des frères?
3. Tu as combien de frères?
4. Tu as des sœurs?
5. Tu as combien de sœurs?
6. Et il y a combien de personnes dans ta famille?

B **Work with a classmate. Ask each other questions about your families in French.**

C **Who is it? Answer in French.**

1. la fille de mon père
2. le fils de mon père
3. le frère de ma mère
4. la sœur de mon père
5. la mère de mon père
6. la fille de mon oncle

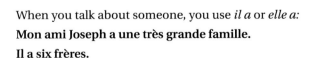

When you talk about someone, you use *il a* or *elle a:*

Mon ami Joseph a une très grande famille.

Il a six frères.

16 · Ma famille • **149**

Tu as *un* frère? Do you have a brother?

Oui, j'ai *un* frère. Yes, I have a brother.

Non, je n'ai pas *de* frère. No, I don't have a brother.

Tu as *une* sœur? Do you have a sister?

Oui, j'ai *une* sœur. Yes, I have a sister.

Non, je n'ai pas *de* sœur. No, I don't have a sister.

Tu as *des* cousins? Do you have cousins?

Oui, j'ai *des* cousins. Yes, I have cousins.

Non, je n'ai pas *de* cousins. No, I don't have cousins.

Write these last three questions and sentences on the chalkboard. Circle the *de* each time. Ask students what word is used after *ne... pas.*

Activités

A. You may prefer to have students work in small groups to ask about their families. Be sensitive to the fact that some students may not be comfortable talking about their families. If so, distribute pictures of families cut from old magazines for all the students to use.

B. In French "half-brother" and "half-sister" are *demi-frère* and *demi-sœur.* Many people would say *mon frère* or *ma sœur* for "stepbrother" or "stepsister" and let it go at that. As for stepparents, *ma belle-mère* and *mon beau-père* are sometimes heard, but these terms are more commonly used for "mother-in-law" and "father-in-law." (*Ma belle-mère* or *mon beau-père* might be used for a stepparent if the natural parent were still alive, but if the latter were deceased, the stepparent might be referred to as *ma mère* or *mon père,* depending on the personal situation.) To be precise about a step relationship, a French person

would say: *le mari de ma mère,
la femme de mon père, le fils (la
fille) du mari de ma mère, le fils
(la fille) de la femme de mon
père.*

C. Answers: 1. ma sœur 2. mon
frère 3. mon oncle 4. ma tante
5. ma grand-mère 6. ma
cousine

**Mon ami Joseph a une très
grande famille.** My friend
Joseph has a very big family.

Il a six frères. He has six brothers.

Activité

A. Gather other pictures of families
for students to talk about. You
can also have students cut out
pictures from old magazines
and have them make their own
"families."

Telling Age

J'ai douze ans. I am twelve
years old.

Et mon frère a quinze ans. And
my brother is fifteen years old.

Et toi, tu as quel âge? And you,
how old are you?

Activité

A Look at this photograph of *la famille Duvalier* from
Toulouse, France. Describe the family in French.

Telling Age

To tell how old you or someone else is, you say:
J'ai douze ans.
Et mon frère a quinze ans.

To ask how old someone is, you say:
Et toi, tu as quel âge?

Do you know what this
greeting card says in French?

150 • *Welcome to French!*

Activités

A Ask each of your classmates his or her age. Tell each one your age.

B Give the ages of some of your friends and relatives.

*C*ulture

The Family in French Culture

Just as in the United States, many French teenagers have step-parents and step-brothers or sisters. In French, however, there are no specific words to express "stepbrother" or "stepsister." In the case of parents, you could say *belle-mère* or *beau-père,* but these terms are confusing. They mean both "stepmother" or "stepfather" and "mother-in-law" or "father-in-law." You would, therefore, say *le mari de ma mère* or *la femme de mon père.*

There are expressions for "half brother" and "half sister." They are *demi-frère* and *demi-sœur.*

French-Moroccan family, Paris, France

16 · Ma famille • 151

Lesson 17

 Video

 Audio

 Transparencies

Workbook

FOCUS

Students will
- use the names of common pets
- ask and respond to questions about likes and dislikes

TEACH

un chien dog
un chat cat
un hamster hamster
une gerboise gerbil

un canari canary
une cage d'oiseau birdcage
un perroquet parrot
une perruche parakeet

des poissons fish (pl.)
un guppy guppy
un poisson rouge goldfish
un aquarium aquarium

Vocabulary

1. Point to each pet and item on the overhead transparency as you name it. Repeat two or three times.

2. Point to each pet and item as you name it, but pause before one as if you forgot it. Signal to the class to respond chorally. Repeat with other items.

3. Point to each pet and item as you name it, but pause before one and call on a student by name to respond. Repeat two or three times.

152

---

17 ◆ Un bon ami

Talking About My Pet

un chien

des oiseaux

un canari

un perroquet

une perruche

une cage d'oiseau

des poissons

un guppy

un poisson rouge

un aquarium

un hamster

un chat

une gerboise

Telling What I Like

—Tu aimes les animaux?

   —Moi, j'adore les animaux.

—Tu as un chien?

   —Non, je n'ai pas de chien. Mais j'ai un chat. J'adore mon petit chat. Il est adorable.

Activités

A   **Answer the following personal questions in French.**

1. Tu aimes les animaux?

2. Tu as un chat ou un chien? Tu aimes ton chat ou ton chien? Il est adorable?

3. Tu as un oiseau? Tu as quel type d'oiseau? Tu as un canari, un perroquet?

4. Tu aimes les poissons? Tu as des poissons? Tu as un aquarium?

B   **Ask a classmate all about his or her pet. Use the following questions as a guide.**

1. Qu'est-ce que tu as? Tu as un chien? Un chat? Un oiseau?

2. Il a quel âge?

3. Il est adorable?

---

4. You may also use the audio or video programs to present the vocabulary.

Telling What I Like

—**Tu aimes les animaux?** Do you like animals?

—**Moi, j'adore les animaux.** I love animals.

—**Tu as un chien?** Do you have a dog?

—**Non, je n'ai pas de chien. Mais j'ai un chat. J'adore mon petit chat. Il est adorable.** No, I don't have a dog. But I have a cat. I adore my little cat. He is adorable.

Dialogue

1. Use the video or audio programs to present the dialogue. Point to the speaker as each line of the dialogue is heard.

2. Have two students model the dialogue. Let the second speaker choose any appropriate response. Repeat with other pairs of students.

Activités

A. Have students work in small groups to ask and answer questions about pets. Encourage students who don't have pets to talk about a friend's or relative's pet.

B. Remind students that if their pet is less than a year old, they can use *mois* to give its age in months.

Telling What My Pet Does

Le chien aboie. Il saute.
The dog barks. He jumps.

Le chat miaule. Il saute aussi.
The cat meows. He jumps also.

Le perroquet parle.
The parrot talks.

Le canari chante.
The canary sings.

Le poisson nage dans l'aquarium.
The fish swims in the aquarium.

Vocabulary

1. Point to each pet description on the overhead transparency as you name it. Repeat two or three times.

2. Point to each pet description as you name it, but pause before one as if you forgot it. Signal to the class to respond chorally. Repeat with other items.

3. Point to each pet description as you name it, but pause before one and call on a student by name to respond. Repeat two or three times.

4. You may also use the audio or video programs to present the vocabulary.

Culture

Prepare several sets of cards with the names of the pets. Have students work in small groups. One person in the group deals out the cards, face down, one per person. Students should ask each other about the pets they "have" including what kind of sound it makes and what activity it does.

le chien: "ouah ouah"
the dog: "bow-wow"

le chat: "miaou"
the cat: "meow"

le mouton: "bê"
the sheep: "baah"

l'oiseau: "cuicui"
the bird: "tweet-tweet"

le cochon: "groin groin"
the pig: "oink-oink"

le canard: "coin coin"
the duck: "quack quack"

154

Telling What My Pet Does

Le chien aboie. Il saute.

Le chat miaule. Il saute aussi.

Le perroquet parle.

Le poisson nage dans l'aquarium.

Le canari chante.

Culture

Animal Talk in French

Every language has its words for animal sounds. In English, a dog says "woof-woof" and a cat says "meow." What do the French animals say?

le chien: "ouah ouah"   **le canard: "coin coin"**

le chat: "miaou"   **l'oiseau: "cuicui"**

le mouton: "bê"   **le cochon: "groin groin"**

Compare these animal sounds with the animal sounds you know in English.

Pour leur assurer un bon départ.

Commencez ici.

Puppy Chow et Chow Chaton fournissent les vitamines, minéraux et éléments nutritifs supplémentaires si importants durant la première année de votre petit compagnon.

What do you think this French ad describes?

Activités

A Tell if the following animals or pets play.

1. le poisson rouge
2. le chien
3. la gerboise
4. le perroquet
5. le hamster
6. le chat

B Match the name of the animal with what it does.

1. un perroquet
2. un chat
3. un oiseau
4. un poisson

a. il chante
b. il nage
c. il parle
d. il saute

17 · Un bon ami • 155

Culture

There are several businesses in France that cater to the French love for their pets. There are dog-sitting agencies, dog-walking services, and even a 24-hour dog hospital in Paris.

ASSESS

Review the lesson and check student progress by using the following:

*   Activities Workbook, Lesson 17

CLOSE

On a piece of paper, ask students to make four columns labeled *Chiens, Chats, Oiseaux, Poissons, Autres* (Others). Make a prediction what the total number of pets in the class-room will be in each category. They should write a number in each col-umn and turn the paper over. Then write the same categories on the board and take a tally of the class, asking each individual about his or her pets. Have students compare their predictions with the actual count.

Culture

French Pets

There is no word in French that means "pet." This does not mean to say, however, that the French do not have pets. In fact, pets are more common in France than in any other European country. The French adore their pets. Cats and dogs are the most popular pets and the French take their dogs everywhere. It is not the least unusual in France to see *un chien* in a restaurant or supermarket.

18 **L***es sports*

Talking About Sports

le base-ball

une équipe

le foot(ball)

un terrain
de foot(ball)

le ballon

le volley(-ball)

la balle

un court de tennis

le tennis

FOCUS

Students will

- use the names of popular sports
- use the forms *tu joues* and *je joue* appropriately

TEACH

le foot(ball) soccer
le volley(-ball) volleyball
le ballon ball
le base-ball baseball
le basket(-ball) basketball
le tennis tennis
la balle ball
le joueur (male) player
la joueuse (female) player
une équipe team
un terrain de foot(ball)
  soccer field
un court de tennis tennis court

It is extremely common to use the short form for these sports in every-day speech:

le foot soccer
le volley volleyball
le basket basketball

18 · Les sports • 157

—**Gilles, tu joues au foot?** Gilles, do you play soccer?

—**Oui, je joue au foot.** Yes, I play soccer.

—**Tu es dans l'équipe de ton école?** Do you play on the school team?

—**Oui. Et c'est une très bonne équipe.** Yes. And it's a very good team.

Vocabulary

Be sure students understand the difference between *le foot(ball)* (soccer) and *le football américain* (football).

1. Point to each item on the over-head transparency as you name it. Repeat two or three times.

2. Point to each item as you name it, but pause before one as if you forgot its name. Signal to the class to respond chorally. Repeat with other items.

3. Point to each item as you name it, but pause before one and call on a student by name to respond. Repeat two or three times.

4. You may also use the audio or video programs to present the vocabulary.

Dialogue

1. Use the video or audio programs to present the dialogue. Point to the speaker as each line of the dialogue is heard. Or model the dialogue yourself, pointing to the appropriate speaker on the overhead transparency.

2. Model the dialogue with one of the more able students.

3. Have two students model the dialogue.

Activités

A. Have students work in pairs and check each other's work.

B. If you don't have a beach ball, use another kind of soft ball or a beanbag.

158

le joueur

la joueuse

le basket(-ball)

—Gilles, tu joues au foot?

   —Oui, je joue au foot.

—Tu es dans l'équipe de ton école?

   —Oui. Et c'est une très bonne équipe.

Activités

A Write up a list of the sports that you enjoy playing.

Je joue au...
J'aime...

B Get a beach ball. One student throws the ball to another. The one who throws the ball asks a question with *Tu joues*. The one who catches the ball answers, *Oui, je joue...* or *Non, je ne joue pas...*

C Answer the following personal questions.

1. Tu aimes les sports?
2. Tu préfères quel sport? Quel est ton sport favori?

158 • *Welcome to French!*

3. Tu joues au _____?

4. Tu es dans l'équipe de ton école?

5. C'est une bonne équipe?

D Give the following information about your favorite sport.

1. Quel est ton sport favori?

2. C'est un sport d'équipe?

3. Il y a combien de joueurs dans l'équipe?

4. Tu joues au _____?

*C*ulture

Le Tour de France

The Tour de France is the most famous bicycle race in the world. It takes place in July. The course is changed every year, but there are always several *étapes* through the Pyrenees and the Alps. The finish line is always in Paris on the Champs-Élysées. In recent years, the course has gone through one or more neighboring countries, including Belgium, Germany, or Spain.

18 · Les sports • 159

C. In class, ask pairs of students to interview each other and to take notes on the answers. For homework, have students expand their notes into complete sentences. Give them this model:

1. **(Marc) aime les sports.**

2. **Il préfère le basket.**

3. **Il joue au basket.**

4. **Il est dans l'équipe de l'école.**

5. **C'est une très bonne équipe.**

Culture

The Tour de France in 1996 was interrupted by snow in some of the mountain areas and several competitors were forced to drop out because of the extreme conditions. Have students research previous winners of the Tour, including the Americans, Greg LeMond and Lance Armstrong.

ASSESS

Review the lesson and check student progress by using the following:

• Activities Workbook, Lesson 18

CLOSE

Ask students to list the names of the sports in the lesson vocabulary under the heads *J'aime* or *Je n'aime pas*. Ask them to list the other items according to whether the school has one or not. Use the heads *L'école a une équipe de* or *L'école n'a pas d'équipe de*.

Expansion

The verb *jouer* can also be used with board games such as *je joue aux échecs* (chess) and *je joue au jeu de dames* (checkers).

Lesson 19

- Video
- Audio
- Transparencies
- Workbook

FOCUS

Students will

- use the names of common clothing items
- use the forms *je porte* and *on porte* appropriately

TEACH

une chemise shirt
un pantalon pants
un (blue) jean jeans
un blouson light jacket
un survêtement sweatsuit
un tee-shirt T-shirt
une blouse blouse
une jupe skirt
un short shorts
des tennis sneakers
des chaussures shoes
une casquette cap

Vocabulary

1. Point to each clothing item on the overhead transparency as you name it. Repeat two or three times.

2. Point to each clothing item as you name it, but pause before one as if you forgot its name. Signal to the class to respond chorally. Repeat with other clothing items.

3. Point to each clothing item as you name it, but pause before one and call on a student by name to name the item. Repeat two or three times.

160

---

19 ◆ Les vêtements

Clothing

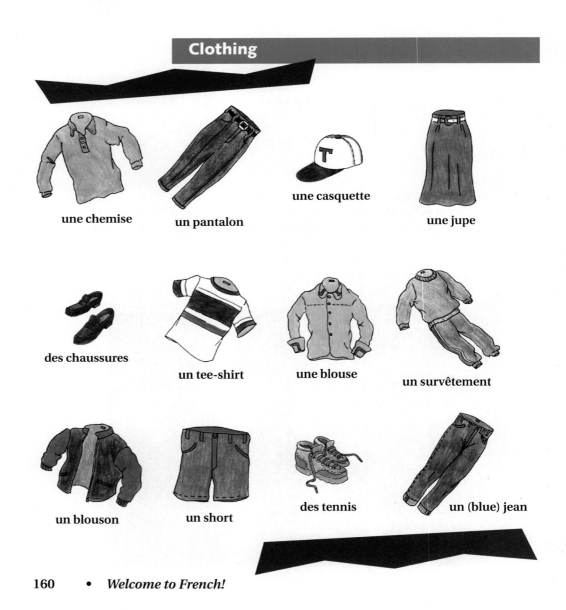

une chemise

un pantalon

une casquette

une jupe

des chaussures

un tee-shirt

une blouse

un survêtement

un blouson

un short

des tennis

un (blue) jean

160 • *Welcome to French!*

The word *on* is very useful in French. It can mean "we," "people," or "one."

> **On joue au tennis.**
>
> **Et quand on joue au tennis on porte des tennis.**

Activités

A In French, tell what you are wearing today.

Aujourd'hui je porte...

Department Store,
Paris, France

B Talk about the dress code in your school. Tell what you wear to class:

On porte _____ en classe.

And tell what you don't wear to class:

On ne porte pas de _____.

4. You may also use the audio or video programs to present the vocabulary.

On joue au tennis. People/We play tennis.

Et quand on joue au tennis on porte des tennis. And when one plays tennis, one wears sneakers.

Activités

A. Tell students to use *un, une,* or *des* with clothing items. For example, *Je porte un jean et une chemise.*

B. Give students other situations and ask what they would wear: *Quand on joue au foot, on porte...* or *En été, on porte...* or *Quand il y a du vent, je porte...* Additional items of clothing are given in the Expansion section.

C **Match the article of clothing with the color.**

a. rouge

b. gris

c. jaune

d. marron

e. bleu

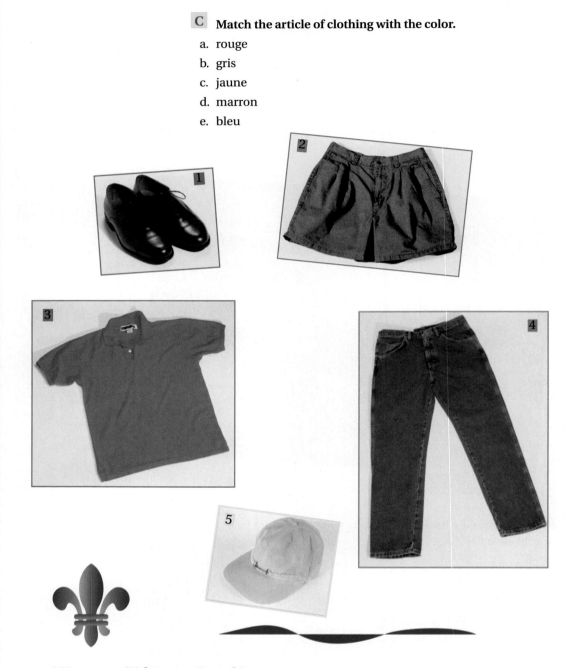

Culture

Clothing Today

Take a look at these photographs of French-speaking students your age. Note that they wear the same clothing that you and your friends do.

Chartres, France

Pointe-à-Pitre, Guadeloupe

19 · Les vêtements • 163

Bring in some pictures of contemporary, traditional, and regional French clothing to class. Stress that it is much more common to see clothing like the kind we wear in the United States. The French, though, do tend to dress up somewhat more than we do. Ask students to describe certain kinds of U.S. traditional clothing (cowboy clothes, Pilgrim clothes, Native American outfits, Amish clothing).

ASSESS

Review the lesson and check student progress by using the following:

- Asking students to describe what a person in a magazine or clothing catalogue is wearing.

- Activities Workbook, Lesson 19

CLOSE

Ask students to draw a boy or girl of the next century and label the clothing in French.

Expansion

You might want to introduce these words to help your students describe clothing:

un maillot de bain bathing suit

des chaussettes socks

des baskets high-top sneakers

un anorak parka

un manteau overcoat

une robe dress

un complet suit (business)

un sac à main purse, handbag

un sweat(shirt) a sweatshirt

Welcome to
Italian!

Italian is the language of the arias of the world's most beautiful operas—*Aida*, *Tosca*, and *Madama Butterfly*. Italian, like Spanish and French, is a Romance language derived from Latin. It is the language of Italy, the country where the original Latin was spoken. Italian is also the language of one section, or canton, of Switzerland.

When we think of Italian culture, the names of many famous artists and writers come to mind—Michelangelo, Dante, Raphael, and Leonardo da Vinci. Italy has given birth to so many writers, artists, philosophers, and musicians that it is often called the "cradle of Western civilization."

Italian is the mother tongue of many Americans of Italian origin. It is also spoken by many people of Italian descent in Argentina, Uruguay, and Chile.

Venice, Italy

Imperia, Italy

164

"Leaning Tower,"
Pisa, Italy

Dolomite Alps, northern Italy

Italian to English

As you study Italian, you will recognize many words of Italian origin. This is particularly true of the language of classical music:

alto	crescendo	solo
andante	libretto	soprano
aria	opera	staccato
basso	piano	

The Italian language also provides us with words for delicious foods and drinks:

cappuccino	pasta	ravioli
espresso	prosciutto	spaghetti
lasagna		

165

Lesson 1

Audio

Transparencies

Workbook

FOCUS

Students will
- use and respond to greetings with peers
- use and respond to greetings with older people

TEACH

—**Ciao, Giovanni!** Hi, Giovanni!

—**Ciao, Maria! Come stai?** Hi, Maria! How are you?

—**Bene, grazie, e tu?** Good, thanks, and you?

—**Non c'è male, grazie.** Not bad, thanks.

—**Buon giorno, signora.** Good day, Ma'am.

—**Buon giorno, signorina. Come sta?** Good day, Miss. How are you?

—**Molto bene, grazie, e Lei?** Very well, and you?

—**Molto bene, grazie.** Very well, thanks.

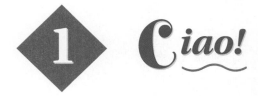

Greeting People

—Ciao, Giovanni!
—Ciao, Maria! Come stai?
—Bene, grazie, e tu?
—Non c'è male, grazie.

When speaking Italian, you must decide between formal and informal speech. The conversation above is between friends. If you were speaking to an adult you did not know well, you would say *Come sta?* rather than *Come stai?* You would also say *E Lei?* instead of *E tu?*

166 • *Welcome to Italian!*

166

—Buon giorno, signora.
　—Buon giorno, signorina. Come sta?
—Molto bene, grazie, e Lei?
　—Molto bene, grazie.

Buon giorno and *buona sera* are more formal greetings than *ciao.* You would say *buon giorno* (A.M.) or *buona sera* (P.M.) when greeting adults, for example.

Buon giorno, signora.　　　**Buona sera, signorina.**

When you address a woman, the titles *signora* or *signorina* are almost always used in Italian. The last name of the person may be added, but it's not necessary. The title, *signore,* however, is seldom used when addressing a man. But if you know the man's name, you could say:

Buon giorno, signor Calabrese.

Attività

A　Get up from your desk and walk around the classroom. Say *buon giorno* to each classmate you meet.

B　Draw and cut out five stick figures. Give each one a name. They will represent your friends, family, and teachers. Greet each of your stick figures properly in Italian.

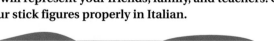

Buon giorno, signora. Good day, Ma'am.

Buona sera, signorina. Good evening, Miss.

Buon giorno, signor Calabrese. Good day, Mr. Calabrese.

Dialogues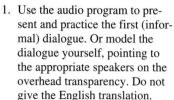

1. Use the audio program to present and practice the first (informal) dialogue. Or model the dialogue yourself, pointing to the appropriate speakers on the overhead transparency. Do not give the English translation.

2. Ask students to greet a neighbor with the proper salutation. Continue until everyone has had a chance.

3. Use the overhead transparency and audio program to present the second (formal) dialogue. Or model the dialogue yourself.

4. To practice formal greetings, walk around the room, greeting various students. Elicit the formal response: *Buon giorno, signora/signor* (your name).

Attività

A. If your furniture is movable, arrange it so that students can move about easily. Greet several students to get them started.

B. Have students label adults as *signor/signora* (+ name). Be sure they use the appropriate formal and informal greetings. After they greet their own stick figures, ask them to circulate around the room and greet other students' stick figures.

Bene, grazie. Fine, thanks.

Molto bene. Very well.

Benissimo. Very well.

Abbastanza bene. Pretty well.

Non c'è male. Not bad.

Così così. So-so.

Attività

A. Have students change partners after each conversation so that each has three or four conversations. Encourage the use of students' names and other variations.

B. Elicit that both young people and adults in Italy may shake hands and kiss each other on the cheek when meeting.

ASSESS

Review the lesson and check student progress by using the following:

• Activities Workbook, Lesson 1

CLOSE

Ask students to prepare a brief conversation between two students who meet on the street. Have them illustrate it with pictures cut out from old magazines.

Expansion

A. You might want to introduce another common way of asking how someone is or how things are going: *Come va?*

B. The numbers are taught in Lesson 4. Rather than teach all of the numbers at once, it is recommended that you teach several numbers while doing each lesson.

As you already know, you can ask *Come stai?* or *Come sta?* to find out how someone is feeling. There are several ways to express how you are feeling or how things are going for you. Some common expressions are:

Bene, grazie.	**Abbastanza bene.**
Molto bene.	**Non c'è male.**
Benissimo.	**Così così.**

Attività

A Work with a classmate. Make up a conversation in Italian. Greet each other and find out how things are going.

B Look at these photographs of people greeting each other in Verona, Italy. Do they do some of the things we do when they greet each other? Do they do some things that are different? Explain.

168 • *Welcome to Italian!*

168

2 *Arrivederci!*

Saying "Good-bye"

—Arrivederci, Carlo!
—Arrivederci, Teresa!

—Ciao, Marco!
—Ciao, Rosangela! A più
tardi.

2 · Arrivederci! • 169

Audio

Transparencies

Workbook

FOCUS

Students will

• use and respond to leave-taking
expressions

TEACH

—**Arrivederci, Carlo!**
Good-bye, Carlo!

—**Arrivederci, Teresa!**
Good-bye, Teresa!

—**Ciao, Marco!** Bye, Marco!

—**Ciao, Rosangela! A più tardi.**
Bye, Rosangela! See you later.

A più tardi. See you later.

A presto. See you soon.

Ci vediamo. See ya!

A domani. See you tomorrow/ 'Til tomorrow.

Dialogue

1. Use the audio program to present the dialogues or model the two brief dialogues yourself, pointing to the appropriate speaker on the transparency. Use appropriate gestures to convey the idea that you are ending an encounter.

2. Model the dialogues with one of the more able students.

3. Have two students model the dialogues.

Attività

A. If your furniture is movable, arrange it so that students can move about easily.

B. Have students repeat the leave-takings with more than one friend if they can.

C. Repeat this activity just before students leave class. Remind students to say *Arrivederci/ ArriveserLa, signor (signora/ signorina)* + your name, and *Ciao/Arrivederci* to another student.

The usual expression to use when saying "good-bye" to someone is:

Arrivederci.

You can also say *arrivederLa* when you want to be very formal.

If you plan to see the person again soon, you can say:

A più tardi.

A presto.

Ci vediamo.

If you plan to see the person the next day, you can say:

A domani.

The informal expression *ciao* can be used both to greet someone or to say "good-bye" to someone. It can mean "hi" or "bye." This popular Italian expression is used in other languages, too. You will hear it frequently in Spain, France, and Germany.

Attività

A Go over to a classmate. Say "so long" to him or her and then return to your seat.

B Work with a friend in class. Say "good-bye" to each other and let each other know that you'll be getting together again soon.

C Say "good-bye" to your teacher in Italian and then say "good-bye" to a friend. Don't forget to use a different expression with each person!

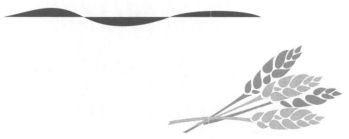

Parliamo di più

—Buon giorno, Carlo.

  —Ciao, Franca. Come stai?

—Bene, grazie, e tu?

  —Non c'è male.

—Ciao, Carlo! A più tardi.

  —Arrivederci, Franca! A presto.

Attività

A Work with a friend. Speak Italian together. Have fun saying as much as you can to one another!

B Look at these photographs of people saying "good-bye" in an Italian section of San Francisco and in Bologna, Italy. Describe what the people are doing.

Bologna, Italy

San Francisco, California

2 · Arrivederci! • 171

—**Buon giorno, Carlo.** Hello, Carlo.

—**Ciao, Franca. Come stai?** Hi, Franca. How are you?

—**Bene, grazie, e tu?** Well, thanks, and you?

—**Non c'è male.** Not bad.

—**Ciao, Carlo! A più tardi.** Bye, Carlo! See you later!

—**Arrivederci, Franca! A presto.** Good-bye, Franca! See you soon.

1. Use the audio program to model the dialogue.

2. Draw and label Carlo and Franca on the chalkboard. Model the review dialogue, pointing to the appropriate speaker on the chalkboard. Or use puppets or stick figures.

3. Model the dialogue with a volunteer, using real names.

4. Have two students model the dialogue, using real names.

Attività

A. Encourage students to use appropriate gestures, such as shaking hands or patting each other on the shoulder when greeting each other, and shaking hands when departing. Have students change partners so that each one has three or four conversations.

B. Elicit students' impressions of the people in the photos. Discuss differences and similarities.

Cultura

Ask students to find the Italian version of their name on the lists. If there is no Italian version, ask them to pick an Italian name for themselves.

ASSESS

Review the lesson and check student progress by using the following:

- Activities Workbook, Lesson 2

CLOSE

Ask students to prepare an ending to the two conversations they wrote in the Close of Lesson 1, by having speakers say "good-bye" to each other.

Expansion

Write Italian names on the chalkboard and work with class to figure out their English equivalents. Point out that masculine names ending in *-o* have an equivalent feminine name ending in *-a: Franco, Franca; Gino, Gina; Paolo, Paola; Carlo, Carla.* Add these names to the list: (masculine) *Alberto, Enrico* (Henry), *Giacomo* (Jack), *Lorenzo* (Lawrence), *Marcello, Mario, Roberto, Tommaso, Vittorio;* (feminine) *Angela, Antonella, Caterina, Francesca, Giulia/Giulietta, Lisa, Rosanna, Silvia.*

Cultura

Common First Names

The following are some common names used for boys and girls in Italian.

Ragazzi

Antonio, Beppino, Carlo, Cesare, Dino, Franco, Gianni, Giorgio, Giuseppe, Luciano, Luigi, Maurizio, Michele, Paolo, Pietro, Riccardo, Sergio, Vincenzo

Ragazze

Anna, Clara, Claudia, Daniela, Domenica, Franca, Gigi, Giovanna, Giulia, Isabella, Luisa, Marcella, Maria, Marta, Patrizia, Pina, Rosangela, Teresa, Vittoria

Can you find the Italian names in these friendship ads below?

● CIAO, SONO UNA RAGAZZA DI 15 ANNI, adoro lo sport, la musica e il cinema; vorrei corrispondere con ragazzi/e di ogni età. Scrivetemi, la risposta è assicurata! Vittoria Callegari, via Lussino 12, 21560 Stretti

● SONO UN RAGAZZO DI QUASI 15 ANNI. Amo ogni cosa che mi possa rallegrare e il giallo (anche i gelati!!). Scrivetemi e vi risponderò. Giulio Mantovani, via Cadorna 15/A, 30020 Roma

● SONO UNA RAGAZZA DI 16 ANNI, ammiratrice di Amedeo Minghi. Vorrei corrispondere con persone che amino la sua musica per scambiarci materiale e magari incontrarci. Donatella Zanchetta, via Valdivisenza 10, 67793 Padova

Milan, Italy

 Italian Online

For more information about Milan and other cities in Italy, go to the Glencoe Web site: glencoe.com

172 • *Welcome to Italian!*

3 **I**n classe

FOCUS

Students will
- use words for common classroom objects
- request common classroom objects

Identifying Classroom Objects

To find out what something is, you ask:

Cos'è? (or) **Che cos'è?**

una scrivania

una sedia

un foglio di carta

un libro

un tavolo

un quaderno

una calcolatrice

un computer

la lavagna

un gesso

un blocchetto

una matita

una gomma

una penna

uno zaino

To ask for something in a polite way, you say:

Un foglio di carta, per favore.

3 · In classe • 173

TEACH

Cos'è? (or) **Che cos'è?**
   What is it?

una penna   pen

una matita   pencil

una gomma   pencil eraser

un libro   book

un quaderno   notebook

un foglio di carta   sheet of paper

un blocchetto   pad

un gesso   chalk

una calcolatrice   calculator

un computer   computer

uno zaino   backpack

una sedia   chair

una scrivania   desk

un tavolo   table

la lavagna   chalkboard

Un foglio di carta, per favore.
   (Give me) a sheet of paper,
   please.

Vocabulary

1. Point to each object on the transparency as you say its name and have students repeat after you. Or have students listen to the audio program. To continue practice, use the actual items, which you have assembled beforehand.

2. After introducing vocabulary, have students close books. Point to an object and ask *Che cos'è?* Model response: *È (una matita).* Then call on various students to respond. Have students repeat *Che cos'è?* Then have them hold up an item and ask you what it is.

3. To introduce the phrase *per favore,* call on a volunteer to hand you various objects you request: *Maria, una penna, per favore.* Be sure to say *grazie* each time. You may want to introduce *Ecco (una penna)* (Here is a pen).

Attività

A. Answers: 1. Una calcolatrice, per favore.   2. Un foglio di carta, per favore.   3. Un quaderno, per favore.   4. Un libro, per favore.   5. Una matita, per favore.   6. Un computer, per favore.

Vary the activity by having students use *ecco, grazie: Anna, una matita, per favore. (Ecco una matita.) Grazie.* Prepare a box with the smaller objects in it. Have students pass this box around and ask their neighbor for an item. Model questions and answers alone and then with another student.

B. Answers: 1. un gesso   2. uno zaino   3. una calcolatrice   4. una sedia

Attività

A   Ask a classmate for the following things in Italian. Don't forget to ask politely!

1.

2.

3.

4.

5.

6.

B   Look at each picture and say in Italian what each person needs.

1.

2.

3.

4.

C Point to something in the classroom and ask a friend what it is.

Cultura

Schools in Italy

In Italy there are eight years of required schooling: five years of *scuola elementare* and three years of *scuola media.*

After finishing middle school, students decide whether or not to go on to four or five years of high school—four or five years of *scuola secondaria superiore.*

When they have completed five years of high school, students take a final exam—*l'esame di maturità.* If they pass the exam, they can enter the university of their choice.

Almost all schools in Italy are public and there is no tuition.

High school exam, Torino, Italy

Cultura

Explain that education in Italy is compulsory until the age of 16. After *la scuola media,* students can continue their education in a *liceo* or an *istituto* for two to five more years, depending on the area of study. If they pass the *esame di maturità,* they may go on to a university. Schoolchildren go to school six days a week and must take oral exams before entering the next grade. School is quite competitive, leaving little time for extracurricular activities, such as intramural athletics, clubs, etc.

ASSESS

Review the lesson and check student progress by using the following:

• Activities Workbook, Lesson 3

CLOSE

Ask students to make a list of the items from the lesson vocabulary that they have in their desks or in their backpacks.

Expansion

Have students locate and cut out pictures of the school vocabulary items from old magazines you have provided. Students will prepare labels for all items and attach them to the pictures. Mount them on poster board or a bulletin board for reference. Labels may be taped to larger classroom items. You may want to add the following items to be labeled:

una cattedra a desk
una bandiera a flag
un calendario a calendar
un dizionario a dictionary
una carta a map
una finestra a window

Lesson 4

FOCUS

Students will

- use and respond to words for numbers
- ask and respond to a request for the price of something

TEACH

Vocabulary

You may want to teach the numbers in groups (1–30, 31–100, etc.) to make them easier for students to learn. Start with 1–10. Do not expect students to learn all the numbers in one lesson. Present numbers as you teach each lesson. The numbers will also be recycled when learning time and dates.

1. Point to each number in order on the overhead transparency as you say its name. Or you may use the audio program to present the numbers.

2. Point to each number in random order on the overhead transparency as you say its name.

3. Point to each number in order, but pause before one as if you forgot its name. Signal the class to say the number chorally. Repeat with a pause before another number three or four times.

4. Point to each number in order and pause before one, but this time point to a student to respond with the number. Repeat three or four times with different students.

176

◆ 4 ◆ Numeri

Counting in Italian

1	uno	20	venti	40	quaranta
2	due	21	ventuno	50	cinquanta
3	tre	22	ventidue	60	sessanta
4	quattro	23	ventitré	70	settanta
5	cinque	24	ventiquattro	80	ottanta
6	sei	25	venticinque	90	novanta
7	sette	26	ventisei		
8	otto	27	ventisette	100	cento
9	nove	28	ventotto	200	duecento
10	dieci	29	ventinove	300	trecento
				400	quattrocento
11	undici	30	trenta	500	cinquecento
12	dodici	31	trentuno	600	seicento
13	tredici	32	trentadue	700	settecento
14	quattordici	33	trentatré	800	ottocento
15	quindici	34	trentaquattro	900	novecento
16	sedici	35	trentacinque		
17	diciassette	36	trentasei	1.000	mille
18	diciotto	37	trentasette	2.000	duemila
19	diciannove	38	trentotto		
		39	trentanove		

Look at the way the numbers one and seven are written in Italian:

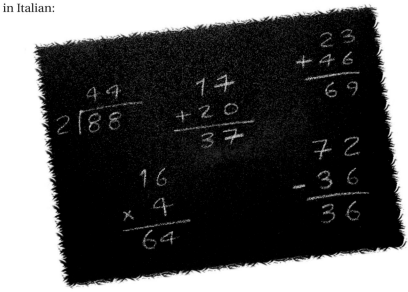

Attività

A Your teacher will write some numbers on the chalkboard. Then he or she will call out the number in Italian and ask a student to circle the correct number.

B Work with a classmate. One of you will count from 20 to 30. The other will count from 40 to 50.

C Have a contest with a friend. See who can count the fastest from 1 to 100 by tens.

D Have a contest with a friend. Count from 100 to 1000 by hundreds.

4 · Numeri • 177

Attività

A. You can also have students call out the numbers and ask other students to circle them.

B. Repeat this activity with other groups of numbers.

C., D. Have students time each other. Challenge students to count backwards by tens from 100; and from 1,000 to 100.

Finding Out the Price

—**Quanto è la calcolatrice, signora?** How much is a calculator, ma'am?

—**Quattro euro.** Four euros.

—**Grazie, signora.** Thank you, ma'am.

1. Model the dialogue yourself, pointing to the appropriate speaker on the overhead transparency. Use props to make the dialogue more realistic.

2. Model the dialogue with one or more able students.

3. Have two students model the dialogue.

4. Or use the audio program to model the dialogue.

Attività

A. Put price tags on the exercise items and have students use them as props. You can extend the exercise by using all the items from Lesson 3.

Sample answer:

—**Quanto è il quaderno, signora?**
—**Cinque euro.**
—**Grazie.**

Prices:

la calcolatrice: quattro euro
la gomma: uno euro
la penna: due euro
la matita: uno euro
lo zaino: venticinque euro

Finding Out the Price

To find out how much something costs, you ask:

—Quanto è la calcolatrice, signora?
—Quattro euro.
—Grazie, signora.

Attività

A **Work with a classmate. One of you will be the customer and the other will be the clerk at a stationery store. Make up a conversation to buy the following things.**

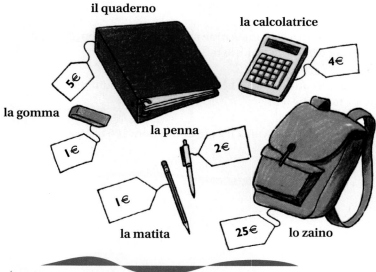

il quaderno

la calcolatrice

4€

5€

la gomma

la penna

1€

2€

1€

la matita

25€   lo zaino

Cultura

Point out that the exchange rate
fluctuates, but that one dollar is
equal to approximately one euro.

Cultura

Money Systems

The Italian monetary unit is the euro.

4 · Numeri • 179

Attività

 Give the amount of each Italian coin and bill pictured below.

1.

2.

3.

4.

180 • *Welcome to Italian!*

180

5 Prego

Speaking Politely

—Buon giorno.
—Buon giorno. Un espresso, per favore.

FOCUS

Students will

- request common foods and drinks in a restaurant setting
- ask and respond to a request for the cost of common foods and drinks

TEACH

—**Buon giorno.** Good day.

—**Buon giorno. Un espresso, per favore.** Good day. An espresso, please.

(The waiter brings the order.)

—**Grazie.** Thanks.

—**Prego.** You're welcome.

(The waiter brings the order.)
—Grazie.
　—Prego.

5 · Prego • 181

(A little later.)

—Quanto è il espresso, per favore? How much is the espresso, please?

—Due euro. Two euros.

Per piacere. Please.

Dialogue

1. Use the audio program to present the dialogue. Point to the appropriate speaker as each line is heard. Or model the dialogue yourself, pointing to the appropriate speaker on the overhead transparency. Do not translate into English.

2. Model the dialogue with one of the more able students.

3. Have two students model the dialogue.

Attività

A. If students need more practice with the basic dialogue, have them change partners after the first reading so that each student practices the dialogue three or four times.

B. Answers: 1. Un caffè, per favore. 2. Un tè, per favore. 3. Un espresso, per favore. 4. Un cappuccino, per favore. 5. Una limonata, per favore. 6. Un'aranciata, per favore. 7. Una cola, per favore.

Arrange the classroom furniture, so that the "customer" is seated at a restaurant "table" or standing at a "counter."

(A little later.)
—Quanto è il espresso, per favore?
—Due euro.

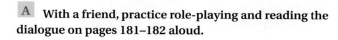

Another way to say "please" is:

Per piacere.

Attività

A With a friend, practice role-playing and reading the dialogue on pages 181–182 aloud.

B You are at a *caffè* in Venezia Lido, Italy. Order the following things. Ask a classmate to be the server.

1. un caffè

2. un tè

3. un espresso

4. un cappuccino

182 • *Welcome to Italian!*

5. una limonata

6. un'aranciata

7. una cola

C You would like to order the following foods at an Italian restaurant. Be polite when you order them!

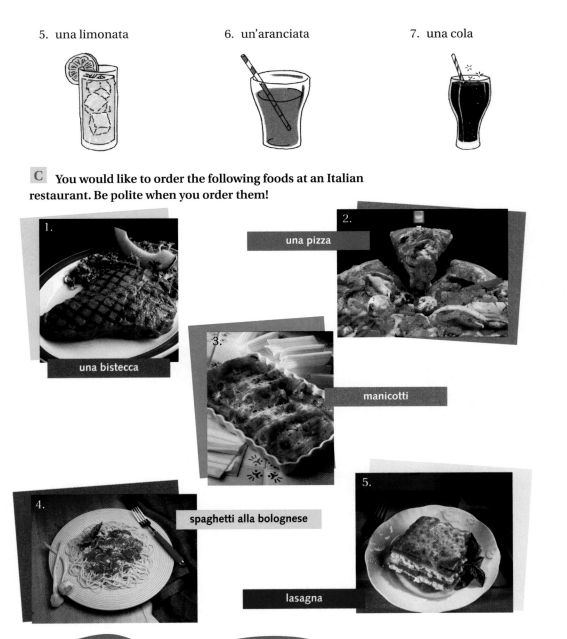

1. una bistecca

2. una pizza

3. manicotti

4. spaghetti alla bolognese

5. lasagna

Cultura

Bring in pictures of Italian foods or a well-illustrated Italian cookbook. Discuss the various types of pastas, cheeses, and sauces. Find out if any of the students has an Italian relative or friend who could talk to the class about Italian cuisine or eating customs.

ASSESS

Review the lesson and check student progress by using the following:

- Give students the basic dialogue with some blanks, and ask them to fill in the blanks.

- Activities Workbook, Lesson 5

CLOSE

On the chalkboard, write the introductory dialogue lines in the wrong order. Ask students to write them in a logical order.

Expansion

Have students design a menu for an Italian café or restaurant. Photocopy the result and have students use it to role-play a group ordering a meal. Teach other common drinks and foods:

un'acqua minerale   mineral water

un succo di frutta   fruit juice

un panino   sandwich

una pizetta   small pizza

un gelato   ice cream

You may also want to teach this polite and frequently used expression:

- **Vorrei...**   I'd like . . . .

*C*ultura
Foods of the Italian World

Italian cuisine, *la cucina italiana,* is considered one of the best in the entire world. Italian or Italian-American cooking is very popular everywhere in the United States. When we think of Italian food, we think of pasta. Pasta is made by mixing flour and water or flour and eggs in different proportions. You can add a variety of delicious sauces to the pasta.

Pasta comes in a wide range of shapes, sizes, thickness, and textures. All have different names. How many of these pastas do you know?

capellini	ravioli
farfalle	spaghetti
lasagne	tortellini
linguine	vermicelli (or) spaghettini
maccheroni	ziti
penne	

6 Che ora è?

Telling Time

To find out the time, you ask:

Che ora è? (or) **Che ore sono?**

To tell the time, you say:

È l'una.   **Sono le due.**   **Sono le tre.**   **Sono le quattro.**

Sono le cinque.   **Sono le sei.**   **Sono le sette.**   **Sono le otto.**

Sono le nove.   **Sono le dieci.**   **Sono le undici.**   **Sono le dodici.**

6 · Che ora è? • 185

Lesson 6

Audio

Transparencies

Workbook

FOCUS

Students will

- ask and respond to requests for the time
- give the time of events

TEACH

Che ora è? (or) **Che ore sono?**
  What time is it?

È l'una.   It is one o'clock.

Sono le due.   It is two o'clock.

Sono le tre.   It is three o'clock.

Sono le quattro.   It is four o'clock.

Sono le cinque.   It is five o'clock.

Sono le sei.   It is six o'clock.

Sono le sette.   It is seven o'clock.

Sono le otto.   It is eight o'clock.

Sono le nove.   It is nine o'clock.

Sono le dieci.   It is ten o'clock.

Sono le undici.   It is eleven o'clock.

Sono le dodici.   It is twelve o'clock.

185

È l'una e cinque. It is 1:05 (five minutes after one).

Sono le due e dieci. It is 2:10.

Sono le cinque e quaranta. It is 5:40.

Sono le sei e un quarto. Sono le sei e quindici. It is 6:15 (a quarter after six).

Sono le sette e mezzo. Sono le sette e trenta. It is 7:30. (It is half past seven.)

Vocabulary

1. You may want to teach a few time expressions at a time, rather than all in one lesson. Begin with times on the hour, then the quarter and half-hour, then minutes past the hour. A toy clock or one made with movable hands to illustrate the time expressions is a useful prop.

2. Using the overhead transparency, ask *Che ora è?* or *Che ore sono?* Point to each clock as you say the time and have students repeat after you. Or have students listen to the audio program as you point to the appropriate clock.

3. Using the clock, ask *Che ora è?/Che ore sono?,* changing the hours and eliciting individuals to respond. If you do not have a clock, draw one on the chalkboard. Repeat until all students have had an opportunity to respond.

   Repeat this procedure with the times, giving the number of minutes after the hour.

Attività

A. Answers: 1. Sono le due e un quarto. 2. Sono le undici. 3. Sono le otto. 4. Sono le quattro e mezzo. 5. È l'una e venticinque.

   Have students do this activity in pairs, taking turns asking and giving the time on the clocks shown.

| È l'una e cinque. | Sono le due e dieci. | Sono le cinque e quaranta. | Sono le sei e un quarto. Sono le sei e quindici. | Sono le sette e mezzo. Sono le sette e trenta. |

Attività

A Give the following times in Italian.

186 • *Welcome to Italian!*

186

B Walk up to a classmate and ask for the time. Your classmate will answer you.

Telling At What Time

To find out at what time something takes place, you ask:
A che hora è la lezione?

To tell at what time something takes place, you answer:
La lezione è alle nove e trenta.

Attività

A Tell at what time you have the following classes. Note that these words are cognates. They are very similar in both Italian and English.

1. la lezione di matematica
2. la lezione di storia
3. la lezione d'educazione fisica
4. la lezione di biologia
5. la lezione d'italiano
6. la lezione d'inglese

B Draw pictures of some of your daily activities such as getting up in the morning, eating breakfast, walking or riding the bus to school, going to after-school sports, eating dinner, going to bed, etc. Then compare your pictures with those of a classmate. Both of you will tell when you do these activities. Keep track of how many activities you both do at the same time.

6 · Che ora è? • 187

B. Have students draw their own clocks on paper, exchange their paper with another student, and either give the times indicated on their partner's clocks or write them down in words. Circulate among students to monitor answers.

Telling At What Time

A che ora è la lezione? At what time is the class?

La lezione è alle nove e trenta. The class is at 9:30.

Attività

A. Answers: La lezione di/d'è...
   Vary activity by having pairs of students take turns asking each other the time of the classes listed.

B. Some students may benefit from adding a clock to their drawing that shows the time they do the activity.

Cultura

Point out that *mezzogiorno* means mid(dle) day and *mezzanotte* means mid(night).

You may want to explain the use of a comma instead of a colon when writing the time (8,30 = 8:30).

Explain that the 24-hour system is used in Italy (and throughout the world) for official times such as train, bus, and plane schedules, movie schedules, and television and radio programs instead of adding A.M. and P.M. to each hour. For example, 6 P.M. would be 18,00.

ASSESS

Review the lesson and check student progress by using the following:

- Ask students the time at random throughout the class period.
- Activities Workbook, Lesson 6

CLOSE

Provide TV or movie schedules in English and have students convert the times using the 24-hour system. Or bring in an Italian newspaper with a movie schedule and have students read the times shown.

Expansion

You may want to teach your students the other way to express times after the half hour.

Sono le sei meno dieci.
It is ten to six.

Sono le otto meno venti.
It is twenty to eight.

Cultura

Lunch Customs

In Italy, many people still go home for lunch. Businesses close at 1:00 *(all'una)* in the afternoon and open again between 4:30 and 5:00 *(alle quattro e mezzo o alle cinque)*. Because of the traffic problems in the large cities, however, many people now eat where they work or go to a nearby *caffè, trattoria,* or *paninoteca.*

PINOCCHIO PIZZERIA

PINOCCHIO

PIZZERIA - Specialita' carne e pesce alla brace
Chiuso il venerdi'

MILANO: v. V. Foppa, 16
(ang. v. California) ☎ (02) 481 47 73

Bakery,
Naples, Italy

Café near the Pantheon,
Rome, Italy

188 • *Welcome to Italian!*

188

7 | *I giorni della settimana*

Telling the Days of the Week

ITALIA   **GENNAIO**

DOMENICA	LUNEDÌ	MARTEDÌ	MERCOLEDÌ	GIOVEDÌ	VENERDÌ	SABATO	DOMENICA	LUNEDÌ	MARTEDÌ	MERCOLEDÌ	GIOVEDÌ	VENERDÌ	SABATO	DOMENICA	LUNEDÌ	MARTEDÌ	MERCOLEDÌ	GIOVEDÌ	VENERDÌ	SABATO	DOMENICA	LUNEDÌ	MARTEDÌ	MERCOLEDÌ	GIOVEDÌ	VENERDÌ	SABATO	DOMENICA	LUNEDÌ	MARTEDÌ
1	2	3	4	5	6	7	8	9	10	11	12	13	14	15	16	17	18	19	20	21	22	23	24	25	26	27	28	29	30	31

7 · I giorni della settimana • 189

  Audio

Transparencies

Workbook

FOCUS

Students will
- use the names of the days of the week
- ask and respond to questions about the current day

TEACH

lunedì Monday
martedì Tuesday
mercoledì Wednesday
giovedì Thursday
venerdì Friday
sabato Saturday
domenica Sunday

—**Che giorno è oggi?** What day is today?

—**È lunedì. Oggi è lunedì.** It's Monday. Today is Monday.

—**Che giorno è domani.** What day is tomorrow?

—**È martedì. Domani è martedì.** It's Tuesday. Tomorrow is Tuesday.

Vocabulary/Dialogue

1. Point to each day of the week on the overhead transparency as you name it. Repeat two or three times.

2. Point to each day as you name it, but pause before one as if you forgot it. Signal to the class to respond chorally. Repeat with other days.

3. Point to different days on the calendar and ask and answer: *Che giorno è?* (for example, pointing to Monday) *È lunedì? Sì, è lunedì.* Repeat with other students.

4. Use the dialogue expressions to ask the day and to answer.

5. You may also present the vocabulary and dialogue with the audio program.

Attività

A. Answers: 1. Oggi è...
2. Domani è... 3. Sabato, domenica

You may want to have students answer the questions orally in class and prepare the answers for homework.

Cultura

Explain that Italian students attend school from early September through June and that they have school on Saturday. However, they have many more vacation days than most American students. Discuss with class whether they would opt for this type of schedule.

Finding Out and Giving the Day

—Che giorno è oggi?
 —È lunedì.
  (or) Oggi è lunedì.

—Che giorno è domani?
 —È martedì.
  (or) Domani è martedì.

Attività

A Answer the following questions in Italian.

1. Che giorno è oggi?
2. E domani? Che giorno è?
3. Quali sono i giorni del week-end, del fine settimana?

Cultura
Italian-American Festivals

There are wonderful Italian street fairs held in many cities of the United States where there is a large Italian-American population. Many of these fairs are organized by the local Italian parish church. Quite often the *festa* is in honor of the patron saint of the parish.

A famous *festa italiana* is the Feast of San Gennaro, celebrated each summer in Little Italy, a section of New York City.

190 • *Welcome to Italian!*

190

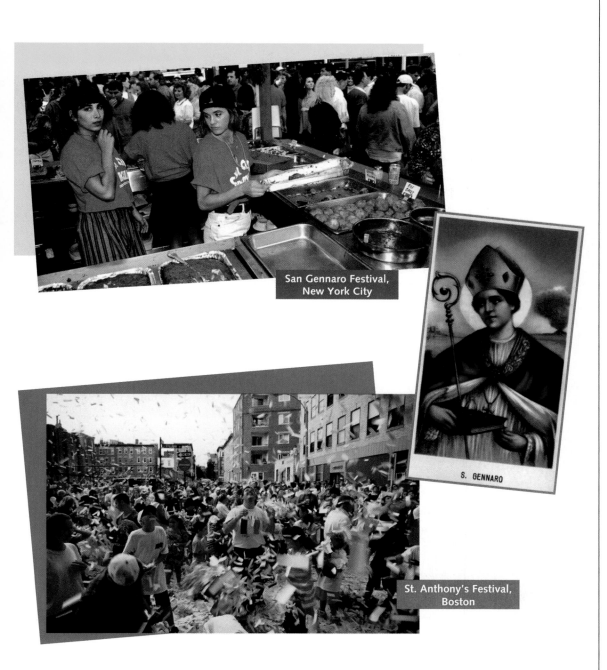

San Gennaro Festival,
New York City

S. GENNARO

St. Anthony's Festival,
Boston

Review the lesson and check student progress by using the following:

- Activities Workbook, Lesson 7

1. Have students draw one activity that they are going to do the next weekend. Have them label it with the day of the week and the time they are going to be doing it.

2. Have students prepare a weekly class schedule *(un orario),* including all classes and times: *italiano 10, 10-10,55.* Then call on students and ask: *A che ora è la lezione d'inglese?* (When is your English class?) Encourage them to answer in full sentences to practice expressions and pronunciation: *La lezione d'inglese è alle…).*

3. To review times and days of the week, have pairs of students describe their schedules: *Il lunedì la lezione di storia è alle due.* Point out the use of *il* before the days of the week except *la domenica* to express "on Mondays," "on Tuesdays,"etc.

Expansion

Have students research the many holidays in Italy. Good sources of information are the library, on-line resources, people who have lived in the country, and its embassy or consulate. List the holidays on the chalkboard and compare to the number of holidays we celebrate in the United States.

Lesson 8

Audio Audio

Transparencies Transparencies

Workbook Workbook

FOCUS

Students will

- use the names of the months of the year and the seasons
- ask and respond to requests for the date

TEACH

gennaio January

febbraio February

marzo March

aprile April

maggio May

giugno June

luglio July

agosto August

settembre September

ottobre October

novembre November

dicembre December

la primavera spring

l'estate summer

8 Mesi e stagioni

Telling the Months

GENNAIO	FEBBRAIO	MARZO	APRILE	MAGGIO	GIUGNO
1 2 3 4 5 6 7 8 9 10 11 12 13 14 15 16 17 18 19 20 21 22 23 24 25 26 27 28 29 30 31	1 2 3 4 5 6 7 8 9 10 11 12 13 14 15 16 17 18 19 20 21 22 23 24 25 26 27 28 29	1 2 3 4 5 6 7 8 9 10 11 12 13 14 15 16 17 18 19 20 21 22 23 24 25 26 27 28 29 30 31	1 2 3 4 5 6 7 8 9 10 11 12 13 14 15 16 17 18 19 20 21 22 23 24 25 26 27 28 29 30	1 2 3 4 5 6 7 8 9 10 11 12 13 14 15 16 17 18 19 20 21 22 23 24 25 26 27 28 29 30 31	1 2 3 4 5 6 7 8 9 10 11 12 13 14 15 16 17 18 19 20 21 22 23 24 25 26 27 28 29

LUGLIO	AGOSTO	SETTEMBRE	OTTOBRE	NOVEMBRE	DICEMBRE
1 2 3 4 5 6 7 8 9 10 11 12 13 14 15 16 17 18 19 20 21 22 23 24 25 26 27 28 29 30 31	1 2 3 4 5 6 7 8 9 10 11 12 13 14 15 16 17 18 19 20 21 22 23 24 25 26 27 28 29 30 31	1 2 3 4 5 6 7 8 9 10 11 12 13 14 15 16 17 18 19 20 21 22 23 24 25 26 27 28 29 30	1 2 3 4 5 6 7 8 9 10 11 12 13 14 15 16 17 18 19 20 21 22 23 24 25 26 27 28 29 30 31	1 2 3 4 5 6 7 8 9 10 11 12 13 14 15 16 17 18 19 20 21 22 23 24 25 26 27 28 29 30	1 2 3 4 5 6 7 8 9 10 11 12 13 14 15 16 17 18 19 20 21 22 23 24 25 26 27 28 29 30 31

Telling the Seasons

la primavera

l'estate

192 • *Welcome to Italian!*

192

l'autunno

l'inverno

Finding Out and Giving the Date

—Qual è la data di oggi?
—Oggi è il primo aprile.

Primo is used for the first of the month. For other days, you use *due, tre, quattro,* etc.: *il due maggio.*

Attività

A Each of you will stand up in class and give the date of your birthday in Italian. Listen and keep a record of how many of you were born in the same month.

B Based on the information from *Attività A,* tell in Italian in which months most of the students in the class were born. Tell in what month the fewest were born.

8 · Mesi e stagioni • 193

---

l'autunno autumn
l'inverno winter

—**Qual è la data di oggi?** What is today's date?

—**Oggi è il primo aprile.** Today is the first of April.

Vocabulary

1. Introduce by pointing to each month and season on the over-head transparency as you name them. Repeat two or three times, with students repeating after you or have the class listen to the audio program. Recycle the days of the week as you do this lesson.

2. Say a month and have students give the next month.

3. Say a season and have students respond with the corresponding months.

   Repeat this procedure with the seasons.

Finding Out and Giving the Date

1. Model the brief dialogue your-self, using a calendar.

2. Model the dialogue with one of the more able students.

3. Have two students model the dialogue.

4. You may also present the dia-logue with the audio program.

Attività

A. To make it easier to tally the birthdays, write the months on the chalkboard and have a stu-dent make a mark under each month for each birthday.

B. You may want to introduce *Quando è il tuo compleanno?* (When is your birthday?) Write it on the board above the list of months. Students respond: *Il mio compleanno è il ____.*

C. Post the finished calendar in the classroom.

D. Answers: 1. l'inverno 2. la primavera 3. la primavera 4. l'estate

Review the lesson and check student progress by using the following:

- Activities Workbook, Lesson 8

CLOSE

Ask students to write the month in Italian that these holidays occur in:

- Labor Day
- Valentine's Day
- Halloween
- Presidents' Day
- Mother's Day
- Thanksgiving Day
- Father's Day
- Independence Day
- New Year's Day

Expansion

A. Some Italian-language calendars record the name of the saint associated with each day. Try to locate one and have students identify their saint's day based on their name, or the name they chose in Lesson 2.

B. Have a party with an Italian theme. Help students decorate the class. You may want to play Italian music and serve Italian foods.

C Work in groups of two or three. Each group is responsible for drawing a calendar for one month of the year. Include the dates of classmates' birthdays.

D In which season of the year is . . . ?

1. dicembre
2. maggio
3. aprile
4. luglio

Look at the ad below. Tell when each Italian film is shown.

194 • *Welcome to Italian!*

9 **I***l tempo*

Describing the Weather

—Che tempo fa oggi?
  —Fa bello. Fa bel tempo.
     C'è sole.

—Fa cattivo tempo.
  Fa brutto.
  Piove.

9 · *Il tempo* • 195

 Audio

 Transparencies

 Workbook

FOCUS

Students will

• use some common weather expressions

TEACH

—**Che tempo fa oggi?** What's the weather like today?

—**Fa bello. Fa bel tempo.** It's nice (weather). It's beautiful weather.

C'è sole. It's sunny.

—**Fa cattivo tempo.** It's bad weather.

Fa brutto. It's nasty.

Piove. It's raining.

Tira vento. It's windy.

Nevica. It's snowing.

Fa caldo. Non fa fresco. It's hot. It's not cool.

Fa freddo. It's cold.

Vocabulary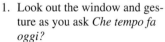

1. Look out the window and gesture as you ask *Che tempo fa oggi?*

2. Point to each picture on the overhead transparency as you state the weather expression associated with it. (Point to the sunny weather for *C'è sole. Fa bello. Fa bel tempo,* and so on.) Repeat two or three times.

3. Point to each picture as you give the weather expression, but pause before one as if you forgot it. Repeat with other pictures. You may also use pictures from magazines, photos, or flashcards.

195

4. Point to each picture again as you give the weather expression, but pause before one and point to a student to respond. Repeat with other pictures and other students.

5. You may also present the vocabulary with the audio program.

Attività

A. Have students work in pairs to ask and give the weather information. Have them change partners so that each has three or four conversations.

B. You may want to have students describe the weather orally and write it for homework.

C. Have students describe their pictures in small groups for more efficient individual practice. Monitor answers. Expand the activity by having students illustrate their favorite holiday (with symbols, weather scenes, etc.) Have them indicate the day and date, the season, and the weather: *È il quattordici febbraio. È l'inverno. Fa freddo.* You may want to let other students guess the season and weather.

Cultura

Explain that for Italians, the month of August is synonymous with vacation, known as *il ferragosto* (meaning the August feast-festival). Thousands of businesses and factories close, and millions of workers go on vacation together. Highways are clogged, and beaches and tourist spots are packed. Those who remain in the deserted cities are left with few stores open and insufficient services. Ask for students' impressions of this kind of national vacation time and whether there is a particular month in which Americans vacation.

Tira vento.

Nevica.

Fa caldo. Non fa fresco.

Fa freddo.

Attività

A Tell in Italian what the weather is like today.

B Work in groups of four. Write in Italian the name of each season on a separate sheet of paper. Put the papers in a pile. Each of you will pull one sheet from the pile. Then describe the weather of the season written on the sheet.

C Draw a picture of your favorite type of weather. Then describe your picture to the class in Italian.

196 • *Welcome to Italian!*

196

Cultura

Seasons in Italy

Italy enjoys a wonderful climate. In the winter, skiers flock to ski resorts such as Cortina d'Ampezzo. In summer, sun-lovers enjoy the beaches of the Mediterranean or the Adriatic such as Portofino or Venezia Lido.

Can you tell what the weather is like today in northern Italy and in southern Italy from this weather map below? How about tomorrow's weather?

Portofino, Italy

Ski resort, Cervinia, Italy

Review the lesson and check student progress by using the following:

- Ask students to pretend that it is yesterday and to give the weather.

Activities Workbook, Lesson 9

CLOSE

1. Ask students to talk about what the weather is like in their hometowns during the different months (*Tira vento in aprile a Boston*).

2. Ask students to predict tomorrow's weather. Have them use the present tense. Have students correct their prediction if necessary the next day. Reward those who predicted correctly.

Expansion

Using the weather map of Italy, divide the class into small groups and assign each group a major city or region. (If cities aren't indicated on weather map, use a map of Italy to show students where they are located.) Include such cities as *Firenze, Siena, Torino, Bologna, Roma, Napoli, Palermo*. Ask each group to write a forecast for their city, according to the weather map. Then ask *Che tempo fa (a Roma)? Fa molto bello. C'è il sole e fa caldo.* You may want to point out that to say "in (+ city)," you just use *a* before the city's name.

Lesson 10

📼 Audio

🎙 Transparencies

📓 Workbook

FOCUS

Students will

- ask and respond to requests for one's name
- ask and respond to questions about one's nationality

TEACH

—**Buon giorno. Tu sei un amico di Gianni Rossi, non è vero?**
Hi! You're a friend of Gianni Rossi, aren't you?

—**Sì, sono Mark Thomson. E tu sei Luciana, vero?** Yes, I'm Mark Thomson. And you are Luciana, right?

—**Sì, sono Luciana. Luciana Carlucci. Sei americano, Mark?** Yes, I'm Luciana. Luciana Carlucci. Are you American, Mark?

—**Sì, sono americano. Sono di Nuova York.** Yes, I'm American. I'm from New York.

Dialogue

1. Use the overhead transparency and have the students listen to the audio program, pointing to the appropriate speaker as each line is heard. Have students listen again.

2. Or model the dialogue yourself, pointing to the appropriate speaker on the overhead transparency.

3. Have two students model the dialogue, using their real names. Prompt them if necessary.

10 Sono...

Telling Who I Am and Where I'm From

—Buon giorno. Tu sei un amico di Gianni Rossi, non è vero?

    —Sì, sono Mark Thomson. E tu sei Luciana, vero?

—Sì, sono Luciana. Luciana Carlucci. Sei americano, Mark?

    —Sì, sono americano. Sono di Nuova York.

When you hear a question with *sei* in Italian, you answer with *sono*. *Sei* is used to speak to a friend *(tu)* and *sono* is used to speak about yourself *(io)*.

    Sei? → **sono**

When you describe a boy in Italian, you use -o. When you describe a girl, you use -a.

Ricardo non è *italiano*.   Giulia non è *americana*.

Ricardo è *americano*.   Giulia è *italiana*.

Ricardo è *un amico* di Gianni.   Giulia è *un'amica* di Luigi.

Attività

A Work with a classmate. Practice reading aloud the dialogue on page 198. Use as much expression as possible!

B Walk up to a classmate. Pretend that you think that you remember his or her name, but you aren't sure. Then find out if he or she is a friend of someone you know.

C Answer the following questions about yourself.

1. Sei americano(a)?

2. Di dove sei?

3. Sei un amico (un'amica) di Marcello Scotti?

D Draw a picture of a male friend or relative. Give him an Italian name. Then tell as much about him as you can.

E Draw a picture of a female friend or relative. Give her an Italian name. Then tell as much about her as you can.

Ricardo non è italiano. Richard is not Italian.

Ricardo è americano. Richard is American.

Ricardo è un amico di Gianni. Richard is a friend of Gianni.

Giulia non è americana. Julia is not American.

Giulia è italiana. Julia is Italian.

Giulia è un'amica di Luigi. Julia is a friend of Luigi.

Attività

A. Have students substitute their own names.

B. Before doing this activity, model the dialogue with a female and a male student.

   —Ciao! Tu sei un'amica di…, non è vero?

   —Sì, sono un'amica di… Sono Cathy.

   —E tu sei Roberto, non è vero?

   —No, non sono Roberto. Sono Paolo.

C. This activity can be enhanced by the use of photos. Have students bring photos of themselves from home, or use photos taken at school activities if available. Have students give the answers orally in class and write the answers for homework.

D., E. Have students write the information under the drawing and post the results.

Parliamo di più

—**Ciao!** Hi!

—**Ciao!** Hi!

—**Sei un amico di Franco Marotto, non è vero?** You're a friend of Frank Marotto, right?

—**Sì, sono un amico di Franco. Sono Mark Thomson.** Yes. I am a friend of Franco. My name is Mark Thomson.

—**Come stai, Mark?** How are you, Mark?

—**Molto bene, grazie, e tu?** Very well, thanks, and you?

—**Non, c'è male.** Not bad.

—**Sei Luciana, no?** You're Luciana, right?

—**Sì, sono Luciana.** Yes, I'm Luciana.

—**Sei di Roma, Luciana?** You are from Rome, Luciana?

—**No, io sono di Milano. Ma tu sei americano, non è vero?** No, I am from Milan. But you are American, right?

—**Sì, sono di Nuova York.** Yes, I am from New York.

—**Ciao, Mark. A presto.** Bye, Mark. See you soon.

—**Arrivederci, Luciana. Ci vediamo.** Good-bye, Luciana. See you soon.

1. Draw and label Mark and Luciana on the chalkboard. Model the review dialogue yourself, pointing to the appropriate speaker on the chalkboard. If possible, use puppets for this activity.

2. Have two students model the dialogue, using the names Mark and Luciana and their nationalities. Have several other pairs of students model the dialogue.

3. If you have students of other nationalities, have two students model the dialogue using their real names and nationalities.

4. You may also use the audio program to present the dialogue.

200

Parliamo di più

—Ciao!

  —Ciao!

—Sei un amico di Franco Marotto, non è vero?

  —Sì, sono un amico di Franco. Sono Mark Thomson.

—Come stai, Mark?

  —Molto bene, grazie, e tu?

—Non c'è male.

  —Sei Luciana, no?

—Sì, sono Luciana.

  —Sei di Roma, Luciana?

—No, io sono di Milano. Ma tu sei americano, non è vero?

  —Sì, sono di Nuova York.

—Ciao, Mark. A presto.

  —Arrivederci, Luciana. Ci vediamo.

Attività

A Work with a classmate. Practice the above conversation together with a classmate. One will read the part of Mark and the other will read the part of Luciana. Use as much expression as you can.

B Complete the following story about Mark and Luciana.

Mark è di _____. Mark è _____, non è italiano. Mark è un _____ di Franco. Anche Luciana è un'amica di _____. Luciana non è americana. È _____. Non è di Roma. È _____ Milano.

C Work with a classmate. Find out where he or she is from and his or her nationality. Then give the same information about yourself.

200 • *Welcome to Italian!*

D Look at the photograph of Paula Wright. She is from Houston. Tell all about her in Italian.

E Look at this photograph of Bianca Pretti. She is from Venezia. Tell all about her in Italian.

Attività

A. Have students switch partners and use other names and nationalities in the conversation.

B. Answers: Nuova York, americano, amico, Franco, italiana, di

C. Post the results of this activity in the classroom.

D. Most likely answer: *Paula Wright è di Houston. È americana.*

E. Most likely answer: *Bianca Pretti è di Venezia. È italiana. È un'amica di_____.*

ASSESS

Review the lesson and check student progress by using the following:

• Activities Workbook, Lesson 10

CLOSE

Have students in groups of three prepare a conversation between two Americans and an Italian exchange student (male or female). They do not know the student's name or what city he/she is from. In the conversation, they should greet and ask how the person is, find out where they are from, introduce themselves, and ask the appropriate questions to find out more about the student. Call on volunteers to perform in front of the class.

FOCUS

Students will

• ask and respond to questions about what languages they speak and what they study

TEACH

—**Parli inglese, David?** Do you speak English, David?

—**Sì, parlo inglese.** Yes, I speak English.

—**Parli anche l'italiano?** Do you speak Italian, too?

—**Sì, parlo un po', non molto.** Yes, I speak a little, not much.

—**Studi l'italiano a scuola?** Do you study Italian in school?

—**Sì, la lezione d'italiano è molto interessante.** Yes, Italian class is very interesting.

Dialogue

1. Use the overhead transparency and audio program to present the dialogue. Point to the speaker as each line of the dialogue is heard. Or model the dialogue yourself, pointing to the appropriate speaker on the transparency.

2. If you have students who speak other languages, have two students model the dialogue using their real names and the languages they speak.

Parli? Do you speak?

parlo I speak

Studi? Do you study?

studio I study

italiano Italian

francese French

202

11 ▶ Parlo italiano

—Parli inglese, David?

   —Sì, parlo inglese.

—Parli anche l'italiano?

   —Sì, parlo un po', non molto.

—Studi l'italiano a scuola?

   —Sì, la lezione d'italiano è molto interessante.

When you hear a question with *parli* or *studi*, you answer with *parlo* or *studio*. *Parli* and *studi* are used when speaking to a friend *(tu)* and *parlo* and *studio* are used when speaking about yourself *(io)*.

     Parli? → **parlo**   **Studi?** → **studio**

Look at the Italian names of these languages. You can probably guess the meaning of each as all of these words are cognates.

italiano	russo
francese	polacco
portoghese	arabo
cinese	greco
giapponese	latino

What languages are taught at this school in Miami?

Attività

A Walk around the room and greet a classmate. Find out what language(s) he or she speaks. Then tell your class-mate what language(s) you speak.

B Get a beach ball. One person throws the ball to another and asks, *Parli italiano?* The person who catches the ball answers, *Sì, parlo...* or *No, non parlo...*

C If you speak a language other than English at home, tell the class what language you speak.

D Answer the following questions.

1. Studi la matematica? È facile o difficile la lezione di matematica?

2. Studi l'italiano a scuola? È facile o difficile la lezione d'italiano?

PADOVAN LANGUAGE INSTITUTE

YOUR PASSPORT TO FLUENCY

CORSI DI:

- SPAGNOLO
- FRANCESE
- PORTOGHESE
- ITALIANO
- RUSSO
- TEDESCO

INGLESE DA LIVELLO 0 A LIVELLI AVANZATI
Preparazione al TOFEL
Tutti i livelli. Lezioni private o in gruppo.

Impara di più, in meno tempo con il Metodo Padovan!

CHIAMA OGGI STESSO!

(305) 375-0315

(dietro la chiesa)

CUCINA GIAPPONESE
ROKKO 六甲
Domenica Riposo
00187 ROMA
Via Rasella, 138 .... ☎ (06) **4 88 12 14**

Ristorante Cinese
RU YI 如意樓
L'ATMOSFERA CINESE IN UN AMBIENTE ELEGANTE
ARIA CONDIZIONATA
ROMA Via Valadier, 14 (in Prati)
☎ (06) **3 21 58 04**

11 · Parlo italiano • 203

---

portoghese Portuguese
cinese Chinese
giapponese Japanese
russo Russian
polacco Polish
arabo Arabic
greco Greek
latino Latin

Attività

A. If your furniture is movable, arrange it so that students can move about easily.

B. If you don't have a beach ball, use another kind of soft ball or a beanbag. Students should respond with either *Sì, parlo italiano* or *No, non parlo italiano.*

C. Be sensitive to the fact that some students may speak non-standard dialects at home.

D. Possible answers: 1. Sì, studio (or) No, non studio matematica. È facile (or) È difficile la lezione di matematica. 2. Sì, studio (or) No, non studio l'italiano a scuola. È facile (or) È difficile la lezione d'italiano.

ASSESS

Review the lesson and check student progress by using the following:

- Activities Workbook, Lesson 11

CLOSE

Ask students to write a dialogue between a younger Italian cousin they have never met, an Italian exchange student they would like to know better, or between a new student who speaks a few languages.

Expansion

Ask students to use a map or globe to plan an imaginary trip around the world. Have them prepare an itinerary and list the three languages that would be the most useful for them to know on the trip.

Welcome to
LATIN!

Roman aqueduct,
Nîmes, France

Latin is the mother tongue of all the Romance languages. The original home of Latin was Latium, a small district on the western coast of Italy. The chief city of Latium was Rome.

The Romans were often threatened by warlike neighbors. Unwilling to accept defeat, they sent out legions to conquer their enemies. By the middle of the third century B.C., the Romans had conquered all of Italy. Their legions continued beyond the Mediterranean Sea and the Alps. Rome soon became the capital of a tremendous empire and the center of a great civilization.

The Latin language spoken by the Roman armies was also the language of some of the western world's greatest writers and orators. Latin was the language of Vergil, Cicero, Catullus, Ovid, and Pliny. Even after the fall of the Roman Empire, Latin continued to be the language of a large part of Europe. It finally evolved into the modern Romance languages: French, Italian, Portuguese, Rumanian, and Spanish.

Colosseum, Rome, Italy

Roman theater,
Aphrodisia, Turkey

Appian Way,
Rome, Italy

Latin to English

Although English is not a Romance language, some 50% of all English words come from Latin. As you study Latin, you will learn Latin derivatives. Latin derivatives are words used in English that have Latin origins. Some examples are:

audīre (to hear) audio, audible, audience, audition
fortūna (fortune) fortunate, misfortune
grātia (favor, thanks) grace, gracious
liberāre (to free) liberal, liberator
medicus (doctor) medical, medicine

205

Lesson 1

- Audio
- Transparencies
- Workbook

FOCUS

Students will

- use and respond to greetings
- introduce themselves and respond to introductions
- say "good-bye"

TEACH

—**Salvē.** Hello (Hi).

—**Salvē.** Hello (Hi).

—**Quis es?** Who are you?

—**Sum Marcus.** I'm Marcus.

—**Et ego sum Anna.** And I'm Anna.

—**Valē, Anna.** Good-bye, Anna.

—**Valē.** Good-bye.

es? you are?

sum I am

Ego sum Rōmāna. I am a Roman girl.

Dialogue

1. Use the audio program or overhead transparency to model the dialogue. Do not give the English translation.

2. Have several pairs of students model the dialogue. Have students think of as many ways as they can to greet people in English. Look at the list of Latin first names included in this lesson and let students choose one.

206

1 ◆ Salvē et Valē

Greeting People

—Salvē.
  —Salvē.
—Quis es?
  —Sum Marcus.
—Et ego sum Anna.
  —Valē, Anna.
—Valē.

When you hear a question with *es* in Latin, you answer with *sum*. *Es* is used to speak to one person and *sum* is used to speak about yourself.

es? → sum

For emphasis, you can add *ego* with *sum*, but it isn't generally needed:

Ego sum Rōmāna.

Verba Latīna

The word "egoist" comes from the Latin word *ego*. What is an egoist, and what does it mean to have a big ego?

Egoist

Agenda

A Get up from your desk and walk around the classroom. Say *Salvē* to each of your classmates and then say *Valē.*

B Get a beach ball. One person throws the ball as he or she asks *Quis es?* The one who catches the ball answers *Sum...*

Cultūra

Common First Names

Here are some Latin first names that were popular in the days of the Romans.

Puerī

Aemilius, Augustus, Claudius, Cornēlius, Davus, Fabius, Gāius, Horātius, Lūcius, Marcus, Maximus, Paulus, Publius, Quintus, Sextus, Tullus

Puellae

Aelēna, Aemilia, Anna, Aurēlia, Caecilia, Clāra, Claudia, Cornēlia, Fabia, Flavia, Glōria, Jūlia, Lāvīnia, Messalina, Sophia, Tullia

1 · Salvē et Valē • 207

3. *Salvē, valē,* and *avē* can all be used to say "hello" or "good-bye" (much like *aloha* in Hawaiian). They are actually singular imperative forms and literally mean "Be strong" or "Be well." The plural is formed by adding *-te* to the end (*Salvēte, Valēte, Avēte*).

4. Long marks, or macrons, are used only on vowels and only for beginning Latin students. The Romans didn't use them. They are valuable for pronunciation purposes (pay attention to *e* and *i*), but not worth fretting about otherwise.

5. Students might want to know some additional expressions or phrases, such as: How's it going?, What's up? (*Quid agis?*); Fine, thanks (*Valēo, grātias; Rectē, gratiās*); Not bad (*Nōn male*); Not good (*Nōn bene*); So-so (*Variē*); And you? (*Et tu?*).

Verba Latīna

Ask students if they can think of other words that come from *ego* (such as egotist, egotistical, egocentric, egomaniac, ego trip).

Agenda

A. If your furniture is movable, arrange it so that students can move about easily. Greet several students to get them started. Teach them the additional words and phrases if they are interested. Teach and use the plural forms *Salvēte* or *Valēte* if you greet a group of students.

B. If you have introduced additional expressions, continue with the beach ball game and have students ask *Quid agis?*

Cultūra

Roman clothing for women and girls consisted of underwear, an under tunic (with or without sleeves) called a *tunica,* and a dress *(stola).* Sometimes women wore a shawl *(palla)* on top. Roman men and boys wore a loincloth and a tunic *(tunica).* If the man was also a citizen, he was allowed to wear a toga, a long piece of cloth wrapped around the body and draped over the arm.

ASSESS

Review the lesson and check student progress by using the following:

- Ask individual students their names, and if taught, "How it's going?"
- Ask students what an "egoist" is.
- Activities Workbook, Lesson 1

CLOSE

Ask students to prepare a brief conversation between two people who meet on the street. Have pairs of students speak their dialogues in front of the class.

Here is a mosaic of a Roman man and two Roman women. A mosaic was a popular form of art in Roman times. It was made of colored pieces of stone or glass. This mosaic shows the Roman poet Vergil holding a papyrus roll. The two women on either side are Muses, who were goddesses of the arts.

The man—*vir Rōmānus*—is wearing the typical Roman clothing for an adult male—a *toga* over a tunic. The women—*fēminae Rōmānae*—are wearing the typical Roman clothing for an adult female—a *stola* over a tunic.

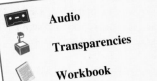

2 ◆ Numerī

Counting in Latin

1	ūnus	6	sex	11	ūndecim
2	duo	7	septem	12	duodecim
3	trēs	8	octō		
4	quattuor	9	novem	20	vīgintī
5	quinque	10	decem	100	centum
				1000	mille

Duo et trēs sunt quinque.

Quattuor et octo et sex et duo sunt vīgintī.

Agenda

A Count from one to ten in Latin.

B Make up some simple addition problems and ask a classmate for the answers.

FOCUS

Students will

- learn and use cardinal numbers
- learn about Roman numerals

(The English equivalents of the numbers are given as Arabic numerals.)

TEACH

Vocabulary

If students are interested, the numbers from 13–19 are as follows: *tredecim* (13), *quattuordecim* (14), *quīndecim* (15), *sēdecim* (16), *septemdecim* (17) *duodēvīgintī* (18), *ūndevīgintī* (19); after 20, use combinations of earlier numbers: *vīgintī ūnus* or *ūnus et vīgintī* (21), *trīgintā* (30).

1. Point to each number in order/in random order on the overhead transparency as you say its name. Signal to the class to say the number chorally.

2. Use the audio program to present the vocabulary.

Agenda

A. Write several numbers on the board. Point to each number and ask students to say the Latin word aloud.

B. Have students count to 12 (or more if you provided the expanded numbers list) by even and then by odd numbers.

Cultūra

Writing Numbers in Latin

The number system we use today is the Arabic system (1, 2, 3, etc.). The Romans used the Roman system shown below.

I	IV
II	V
III	

The Romans used only a limited number of letters to express numerals:

I	1	C	100
V	5	D	500
X	10	M	1000
L	50		

They combined or put letters together to form other numerals:

II	2	XI	11
IV	4	CLXIV	164

Arch of Titus, Rome, Italy

Roman numerals are still frequently used on monuments and buildings. They also are used for decorative purposes. What is the Arabic numeral for the Roman numeral on this house?

210 • *Welcome to Latin!*

Agenda

A Give the Arabic numerals for each of the following Roman numerals.

1. II
2. IX
3. VI
4. XL

5. LX
6. XXV
7. XXVI
8. DL

B Try to think of at least two places where you would normally see Roman numerals used today.

Verba Latīna

Latin numbers provide us with many words in English. Let's take a look at a few of them. Tell what each of the following words means and then give the Latin numeral from which it is derived:

centennial	dual	quintuplets	unison
centipede	duet	trio	unite
century	millionaire	tripod	
decimal	octave	triple	

Ball III, Strike II

2 · Numerī • 211

Agenda

A. Answers: 1. 2 2. 9 3. 6 4. 40 5. 60 6. 25 7. 26 8. 550
Play a game similar to tic-tac-toe. Have students make a 3 x 3 grid on a piece of paper and fill in the 9 spaces with a number (written Roman numerals). Call out numbers at random and see who is the first to get three in a row.

B. Point students toward the first few pages of any textbook to see lowercase Roman numerals used; also the next time they go to the movies, look for the year the film was made. Buildings, monuments, bridges, and other structures often have Roman numerals giving the year they were built. Some clock faces have Roman numerals.

Verba Latīna

- Point out (or elicit) that the Latin words for 10 *(decem)*, 100 *(centum)*, and 1,000 *(mille)* are used as prefixes for the metric system.
- Ask students to think of other English words with Latin numbers as a root.

Review the lesson and check student progress by using the following:

- Ask simple arithmetic questions.
- Ask students how old an octogenarian is, and how they can tell.
- 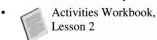 Activities Workbook, Lesson 2

CLOSE

Have students bring a $1 bill to class, or hand one out (temporarily!) to each student. Have them read the individual digits of the serial number aloud in Latin.

Look at the numbers below in three Romance languages. Which do you think are the most similiar to the original Latin?

Latīna	*español*	*italiano*	*français*
ūnus	uno	uno	un
duo	dos	due	deux
trēs	tres	tre	trois
quattuor	cuatro	quattro	quatre
quinque	cinco	cinque	cinq
sex	seis	sei	six
septem	siete	sette	sept
octō	ocho	otto	huit
novem	nueve	nove	neuf
decem	diez	dieci	dix
ūndecim	once	undici	onze

3 Paulus et Clāra

Talking About a Person or Thing

Paulus est amīcus bonus.
Et Paulus est discipulus bonus.

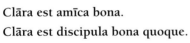

Clāra est amīca bona.
Clāra est discipula bona quoque.

FOCUS

Students will
- learn to describe a boy or a girl
- learn some descriptive adjectives
- ask and answer yes–no questions

TEACH

Paulus est amīcus bonus. Paulus is a good friend.

Et Paulus est discipulus bonus. And Paulus is a good student.

Clāra est amīca bona. Clara is a good friend.

Clāra est discipula bona quoque. Clara is also a good student.

3 · *Paulus et Clāra* • 213

Vīlla est pulchra. The farmhouse /
country house is beautiful.

Sed vīlla est parva. But the farmhouse / country house is small.

Vīlla nōn est magna. The farmhouse / country house is not big.

Casa est parva quoque. The
house is also small.

Casa nōn est magna. The house is
not big.

Sed casa pulchra est. But the
house is beautiful.

**Estne Paulus discipulus
Rōmānus?** Is Paul a Roman
student?

Estne Clāra amīca bona?
Is Clara a good friend?

**Paulusne est discipulus
Rōmānus?** Is Paul a
Roman student?

Sic. Yes.

Ita vērō. Yes.

Minimē. No.

Vocabulary

1. Use the audio program or overhead transparency to present the
   sentences. Do not translate into
   English.

2. If students are interested, teach
   them the word for bad *(malus,
   mala)*. Latin had neither definite
   nor indefinite articles, so feel
   free to use whatever seems most
   natural before a noun.

3. Explain that to ask questions, the
   -ne can be added to any word,
   whichever comes first in the sentence, although it is less likely to
   be seen on short prepositions.

4. Another way to answer "yes" or
   "no" is simply to repeat the verb
   in the sentence, e.g., *Vīllane est
   magna? Est.* or *Nōn est.*

Vīlla est pulchra.

Sed vīlla est parva.

Vīlla nōn est magna.

Casa est parva quoque.

Casa nōn est magna.

Sed casa pulchra est.

To form a question in Latin, you add *-ne* to the first word in
the sentence:

Estne Paulus discipulus Rōmānus?

Estne Clāra amīca bona?

Paulusne est discipulus Rōmānus?

To answer "yes" to a question, you can say:

Sic.

Ita vērō.

To answer "no" to a question, you can say:

Minimē.

214 • *Welcome to Latin!*

214

Agenda

A Answer the following questions in Latin.

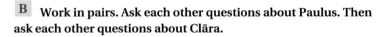

1. Estne Paulus amīcus bonus?
2. Quis est amīcus bonus?
3. Et quis est amīca bona?
4. Quis est discipulus bonus?
5. Quis est discipula bona?
6. Estne vīlla pulchra?
7. Estne vīlla parva?
8. Estne casa magna?

B Work in pairs. Ask each other questions about Paulus. Then ask each other questions about Clāra.

C Work in groups of four. Point to someone in your group as you ask a question with *quis*. Call on someone else from the group to answer. The person who answers must use the name of the person you pointed to.

D Work with a classmate. Make up a conversation using the following as a guide.

—Esne _____?

—Sic, ego sum _____.

—Esne discipulus/discipula?

—Ita vērō. Sum _____.

—Esne discipulus Americanus/discipula Americana?

—Sic, sum _____.

A. Answers: 1. (Sic), Paulus est amīcus bonus.   2. Paulus   3. Clāra   4. Paulus   5. Clāra   6. Vīlla est pulchra.   7. (Sic), vīlla parva est.   8. (Minimē), casa nōn est magna. Casa quoque parva est.
   Have students make up questions and answers about the other characters they have met (Marcus and Anna in Lesson 1). To say that Anna or Clāra is beautiful, say *Anna/Clāra pulchra est.*

B. Students can make up birthdays for these characters using the material in Lesson 2.

C. Encourage students to try to put together as many phrases as they have learned in a variety of ways.

D. Answers will vary.

The literal meaning of *īnsula* is island. Many apartment buildings contained everything that seemed necessary for the tenants.

Cultūra

Houses in the Roman World

There are several words in Latin that mean "house." *Vīlla* is the word for country house. Many wealthy Romans had a house in the country. To escape Rome's bustling activities and noisy streets, they would go to their country house or *vīlla*, particularly in the summer. The J. Paul Getty Museum in California (below) is a modern reconstruction of a Roman *vīlla*.

In the city, people of the working and middle classes lived in *īnsulae*, or apartment buildings. Each *īnsula* was several stories high and had a number of individual apartments and shared cooking areas. On the following page there is a photograph of a model reconstruction of a five-story *īnsula* at Ostia, near Rome.

A *domus* was a self-contained house in the city. Only the nobles and very wealthy Romans had a *domus* in the city. Below is a photograph of an artist's reconstruction of a *domus*. It is based on archaeological remains in Pompeii, Italy.

Latin Online

For more information about Roman life, go to the Glencoe Web site: glencoe.com

INTERIOR OF A ROMAN HOUSE.

A *casa* was a simple cottage for a fisherman or sailor on the Mediterranean coast. Very few examples exist today of these simple cottages. Can you guess why?

3 · Paulus et Clāra • 217

- Ask students if they know some-one who is an alumna or alumnus of a college or university. Tell them the school of which you are an alumnus or alumna.

- Encourage students to think of additional words that might have their roots in one of the Latin words in this lesson. Roots can be confirmed by checking the dictionary.

Verba Latīna

If any of your students speak a language that is not represented here, have them provide the same sentence in the other language and compare it to these.

ASSESS

Review the lesson and check student progress by using the following:

- Ask yes–no questions.
- Activities Workbook, Lesson 3

CLOSE

Describe the different kinds of houses the Romans had and compare them with ours. Look through magazines to try to find a variety of housing styles from around the world.

Verba Latīna

Find the Latin words that come from the following English words.

amicable	magnificent
castle	magnitude
disciple	pulchritude
domicile	villa

Verba Latīna

Looking at the following sentences. Which language seems closest to Latin?

Latin: *Paulus est amīcus bonus.*

French: *Paul est un bon ami.*

Spanish: *Pablo es un amigo bueno.* (or) *Pablo es un buen amigo.*

Italian: *Paolo è un amico buono.* (or) *Paolo è un buon amico.*

"Good," isn't it?

4 ◆ Amīcī et Discipulī

Talking About People

Paulus et Cornēlius
sunt amīcī.

Paulus et Cornēlius
sunt discipulī.

Paulus et Cornēlius
amīcī bonī sunt.

Puerī discipulī bonī
sunt.

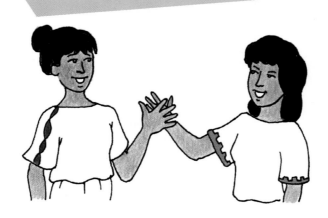

Jūlia et Claudia sunt amīcae.

Puellae sunt amīcae bonae.

Et Jūlia et Claudia sunt
discipulae bonae.

FOCUS

Students will
- learn to describe people
- learn how to form plurals
- learn about Roman schools

TEACH

Paulus et Cornēlius sunt amīcī.
Paulus and Cornelius are friends.

Paulus et Cornēlius sunt discipulī.
Paulus and Cornelius are students.

Paulus et Cornēlius amīcī bonī sunt. Paulus and Cornelius are good friends.

Puerī discipulī bonī sunt.
The boys are good students.

Jūlia et Claudia sunt amīcae.
Julia and Claudia are friends.

Puellae sunt amīcae bonae.
The girls are good friends.

Et Jūlia et Claudia sunt discipulae bonae. And Julia and Claudia are good students.

4 · Amīcī et Discipulī • 219

amīcus   friend (male)

amīcī   friends (male)

amīca   friend (female)

amīcae   friends (female)

discipulus   student (male)

discipulī   students (male)

casa   house

casae   houses

Vocabulary

1. Use the audio program or overhead transparency to present the sentences and vocabulary. Do not translate into English.

2. Give students some additional words that have come into English directly from Latin and have them give the plural. Sometimes, English keeps the Latin plural, other times, it just adds an *s:* antenna, amœba, alga, focus, larva, formula, fungus, stimulus, campus.

Agenda

A. Answers: 1. Paulus et Cornēlius sunt amīcī.   2. (Sic), sunt amīcī bonī.   3. Julia et Claudia sunt amīcae.   4. (Sic), puellae amīcae bonae sunt.   5. Paulus et Cornēlius sunt discipulī bonī.   6. Julia et Claudia sunt discipulae bonae.

Remind students that they know the adjectives for small *(parvus, parva)*, big *(magnus, magna),* and beautiful *(pulchra);* also, bad *(malus, mala)* if you introduced it. They can use these words to make additional questions.

B. Answers: 1. Paulus est discipulus bonus.   2. Paulus et Cornēlius sunt discipulī bonī.   3. Julia est discipula bona.   4. Julia et Claudia sunt discipulae bonae.   5. Paulus est Rōmānus.   6. Julia et Claudia sunt Rōmānae. Introduce *Amēricānus, Americana* to offset *Rōmānus, Rōmāna,* for variety.

220

When you speak or write about more than one person, you must use the plural form. Here's how to form the plural in Latin:

Singular	Plural	Singular	Plural
amīcus	**amīcī**	**amīca**	**amīcae**
discipulus	**discipulī**	**casa**	**casae**

Verba Latīna

Read the following English sentences. Can you tell where the forms "alumnus/alumni" and "alumna/alumnae" come from?

John is an alumnus of Brown University.

Many of his friends are alumni of Brown University.

Erica is an alumna of UCLA.

Many of her friends are alumnae of UCLA.

Can you find the Latin word in this Harvard University seal? What does it mean in English?

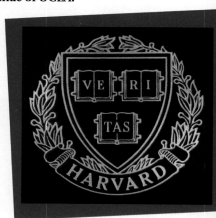

Agenda

A   Answer the following questions in Latin.

1. Quī sunt amīcī?
2. Suntne amīcī bonī?
3. Quae sunt amīcae?
4. Suntne amīcae bonae?
5. Quī sunt discipulī bonī?
6. Quae sunt discipulae bonae?

B   Answer the following questions in Latin.

1. Quis est discipulus bonus?
2. Quī sunt discipulī bonī?
3. Quis est discipula bona?
4. Quae sunt discipulae bonae?
5. Quis est Rōmānus?
6. Quae sunt Rōmānae?

C Here is a portrait of Flavius. Tell as much as you can about him in Latin.

D Here is a portrait of Flavius and Marcus. Tell as much as you can about them in Latin.

E Here is a portrait of Aemilia. Tell as much as you can about her in Latin.

F Here is a portrait of Aemilia and Claudia. Tell as much as you can about them in Latin.

4 · Amīcī et Discipulī • 221

Answers will vary but possibilities are:

C. Flavius est Rōmānus. Flavius nōn est Américānus. Flavius discipulus bonus est. Flavius est quoque amīcus bonus.

D. Flavius et Marcus sunt amīcī bonī. Sunt quoque discipulī bonī. Flavius et Marcus sunt (puerī) Rōmānī.

E. Aemilia est puella Rōmānā. Aemilia pulchra est. Aemilia bona amīca est. Est quoque discipula bona.

F. Aemilia et Claudia sunt Rōmānae. Puellae sunt amīcae bonae. Aemilia et Claudia sunt quoque discipulae bonae.

G. Italy is a beautiful country. Italy is in Europe. Italy is not an island. Italy is a big peninsula.

Spain is also a peninsula. Spain and Italy are peninsulas. Spain and Italy are not islands. Spain and Italy are beautiful countries in Europe.

Britain and Corsica and Sardinia are islands. They are not peninsulas. Britain is a big island. Corsica and Sardinia are small islands.

Answers: 1. patria pulchra 2. paenīnsulae 3. paenīnsula 4. īnsulae 5. magna 6. paenīnsulae 7. īnsulae 8. magna

Verba Latīna

- Encourage students to think of additional words that might have their roots in one of the Latin words in this lesson. Roots can be confirmed by checking the dictionary.

- Point out that the English word "absent" comes almost directly from Latin: the prefix *ab* means "away/away from" and *sunt* means "(they) are" (in Latin, *absunt*).

G **Read the following story and then complete the sentences. Note that many of the words are cognates, which means that they are almost the same in Latin and English.**

Italia est patria pulchra. Italia in Europā est. Italia nōn est īnsula. Italia est paenīnsula magna.

Hispānia quoque paenīnsula est. Hispānia et Italia sunt paenīnsulae. Hispānia et Italia nōn sunt īnsulae. Hispānia et Italia sunt patriae pulchrae in Europā.

Britannia et Corsica et Sardinia īnsulae sunt. Nōn sunt paenīnsulae. Britannia magna īnsula est. Corsica et Sardinia parvae īnsulae sunt.

1. Italia est _____.
2. Italia et Hispānia sunt _____.
3. Sicilia est īnsula. Sicilia non est _____.
4. Sicilia et Corsica sunt _____.
5. Italia non est patria parva. Italia patria _____ est.
6. Italia et Hispānia sunt _____ magnae.
7. Et Sicilia et Corsica sunt _____ parvae.
8. Britannia est īnsula _____.

Verba Latīna

1. Read the story in *Agenda G* again. As you do, make a list of cognates you find.
2. Tell what Latin word these English words come from:

Hispanic   **patriotic**

insular   **peninsular**

Then give a definition of each English word.

Cultūra

Schooling in Roman Times

Students wrote on a wooden tablet called a *tabula*. It was covered with a thin layer of wax. Students scratched their letters on the wax surface with a thin stick of metal, bone, or ivory called a *stilus*. The Roman girl in this painting is holding a *tabula* and a *stilus*.

Roman students were usually escorted to school by a slave who looked after them. This slave was called a *paedagogus*. Another slave, the *capsarius,* carried their books and writing materials. The teacher or *magister* is to the right in this stone relief.

Roman boys and girls started school at about the age of seven. Only children of the middle and professional classes attended school. The very rich were tutored at home. Here, in this painting, a Roman matron teaches her daughter to read.

4 · *Amīcī et Discipulī* • 223

Cultūra

Young schoolchildren learned reading, writing, and simple arithmetic. They could be beaten if they didn't learn their lessons. An abacus helped with arithmetic.

At the age of 12, very bright and/or wealthy boys went to secondary school where they were taught by a *grammaticus.* They studied Greek, history, geography, arithmetic, and literature. If they were interested in law or politics, they also studied public speaking, or oratory.

If girls were wealthy and were not needed to go to work, they were tutored at home.

ASSESS

Review the lesson and check student progress by using the following:

*   Imagine you have just finished the last grade in your school. Say you are an alumnus or alumna of your school.
*   Ask students what "singular" and "plural" mean. Have students give an example.
*   Activities Workbook, Lesson 4

CLOSE

*   Ask students to describe the differences between Roman education and American education.
*   Give students a few sentences to make plural: *Casa est parva, Puella est pulchra, Discipulus est bonus.*

FOCUS

Students will

• learn about Latin word order

• learn the concepts of doer and receiver of an action

TEACH

Paulus Minervam videt. Paulus sees Minerva.

Et Minerva Paulum videt. And Minerva sees Paulus.

Paulus Minervam amat. Paulus likes Minerva.

Minerva Paulum amat. Minerva likes Paulus.

Minerva bonum amīcum Paulum amat. Minerva likes her good friend Paulus.

Paulus bonam amīcam Minervam amat. Paulus likes his good friend Minerva.

Paulus epistulas scrībit. Paulus writes a letter.

5 Amīcus amīcam videt

Word Order

Paulus Minervam videt.

Et Minerva Paulum videt.

Paulus Minervam amat.

Minerva Paulum amat.

Minerva bonum amīcum Paulum amat.

Paulus bonam amīcam Minervam amat.

Paulus epistulas scrībit.

Minerva epistulas legit.

Minerva epistulas legit. Minerva reads the letter.

Vocabulary

1. Use the audio program or overhead transparency to present the sentences. Do not translate into English.

2. When the Romans wrote letters *(epistulae)*, they frequently used abbreviations. A typical letter would begin SVBE (*Si valēs, bene est.* If you are well, it is good.) The equivalent of "How are you? I am fine."

In English, word order is very important. The position of the word in the sentence tells who does the action and who receives the action:

Paul sees Minerva.

The word before the verb "sees" does the action and the word that follows the verb "sees" receives the action. If you reverse them, it changes the meaning completely:

Minerva sees Paul.

In Latin, word order is not important. Latin uses endings to tell who does or receives the action:

Paulus videt Minervam.
Paulus Minervam videt.
Minervam videt Paulus.

Minerva videt Paulum.
Minerva Paulum videt.
Paulum videt Minerva.

Verba Latīna

Tell students that a flexible word order comes in handy for things like poetry. Briefly explain the concepts of doer (subject) and receiver (object/complement) and give some examples in English.

Agenda

A. Answers: 1. Paulus videt Minervam. 2. Paulus videt Minervam. 3. Minerva videt Paulum. 4. Minerva videt Paulum. 5. Paulus amat Minervam. 6. Minerva amat Paulum. 7. Paulus epistulas scrībit. 8. Minerva epistulas legit.

B. If students want to say I live in America, they can say *Habitō in Americā.*

C. You may have students read the story aloud in pairs.

D. Looking at the map, have students identify islands and peninsulas. Make up questions and answers using *Ubi est / Ubi sunt* and *Est in (Europā, Asiā, Italiā, Britanniā,* etc.)

Regardless of the word order, the message is clear because the endings tell who does or receives the action.

Doer	*Receiver*
Paulus	**Paulum**
discipulus	**discipulum**
Minerva	**Minervam**
puella	**puellam**

Verba Latīna

Explain the meaning of the following English words:

epistle	**scribe**
legible	**video**

What Latin word does each one come from?

Agenda

A **Answer the following questions in Latin.**

1. Quis videt Minervam?
2. Quem videt Paulus?
3. Quis videt Paulum?
4. Quem videt Minerva?
5. Quem amat Paulus?
6. Quis amat Paulum?
7. Quis scrībit epistulas?
8. Quis legit epistulas?

B **Read the following story about Cornēlius and Anna.**

Cornēlius et Anna in Italiā habitant. Italiā est patria pulchra. Cornēlius et Anna suam patriam amant. Quem amant Cornēlius et Anna?

C **Read the story once again. Then answer the question in the story.**

D **Here is a map of Italy and Sicily at the time of the Roman Empire. Working in pairs, say as much as you can in Latin about the map. You can also ask each other where a place is using *Ubi est...***

ITALIA

Verba Latīna

- Learning to guess meaning from roots is an important skill. Ask students where the following words come from: scribble, illegible, amatory.
- Try to elicit the same root word in the Latin words *amīcus* and *amat*.

ASSESS

Review the lesson and check student progress by using the following:

- Ask why word order matters in English but not in Latin.
- Have students make up a three-word sentence and scramble the word order. Each then writes it on the chalkboard and has class-mates or a partner translate it.
- 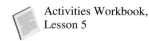 Activities Workbook, Lesson 5

CLOSE

Ask students to think about Roman schools, clothing, houses, and language. Would they have liked to live in Roman times? Why or why not?

Verba Latīna

In the reading selection in *Agenda B,* you came across the Latin word *habitant.* Guess at its meaning from the context of the sentence. The following English words are derived from *habitant:* inhabitant, habitation, to habitate. Do you know what these words mean? If not, look them up in a dictionary.

5 · *Amīcus amīcam videt* • 227

Welcome to
GERMAN!

Heidelberg Castle, Germany

German is the language of these famous composers of beautiful classical music: Bach, Beethoven, Wagner, Strauss, Brahms, Mozart, and Haydn. German is the language of Germany, Austria, and most of Switzerland. It is also the language of two European principalities: Liechtenstein and Luxembourg.

Many Americans are of German descent. Their ancestors came to this country for economic, political, or religious reasons. In areas of Pennsylvania, Ohio, and Indiana, many people still speak Pennsylvania Dutch. The word "Dutch" comes from the German word *Deutsch* which means "German." The "Dutch" spoken by these people is actually a form of German, not the Dutch language spoken in the Netherlands.

Neuschwanstein Castle,
Germany

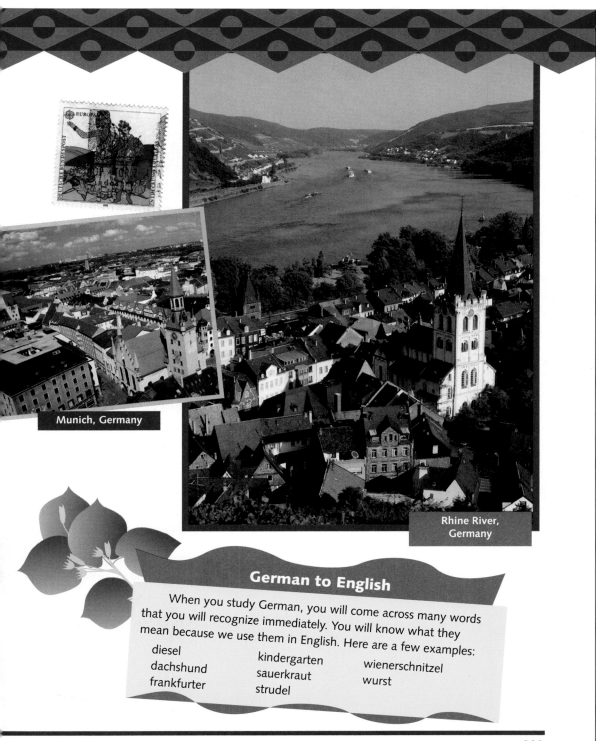

Munich, Germany

Rhine River, Germany

German to English

When you study German, you will come across many words that you will recognize immediately. You will know what they mean because we use them in English. Here are a few examples:

diesel
dachshund
frankfurter

kindergarten
sauerkraut
strudel

wienerschnitzel
wurst

229

Lesson 1

 Audio

 Transparencies

 Workbook

FOCUS

Students will

• use and respond to greetings with peers

• use and respond to greetings with older people

TEACH

—**Tag, Hans.** Hello, Hans.

—**Tag, Eva. Wie geht's?** Hello Eva. How are you?

—**Gut, danke. Und dir?** Fine, thanks. And you?

—**Nicht schlecht, danke.** Not bad, thanks.

Dialogue

1. Use the audio program or the overhead transparency to present the dialogue. Point to the speaker as each line of the dialogue is heard. Or model the dialogue yourself, pointing to the appropriate speaker on the overhead transparency.

2. Model the dialogue with one of the more able students.

3. Have two students model the dialogue.

Guten Tag, Herr Braun. Good day, Mr. Brown.

Guten Tag, Frau Wagner. Good day, Mrs. Wagner.

Guten Tag, Fräulein Schmitt. Good day, Miss Schmitt.

Begrüßung

Greeting People

—Tag, Hans.

    —Tag, Eva. Wie geht's?

—Gut, danke. Und dir?

    —Nicht schlecht, danke.

Guten Tag is a more formal greeting than *Tag.* You would say *Guten Tag* when greeting adults, for example. You would also use the person's title and name:

    Guten Tag, Herr Braun.

    Guten Tag, Frau Wagner.

    Guten Tag, Fräulein Schmitt.

Aktivitäten

A Get up from your desk and walk around the classroom. Say *Guten Tag* to each classmate you meet.

B Work with a classmate. Make up a conversation in German. Greet each other and find out how things are going.

When speaking German, you must decide between formal and informal speech. The conversation on page 230 is between friends. If you were speaking to an adult whom you did not know well, you would say *Wie geht es Ihnen?* rather than *Wie geht's?* You would also say *Und Ihnen?* instead of *Und dir?*

Formal	*Informal*
Wie geht es Ihnen?	**Wie geht's?**
Sehr gut. Und Ihnen?	**Sehr gut. Und dir?**

—Guten Tag, Frau Müller. Wie geht es Ihnen?

—(Es geht mir) sehr gut, danke. Und Ihnen?

—Sehr gut, danke.

Note that the most common answer to the formal *Wie geht es Ihnen?* is:

Es geht mir sehr gut, danke.

There are several different responses to the informal *Wie geht's?* They are:

Es geht.   **Ganz gut.**   **Nicht schlecht.**

A. If your furniture is movable, arrange it so that students can move about easily. Greet several students to get them started.

B. Have students change partners after each conversation so that each has three or four conversations. Encourage the use of students' names and other variations.

Formal

Wie geht es Ihnen? How are you?

Sehr gut. Und Ihnen? Very good. And you?

Informal

Wie geht's? How are you?

Sehr gut. Und dir? Very good. And you?

—**Guten Tag, Frau Müller. Wie geht es Ihnen?** Good day, Mrs. Müller. How are you?

—**(Es geht mir) sehr gut, danke. Und Ihnen?** Fine, thanks. And you?

—**Sehr gut, danke.** Very well, thanks.

1. Use the audio program or the overhead transparency to present the dialogue.

Es geht. It goes well. (Everything's OK.)

Ganz gut. Quite good.

Nicht schlecht. Not bad.

Aktivitäten

A. After students greet their stick figures, ask them to move about the room and greet other students' stick figures.

B. Elicit that both young people and adults in German-speaking countries may shake hands when meeting.

C. Explain that informal speech is used with children, family, close friends, and pets. Teenagers are addressed by strangers with *Sie* when they turn 14.

Aktivitäten

A Draw and cut out five stick figures. Give each one a name. They will represent your friends, family, and teachers. Greet each of your stick figures properly in German.

B Work with a classmate. Make up a conversation in German. Greet each other and find out how things are going.

C Look at these photographs below of German-speaking people greeting each other. Do they do some of the things we do when they greet each other? Do they do some things that are different? Explain.

Kultur

Germantown, USA

In many U.S. cities that have a large population of German descent, there is a section of the city called Germantown. In the Germantown section, you will find German delicatessens, butcher shops, and pastry shops. There will often be a good German restaurant.

German restaurant, San Francisco

German bakery, Chicago

Kultur

Assign students to small groups and ask them to identify a German-speaking actor, musician, politician, or athlete. Ask them to identify his or her ethnic group, if they can. Afterward, compile a list of the German-origin personalities on the chalkboard.

ASSESS

Review the lesson and check student progress by using the following:

- Activities Workbook, Lesson 1

CLOSE

Ask students to write a brief conversation between the students who meet on the street. Have them illustrate it with pictures cut out from old magazines.

Expansion

Explain that in Switzerland, people greet each other with *Grüezi*, whereas in Austria, it's *Servus* or *grüß Gott*. On the telephone, people say their last name, instead of "hello." For example: *Hier Schmitt*.

Lesson 2

 Audio

 Transparencies

 Workbook

FOCUS

- Students will use and respond to leave-taking expressions

TEACH

—**Auf Wiedersehen, Ingrid.**
 Good-bye, Ingrid.

—**Auf Wiedersehen, Dieter.**
 Good-bye, Dieter.

—**Tschüs.** Bye.

—**Tschüs.** Bye.

Bis später. Until later.

Bis nacher. Until later.

Bis bald. See you soon.

Bis gleich. See you soon.

Bis morgen. Until tomorrow.

Tschau. Bye.

Dialogue

1. Use the audio program to present the dialogue or model the brief dialogues yourself, pointing to the appropriate speaker on the overhead transparency. Use appropriate gestures to convey the idea that you are ending an encounter.

2. Model the dialogues with one of the more able students.

3. Have two students model the dialogue.

Aktivitäten

A. If your furniture is movable, arrange it so that students can move about easily.

B. Have students repeat the leave-takings with more than one friend if they can.

234

---

2 ◆ Verabschieden

Saying "Good-bye"

—Auf Wiedersehen, Ingrid.
 —Auf Wiedersehen, Dieter.

—Tschüs!
—Tschüs!

234 • *Welcome to German!*

The usual expression to use when saying "good-bye" to someone is:
Auf Wiedersehen.

If you plan to see the person again soon, you can say:
Bis später.   **Bis nachher.**

If you plan to see the person again very soon, you can say:
Bis bald.   **Bis gleich.**

If you plan to see the person the next day, you can say:
Bis morgen.

Two very informal expressions that you frequently hear people use are:
Tschüs.   **Tschau.**

Tschau is similar to the Italian expression *(ciao)* that is used in several European languages.

Aktivitäten

A Go over to a classmate. Say "so long" to him or her and then return to your seat.

B Work with a classmate. Say *tschüs* to one another and let each other know that you'll be getting together again soon.

C Say "good-bye" to your teacher in German and then say "good-bye" to a friend. Don't forget to use a different expression with each person!

Mehr Sprechen

—Tag, Dieter.
　—Tag, Ingrid. Wie geht's?
—Gut, danke. Und dir?
　—Nicht schlecht, danke.
—Tschüs, Dieter.
　—Tschüs, Ingrid. Bis später.

Danke

C. Repeat this activity just before the end of the class. Have students say *Auf Wiedersehen, Herr/Frau* (your name) chorally, and *Tschüs* to another student.

Mehr Sprechen

—**Tag, Dieter.** Hello, Dieter.
—**Tag, Ingrid. Wie geht's?** Hello, Ingrid. How are you?
—**Gut, danke. Und dir?** Good, thanks. And you?
—**Nicht schlecht, danke.** Not bad, thanks.
—**Tschüs, Dieter.** Bye, Dieter.
—**Tschüs, Ingrid. Bis später.** Bye, Ingrid. Until later.

1. Use the audio program to model the dialogue.
2. Draw and label Dieter and Ingrid on the chalkboard. Model the review dialogue youself, pointing to the appropriate speaker on the chalkboard.
3. Model the dialogue with one of the more able students, using real names.

Aktivitäten

A. Encourage students to use appropriate gestures, such as shaking hands and waving.

B. Discuss which leave-taking behaviors are similar to or different from what we do.

Kultur

Ask students to find the German version of their name on the lists. If there is no German version, ask them to pick a German name for themselves.

ASSESS

Review the lesson and check student progress by using the following:

• Activities Workbook, Lesson 2

235

Ask students to prepare an ending to the conversation they prepared in Lesson 1 by having the students say "good-bye" to each other.

Expansion

Have students prepare some clip-on name badges with the name of *Mädchen* and *Jungen* given. In small groups, have them engage in several conversations as the people whose names they have drawn. After a few minutes, collect the name badges and have students draw again and repeat the activity. Some of the famous names you can use in this activity are the following:

Johannes Brahms, German composer

Johann Sebastian Bach, German composer

Martin Luther, German theologist

Wolfgang Amadeus Mozart, Austrian composer

Arnold Schwarzenegger, Austrian-born actor

Albert Einstein, German-born physicist

Wernher von Braun, German-born scientist

Jacob and Wilhelm Grimm, German poets and collectors of fairytales

Boris Becker, German athlete

Bettina von Arnim, German author

Katarina Witt, German athlete

Steffi Graf, German athlete

Clara Schumann, German pianist and composer

Alma Mahler, German pianist and composer

Marlene Dietrich, German actress

Annette von Droste-Hülshoff, German poet

Gabriele Münter, German-born painter

Aktivitäten

A Work with a friend. Speak German together. Have fun saying as much as you can to one another!

B Look at these two photographs of German-speaking people saying "good-bye." Describe what the people are doing.

Kultur

Common First Names

The following are some common names used for boys and girls in German.

Jungen

Alexander, Bernd, Christoph, Dieter, Erich, Ernst, Fritz, Hans, Jochen, Jürgen, Klaus, Konrad, Martin, Max, Michael, Otto, Paul, Peter, Richard, Rudi, Stefan, Thomas, Willi

Mädchen

Anna, Beate, Brigitte, Christa, Christel, Dagmar, Elisabeth, Elke, Eva, Helga, Ingrid, Jutta, Luise, Margret, Monika, Paula, Petra, Rosa, Sabine, Susanne, Sylvia, Ursula

3 **I**m Klassenzimmer

Identifying Classroom Objects

To find out what something is, you ask:

Was ist das?

Das ist _____.

eine Tafel

ein Stuhl

ein Schreibtisch

ein Stück Papier

ein Computer

ein Buch

ein Tisch

ein Schwamm

eine Kreide

ein Heft

ein Rechner

ein Block

ein Bleistift

ein Radiergummi

ein Kugelschreiber

ein Rucksack

To ask for something in a polite way, you say:

Ein Stück Papier, bitte.

FOCUS

Students will

• use words for common classroom objects

• request common classroom objects

TEACH

Was ist das? What is that?

ein Kugelschreiber ballpoint pen
ein Bleistift pencil
ein Radiergummi pencil eraser
ein Schwamm chalk eraser
ein Buch book
ein Block pad of paper
ein Stück Papier sheet of paper
eine Kreide piece of chalk
ein Heft notebook
ein Rechner calculator
ein Computer computer
ein Rucksack backpack
ein Stuhl chair
ein Tisch table
ein Schreibtisch desk
eine Tafel chalkboard

Ein Stück Papier, bitte. A sheet of paper, please.

Vocabulary 📼 🎞️

1. Use the audio program to present the vocabulary or point to each classroom object on the overhead transparency as you say its name. Repeat this step with the actual objects, which you have assembled beforehand.

2. Name each object again, but pause before one as if you forgot its name. Signal the class to say the name chorally. Repeat with a pause before another object three or four times.

3. Name each object again and pause before one, but this time point to a student to respond with the name of the object. Repeat three or four times with different students.

Aktivitäten

A. Answers: 1. ein Rechner
2. ein Stück Papier   3. ein Heft
4. ein Buch   5. ein Bleistift
6. ein Computer

Prepare a box with the smaller items in it. Have students pass this box around and ask for the objects.

Aktivitäten

A **Ask a classmate to identify the following items in German. Don't forget to ask politely! Your classmate will answer.**

1.

2.

3.

4.

5.

6.

B Look at each picture and say in German what each person needs.

1.   2.

C Point to something in the classroom and ask a classmate what it is.

Kultur

Schools in Germany

In Germany there are three types of high school. When a student finishes elementary school, *die Grundschule,* he or she must decide what type of high school to attend. *Das Gymnasium* is for students who want an academic preparation. *Die Realschule* is for commercial or vocational preparation. *Die Hauptschule* is for general studies.

To complete studies in the *Gymnasium* and receive *das Abitur*—the *Gymnasium* diploma—you must study for nine years. *Das Abitur* is called *das Abi* in student jargon. The *Realschule* requires six years of study and the *Hauptschule* five years.

B. Answers: 1. ein Stück Kreide
2. ein Rucksack

For students needing special help, you can list the objects needed on a piece of paper and have students match the pictures with the words.

C. Have students make up mini-conversations. An example could be:

—**Was ist das?**

—**Das is ein Rechner.**

Kultur

Bring in pictures of students in classrooms in Germany.

ASSESS

Review the lesson and check student progress by using the following:

• Activities Workbook, Lesson 3

CLOSE

Ask students to make a list of the items from the lesson vocabulary that they have in their desks or in their backpacks.

Expansion

Ask a small group to locate and cut out pictures of school supplies from old magazines. Have the group prepare labels for them and attach them to the pictures. Mount the pictures on a poster or bulletin board for reference. With the computer and classroom furniture, have them attach labels to the objects themselves. You may want to add these items to the objects to be labeled:

eine Fahne a flag
ein Fenster a window
eine Tür a door
eine Wand a wall
eine Decke a ceiling
eine Landkarte a map

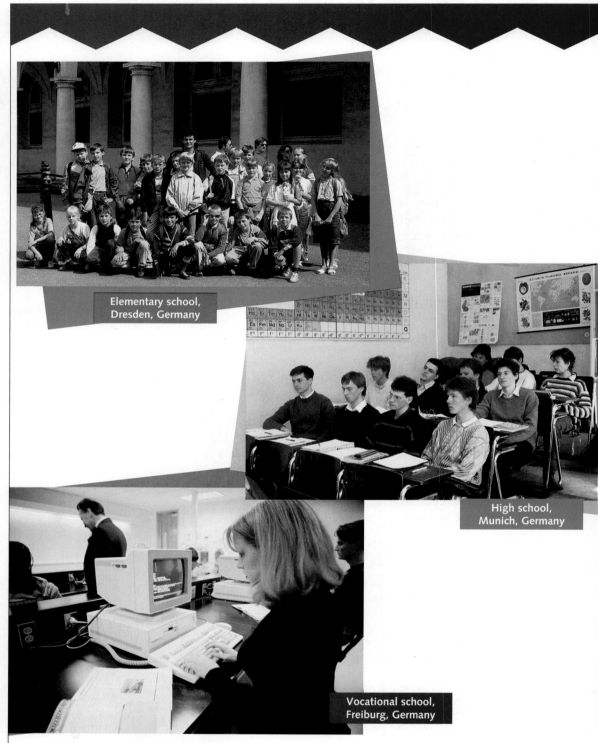

Elementary school,
Dresden, Germany

High school,
Munich, Germany

Vocational school,
Freiburg, Germany

240 • *Welcome to German!*

4 ◆ **D**ie Zahlen

Counting in German

1	eins	16	sechzehn	30	dreißig
2	zwei	17	siebzehn	40	vierzig
3	drei	18	achtzehn	50	fünfzig
4	vier	19	neunzehn	60	sechzig
5	fünf	20	zwanzig	70	siebzig
6	sechs			80	achtzig
7	sieben	21	einundzwanzig	90	neunzig
8	acht	22	zweiundzwanzig		
9	neun	23	dreiundzwanzig	100	(ein) hundert
10	zehn	24	vierundzwanzig	200	zweihundert
		25	fünfundzwanzig	300	dreihundert
11	elf	26	sechsundzwanzig		
12	zwölf	27	siebenundzwanzig	1.000	(ein) tausend
13	dreizehn	28	achtundzwanzig	2.000	zweitausend
14	vierzehn	29	neunundzwanzig		
15	fünfzehn				

FOCUS

...ts will

...e and respond to the words for
...e numbers 1 to 2,000

...sk and respond to a request for
...he price of something

TEACH

Vocabulary

You might want to teach the numbers in two groups (1–30; 31–100) to make them easier for students to learn. Do not wait until all students have mastered numbers before moving on. Reintroduce numbers as you present future lessons.

1. Point to each number in random order on the overhead transparency as you say its name.

2. Point to each number in order, but pause before one as if you forgot its name. Signal the class to say the number chorally. Repeat with a pause before another number three or four times.

3. Point to each number again and pause before one, but this time point to a student to respond with the number. Repeat three or four times with different students.

4. Or use the audio program to present the vocabulary.

Kultur

Writing Numbers in German

In German-speaking countries, the numbers one and seven are written differently. Look at the photographs below to find these numbers. How are they written?

Aktivitäten

A Your teacher will write some numbers on the chalkboard. Then he or she will call out the number in German and ask a student to circle the correct number.

B Work with a classmate. One of you will count from 20 to 30. The other will count from 40 to 50.

C Have a contest with a friend in class. See who can count the fastest from 1 to 100 by tens!

D Work in groups of two. Take turns writing numbers on a piece of paper. Give the number your partner wrote on the paper.

Finding Out the Price

To find out how much something costs, you ask:

—Wieviel kostet der Rechner, Frau Schultz?
  —Vierzehn Euro.
—Danke schön.

Aktivität

A Work with a classmate. One of you will be the customer and the other will be the clerk at a stationery store. Make up a conversation to buy the following things.

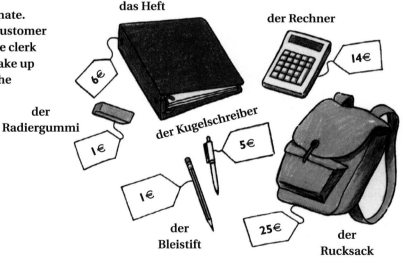

das Heft

der Rechner

der Radiergummi

der Kugelschreiber

der Bleistift

der Rucksack

—**Wieviel kostet der Rechner, Frau Schultz?** How much does the calculator cost, Mrs. Schulz?

—**Vierzehn Euro.** Fourteen euros.

—**Danke schön.** Thank you very much.

1. Model the dialogue yourself, pointing to the appropriate speaker on the overhead transparency. Use props to make the dialogue more realistic.

2. Model the dialogue with one of the more able students.

3. Have two students model the dialogue.

4. Or use the audio program to model the dialogue.

Aktivität

A. Have students make up mini-conversations such as the following:

—**Wieviel kostet das Heft, Herr Braun?**

—**Sechs Euro.**

—**Danke schön.**

Prices:

das Heft: sechs Euro

der Rechner: vierzehn Euro

der Radiergummi: eins Euro

der Kugelschreiber: fünf Euro

der Bleistift: eins Euro

der Rucksack: fünfundzwanzig Euro

Review the lesson and check
student progress by using the
following:

- Aktivität A, Counting
- Aktivität A, Finding Out
  the Price
- 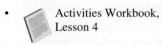 Activities Workbook,
  Lesson 4

CLOSE

In small groups, ask students to
identify the number of:

- numerals 1 on a one-dollar bill
- words "one" on a one-dollar bill

Kultur
Money Systems

The monetary unit of the Federal Republic of Germany and
Austria is the *Euro*.

The Swiss monetary system is based on the Swiss franc, *Franken.* It is divided into 100 *Rappen.*

Aktivität

A Give the amount of each euro pictured below.

1.

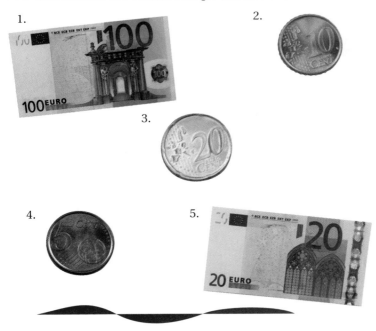

2.

3.

4.

5.

A. Answers: 1. einhundert Euro
2. zehn Cent   3. zwanzig Cent
4. fünf Cent   5. zwanzig Euro

Expansion

In small groups, ask students to do the following calculation:

- Take the number of students in the classroom.
- Subtract the number of Mondays in the current month.
- Add the number of students absent that day.
- Subtract the number of legs a spider has. (eight)
- Add the number of players on a baseball team. (nine)
- Subtract the number of digits in their telephone numbers (without the area code). (seven)

Compare the results that the groups got.

Lesson 5

Audio

Transparencies

Workbook

FOCUS

Students will

- request common foods and drinks in a restaurant setting
- ask and respond to a request for the cost of common foods and drinks

TEACH

—**Guten Tag.** Good day.

—**Guten Tag. Eine Cola, bitte.** Good day. A soda, please.

(The waiter brings the order.)

—**Danke schön.** Thank you.

—**Bitte sehr.** You're welcome.

5 Umgangsformen

Speaking Politely

—Guten Tag.
  —Guten Tag. Eine Cola, bitte.

(The waiter brings the order.)
—Danke schön.
  —Bitte sehr.

246 • *Welcome to German!*

246

(*A little later.*)
—Wieviel kostet die Cola, bitte?
—Drei Euro.

No matter what language you speak, it is important to be polite. The following words mean "please," "thank you," and "you're welcome":

Bitte. **Danke sehr.** **Bitte sehr.**

Danke schön. **Bitte schön.**

Aktivitäten

A With a friend, practice reading the dialogue on pages 246–247 aloud.

B You are at a café in a small German village along the Rhine. Order the following things. Ask a classmate to be the server.

1. eine Tasse Kaffee

2. eine Tasse Tee

3. eine Limonade

4. eine Cola

5. ein Mineralwasser

5 · Umgangsformen • 247

(*A little later.*)
—**Wieviel kostet die Cola, bitte?** How much is the soda, please?
—**Drei Euro.** Three euros.

Dialogue

1. Use the audio program or overhead transparency to present the dialogue. Point to the speaker as each line of the dialogue is heard. Or model the dialogue yourself, pointing to the appropriate speaker on the overhead transparency.

2. Model the dialogue with one of the more able students.

3. Have two students model the dialogue.

Aktivitäten

A. If your students need more practice with the basic conversation, have them change partners after the first reading so that each student practices the conversation three or four times.

B. Answers: 1. Eine Tasse Kaffee, bitte. 2. Eine Tasse Tee, bitte. 3. Eine Limonade, bitte. 4. Eine Cola, bitte. 5. Ein Mineralwasser, bitte.

Arrange the classroom furniture so that the customer is seated at a restaurant "table" or standing at a "counter."

C. Answers: 1. Eine Bratwurst, bitte.   2. Eine Pizza, bitte. 3. Ein Stück Apfelstrudel, bitte. 4. Ein Wienerschnitzel, bitte. 5. Sauerbraten, bitte.   6. Ein Omelett, bitte.

Encourage students to use the alternative expressions for *Bitte schön* (You're welcome). Explain the fact that the appeal of some snack foods, like burgers and fries, is international.

Kultur

Bring in pictures of staple foods of the German-speaking world. Your students may be able to contribute pictures from the library or old magazines at home. Post the pictures around a world map and have students link each picture to the area where the crop is grown, with a length of yarn.

ASSESS

Review the lesson and check student progress by using the following:

- Give students the basic dialogue with some blanks, and ask them to fill in the blanks.
- Activities Workbook, Lesson 5

CLOSE

Give students the sentences of the basic dialogue in the wrong order. Ask them to copy them in an order that makes sense. (Take into account that there may be more than one correct order. For example, someone could ask the cost before ordering a soda.)

C You would like to order the following foods at a German restaurant. Be polite when you order them!

1. eine Bratwurst
2. eine Pizza
3. ein Stück Apfelstrudel
4. ein Wienerschnitzel
5. Sauerbraten
6. ein Omelett

248   •   *Welcome to German!*

248

Kultur

Foods of the German World

The cooking of Germany is extremely varied. Today many Germans are very health conscious. But when we think of typical German fare, we think of German sausage or *Wurst*. One of the most popular is *Bratwurst*. *Bratwurst* comes from Nürnberg and is made with seasoned, spiced pork. *Weisswurst* is made from veal and *Leberwurst* is made from liver.

Bauernwurst is a farmer's sausage, similar to *Knackwurst*. *Knackwurst* is very much like a *Frankfurter,* but a bit rounder. The *Frankfurter* comes from the city of Frankfurt, but it's probably more popular here in the US where it is called a "hot dog."

Small *Frankfurters* are called *Wiener.* In Germany, the word *Wiener* is more commonly used than *Frankfurter.* In Austria, however, the most popular word is *Frankfurter.*

Wurst, regardless of the type, is almost always eaten with a piece of bread and a dab of mustard.

Butcher shop,
Berlin, Germany

Expansion

A. Have students design a menu for a German (for example) restaurant. Photocopy the result and have students use it to role-play a group ordering a meal. You may want to teach these expressions:

- **Zum essen, ein(e)...**
  (To eat, a . . .)
- **Zum trinken, ein(e)...**
  (To drink, a . . .)

B. If there is an ethnic market near you, plan a field trip to it. Ask students to make a "shopping list" of foods they expect to see. Have them check off those that they see. When you return, have students draw and label the foods they saw.

Additional Vocabulary

ein Brot bread

ein Brötchen roll

die Banane banana

der Apfel apple

der Blumenkohl cauliflower

die Milch milk

die Butter butter

der Käse cheese

eine Tafel Schokolade bar of chocolate

der Apfelsaft apple juice

FOCUS

Students will

*   ask and respond to requests for the time
*   give the time of events

TEACH

Wie spät ist es?   What time is it?

Wieviel Uhr ist es?   What time is it?

Es ist eins. Es ist ein Uhr.
   It is one o'clock.

Es ist zwei (Uhr).
   It is two o'clock.

Es ist drei (Uhr).
   It is three o'clock.

Es ist vier (Uhr).
   It is four o'clock.

Es ist fünf (Uhr).
   It is five o'clock.

Es ist sechs (Uhr).
   It is six o'clock.

Es ist sieben (Uhr).
   It is seven o'clock.

Es ist acht (Uhr).
   It is eight o'clock.

Es ist neun (Uhr).
   It is nine o'clock.

Es ist zehn (Uhr).
   It is ten o'clock.

Es ist elf (Uhr).
   It is eleven o'clock.

Es ist zwölf (Uhr).
   It is twelve o'clock.

6 *Die Uhrzeit*

Telling Time

To find out the time, you ask:

Wie spät ist es?

Wieviel Uhr ist es?

To tell the time, you say:

Es ist eins.
Es ist ein Uhr.

Es ist zwei (Uhr).

Es ist drei (Uhr).

Es ist vier (Uhr).

Es ist fünf (Uhr).

Es ist sechs (Uhr).

Es ist sieben (Uhr).

Es ist acht (Uhr).

Es ist neun (Uhr).

Es ist zehn (Uhr).

Es ist elf (Uhr).

Es ist zwölf (Uhr).

250   •   *Welcome to German!*

Es ist ein Uhr fünf.

Es ist zwei Uhr zehn.

Es ist fünf Uhr vierzig.

Es ist sechs Uhr fünfzehn.

Es ist halb acht.
Es ist sieben Uhr dreißig.

Kultur

The 24-Hour Clock

In German, the 24-hour clock is used for schedules, radio and TV program guides, and for any official business.

Es ist vierzehn Uhr.

Es ist achtzehn Uhr.

In more informal situations, the 12-hour clock is used.

Es ist sieben Uhr.

Es ist elf Uhr.

When writing the time in numerals, German uses a period (.) rather than a colon (:).

9.00	**9:00**
19.00	**19:00**

Look at this German Christmas schedule of events. What do you notice about the times?

Programm

Christkindlesmarkt auf dem Hauptmarkt zu Nürnberg

28. November bis 24. Dezember

Freitag	28. Nov.	17.30	Eröffnungsfeier Opening Ceremony
Samstag	29. Nov.	17.00	
Sonntag	30. Nov.	15.00	
	und	17.00	
Montag	1. Dez.	19.00	
Dienstag	2. Dez.	19.00	Posaunenchor
Mittwoch	3. Dez.	18.00	Trombone concert
Donnerstag	4. Dez.	19.00	
Freitag	5. Dez.	19.00	
Samstag	6. Dez.	17.00	
Sonntag	7. Dez.	15.00	
	und	17.00	
Montag	8. Dez.	17.00	Kinderbescherung mit Kindersingen Distribution of Christmas presents among children with singing of carols
Dienstag	9. Dez.	17.00	
Mittwoch	10. Dez.	17.00	
Donnerstag	11. Dez.	18.15	Lichterzug · Lantern procession
Freitag	12. Dez.	19.00	
Samstag	13. Dez.	17.00	
Sonntag	14. Dez.	15.00	
	und	17.00	
Montag	15. Dez.	19.00	
Dienstag	16. Dez.	19.00	
Mittwoch	17. Dez.	18.00	Posaunenchor ·
Donnerstag	18. Dez.	19.00	Trombone concert
Freitag	19. Dez.	19.00	
Samstag	20. Dez.	17.00	
Sonntag	21. Dez.	15.00	
	und	17.00	
Montag	22. Dez.	19.00	
Dienstag	23. Dez.	19.00	

6 · *Die Uhrzeit* • 251

Es ist ein Uhr fünf. It is 1:05.

Es ist zwei Uhr zehn. It is 2:10.

Es ist fünf Uhr vierzig. It is 5:40.

Es ist sechs Uhr fünfzehn. It is 6:15 (a quarter after six).

Es ist halb acht. Es ist sieben Uhr dreißig. It is 7:30 (halfway to eight).

Vocabulary

1. Ask *Verzeihung, wie spät ist es?* with appropriate gestures. Respond, using a clock with movable hands, with the hours from 1 to 12.

2. Using the clock, repeat the hours from 1 to 12. However, pause before saying one hour and signal the class to respond chorally. Repeat this step with several other hours.

3. Using the clock, repeat the hours from 1 to 12. Pause before saying one hour and point to a student to respond. Repeat this step with other hours and other students.

   Repeat this procedure with the times giving the number of minutes after the hour.

4. You may also present these times with the audio program and the overhead transparency.

Kultur

Some students may benefit from adding a clock that shows the time they do the activity to their drawing. You may want to teach these expressions:

- **morgens** in the morning
- **nachmittags** in the afternoon
- **nachts** at night

Es ist vierzehn Uhr. It is 14:00 (2:00 P.M.).

Es ist achtzehn Uhr. It is 18:00 (6:00 P.M.).

Es ist sieben Uhr morgens. It is 7:00 A.M.

Es ist elf Uhr nachts. It is 11:00 P.M.

251

Aktivität

A. Answers: 1. Es ist halb drei.
   2. Es ist zwölf Uhr zwanzig.
   3. Es ist sieben Uhr fünfzig.
   4. Es ist fünf Uhr fünfunddreißig.
   5. Es ist vier Uhr.

   If you don't have a classroom clock, draw one on the chalkboard with the correct time for students to refer to.

Telling At What Time

—**Um wieviel Uhr findet das Konzert statt?**   At what time does the concert start?

—**Das Konzert beginnt um neun Uhr.**   The concert begins at nine o'clock.

Use the audio program to present the dialogue.

A. Answers: 1. Um wieviel Uhr findet das Konzert statt? Das Konzert beginnt um...   2. Um wieviel Uhr findet der Film statt? Der Film beginnt um...   3. Um wieviel Uhr findet die Party statt? Die Party beginnt um...   4. Um wieviel Uhr findet das Theaterstück statt? Das Theaterstück beginnt um...

ASSESS

Review the lesson and check student progress by using the following:

- Ask students the time at random throughout the class period.
- Activities Workbook, Lesson 6

CLOSE

Using a weekly television guide from a newspaper, have your students make a TV-watching schedule for the weekend. Limit to a total of five to six hours. Have them list the time and the programs using the 24-hour clock.

Aktivität

A Give the time.

Telling At What Time

—Um wieviel Uhr findet das Konzert statt?

 —Das Konzert beginnt um neun Uhr.

Aktivität

A Work with a classmate. One of you will ask at what time the following takes place. The other will answer.

1. das Konzert
2. der Film
3. die Party
4. das Theaterstück

252   •   *Welcome to German!*

▶️◀️ Audio

🏗️ Transparencies

📄 Workbook

7 **D**ie Tage

Telling the Days of the Week

Sonnabend is also used for Saturday.

To find out and give the day, you say:

—Welcher Tag ist heute?
—Heute ist Montag.

FOCUS

Students will
- use the names of the days of the week
- ask and respond to questions about the current day

TEACH

Montag Monday
Dienstag Tuesday
Mittwoch Wednesday
Donnerstag Thursday
Freitag Friday
Samstag / Sonnabend Saturday
Sonntag Sunday

—**Welcher Tag ist heute?** What day is today?
—**Heute ist Montag.** Today is Monday.
—**Und welcher Tag ist morgen?** And what day is tomorrow?
—**Morgen ist Dienstag.** Tomorrow is Tuesday.

Vocabulary/ Dialogue

1. Point to each day of the week on the overhead transparency as you name it. Repeat two or three times.
2. Point to each day as you name it, but pause before one as if you forgot it. Signal the class to respond chorally. Repeat with other days.
3. Point to each day as you name it, but pause before one and point to a student to respond. Repeat with other days and other students.

7 · Die Tage • 253

253

4. Use the dialogue expressions to ask the day and to answer.

5. You may also present the vocabulary and the dialogue with the audio program.

Aktivität

A. Answers: 1. Heute ist...
2. Morgen ist...

You may want to have students answer the questions orally in class and prepare the answers for homework.

Kultur

Discuss how students would like to celebrate Carnival or *Fasching*. What costumes would they like to wear?

—Und welcher Tag ist morgen?
—Morgen ist Dienstag.

Aktivität

A **Answer the following questions in German.**

1. Welcher Tag is heute?
2. Und welcher Tag ist morgen?

Kultur

Carnival

The celebration of Carnival is a happy time in most German-speaking areas. In Austria, Bavaria, and southern Germany, Carnival is called *der Fasching*. In Switzerland and the Black Forest area, it is called *die Fastnacht*. Along the Rhine River, it is called *der Karneval.*

Regardless of the word used, it is a time to make merry. People wear crazy costumes. They parade through the streets or they go to private parties or masked balls called *Maskenbälle*. The height of Carnival is the Sunday, Monday, and Tuesday before Ash Wednesday. Ash Wednesday is the first day of Lent, a time for fasting.

German Online

For more information about Carnival and other German celebrations, go to the Glencoe Web site: glencoe.com

Carnival, St. Gallen, Switzerland

German carnival masks

Garmisch Carnival, Bavaria, Germany

Review the lesson and check student progress by using the following:

• Activities Workbook, Lesson 7

CLOSE

Have students draw one activity that they are going to do next weekend. Have them label it with the day of the week and the time that they are going to be doing it.

Expansion

Have students research holidays in Germany. Good sources of information are the library, Internet on-line resources, people who have lived in the country, and its embassy or consulate. Have students list the holidays and compare the number to the number of holidays we celebrate in the United States.

7 · *Die Tage* • 255

Lesson 8

FOCUS

Students will

• use the names of the months of the year and the seasons

• ask and respond to questions for the date

TEACH

Januar/Jänner January

Februar February

März March

April April

Mai May

Juni June

Juli July

August August

September September

Oktober October

November November

Dezember December

der Frühling (im Frühling)
spring (in spring)

der Sommer (im Sommer)
summer (in summer)

der Herbst (im Herbst)
fall (in fall)

der Winter (im Winter)
winter (in winter)

Vocabulary

1. Point to each month on the overhead transparency as you name it. Repeat two or three times.

2. Point to each month as you name it, but pause before one as if you forgot it. Signal the class to respond chorally. Repeat with other months.

256

Die Monate und die Jahreszeiten

Telling the Months

JANUAR	FEBRUAR	MÄRZ	APRIL	MAI	JUNI
1 2 3 4 5 6	1 2 3	1 2	1 2 3 4 5 6	1 2 3 4	1
7 8 9 10 11 12 13	4 5 6 7 8 9 10	3 4 5 6 7 8 9	7 8 9 10 11 12 13	5 6 7 8 9 10 11	2 3 4 5 6 7 8
14 15 16 17 18 19 20	11 12 13 14 15 16 17	10 11 12 13 14 15 16	14 15 16 17 18 19 20	12 13 14 15 16 17 18	9 10 11 12 13 14 15
21 22 23 24 25 26 27	18 19 20 21 22 23 24	17 18 19 20 21 22 23	21 22 23 24 25 26 27	19 20 21 22 23 24 25	16 17 18 19 20 21 22
28 29 30 31	25 26 27 28 29	24 25 26 27 28 29 30 31	28 29 30	26 27 28 29 30 31	23 24 25 26 27 28 29 30

JULI	AUGUST	SEPTEMBER	OKTOBER	NOVEMBER	DEZEMBER
1 2 3 4 5 6	1 2 3	1 2 3 4 5 6 7	1 2 3 4 5	1 2	1 2 3 4 5 6 7
7 8 9 10 11 12 13	4 5 6 7 8 9 10	8 9 10 11 12 13 14	6 7 8 9 10 11 12	3 4 5 6 7 8 9	8 9 10 11 12 13 14
14 15 16 17 18 19 20	11 12 13 14 15 16 17	15 16 17 18 19 20 21	13 14 15 16 17 18 19	10 11 12 13 14 15 16	15 16 17 18 19 20 21
21 22 23 24 25 26 27	18 19 20 21 22 23 24	22 23 24 25 26 27 28	20 21 22 23 24 25 26	17 18 19 20 21 22 23	22 23 24 25 26 27 28
28 29 30 31	25 26 27 28 29 30 31	29 30	27 28 29 30 31	24 25 26 27 28 29 30	29 30 31

In Austria, January is called *Jänner*.

Telling the Seasons

der Frühling (im Frühling)

der Sommer (im Sommer)

256 • *Welcome to German!*

der Herbst (im Herbst)

der Winter (im Winter)

Aktivitäten

A Make your own calendar in German. Label the months and the days of the week. Do it in the German style starting the week with Monday.

B Each of you will stand up in class and give in German the month in which you were born. Listen and keep a record of how many of you were born in the same month.

C Based on the information from *Aktivität B,* tell in German in which month most of the students in the class were born. Tell in which month the fewest were born.

D In which season of the year is . . . ?

1. Mai
2. Januar
3. August
4. Oktober

8 · *Die Monate und die Jahreszeiten* • 257

3. Point to each month as you name it, but pause before one and point to a student to respond. Repeat with other months and other students.

Repeat this procedure with the seasons.

4. You may also present the vocabulary with the audio program.

Aktivitäten

A. Post the finished calendar in the classroom.

B. To make it easier to tally the birthdays, write the months on the chalkboard and have a student make a mark under each month for each birthday.

C. Review numbers by having students count the number of students who have a birthday each month in German.

D. Answers: 1. im Frühling 2. im Winter 3. im Sommer 4. im Herbst

ASSESS

Review the lesson and check student progress by using the following:

• Activities Workbook, Lesson 8

CLOSE

Ask students to write the month in which these holidays occur:

• Christmas
• Halloween
• President's Day
• Mother's Day
• Thanksgiving
• Father's Day

Expansion

Celebrate the next German holiday. Have students decorate the classroom. You may want to play music and even serve special food if it is feasible.

Lesson 9

 Audio

 Transparencies

Workbook

FOCUS

Students will

* use some common weather expressions

TEACH

—**Wie ist das Wetter?** What is the weather like?

—**Das Wetter ist schön.** The weather is beautiful.

Es ist schön. It's beautiful.

Es ist sonnig. It's sunny.

—**Das Wetter ist nicht schön.** The weather isn't nice.

Es ist schlecht. It's nasty.

Es ist bewölkt. It's cloudy.

Es regnet. It's raining.

---

9 ◆ **D**as *Wetter*

Describing the Weather

—Wie ist das Wetter?
  —Das Wetter ist schön.
    Es ist schön.
    Es ist sonnig.

—Das Wetter ist nicht schön.
  Es ist schlecht.
  Es ist bewölkt.
  Es regnet.

258 • *Welcome to German!*

Es ist windig.

Es schneit.

Es ist nicht warm. Es ist heiß.

Es ist nicht kühl. Es ist kalt.

Aktivitäten

A Tell in German what the weather is like today.

B Work in groups of four. Write in German the name of each season on a separate sheet of paper. Put the papers in a pile. Each of you will pull one sheet from the pile. Then describe the weather of the season written on the sheet.

C Draw a picture of your favorite type of weather. Then describe your picture to the class in German.

9 · Das Wetter • 259

Es ist windig. It's windy.

Es schneit. It's snowing.

Es ist nicht warm. It's not warm.
Es ist heiß. It's hot.

Es ist nicht kühl. It's not cool.
Es ist kalt. It's cold.

Vocabulary

1. Look out the window and gesture as you ask, *Wie ist das Wetter?* (How is the weather?)

2. Point to each picture on the overhead transparency as you give the weather expression associated with it. (Point to the sunny weather for *Es ist sonnig.* Point to the rain, wind, and snow for *Es regnet, es ist windig, es schneit.*) Repeat two or three times.

3. Point to each picture as you give the weather expression, but pause before one as if you forgot it. Signal the class to respond chorally. Repeat with other pictures.

4. Point to each picture as you give the weather expression, but pause before one and point to a student to respond. Repeat with other pictures and other students.

5. You may also present the vocabulary with the audio program.

Aktivitäten

A. Have students work in pairs to ask and give the weather information. Have them change partners so that each has three or four conversations.

B. You may want to have students describe the weather orally in class and write it for homework.

C. Have students describe their pictures in small groups for more efficient individual practice.

Review the lesson and check student progress by using the following:

- Ask students to pretend that it is yesterday and to give the weather.

- Activities Workbook, Lesson 9

CLOSE

Ask students to predict tomorrow's weather. Have them use the present tense. Have students correct their prediction, if necessary, the next day. Reward those who predicted correctly.

Expansion

A. Ask students to keep a weather calendar for one week. Use the vocabulary in Lessons 7 and 8 to make a calendar with large boxes for the days. Appoint a different group to observe and write the weather every day in the calendar boxes.

B. Ask a small group of students to write and record a world weather report in German. Have them report the weather in cities such as Berlin, Munich, Vienna, Basel, and so on. You can get information from major newspapers, cable television weather channels, and on-line resources.

Tell students if they do not begin their sentence with *Es ist...*, they must invert the word order. Give them the following examples:

Es ist sehr kalt in Berlin.

In Berlin ist es sehr kalt.

Heute ist es sehr kalt in Berlin.

Kultur
Vacation Spots

In the south of Germany, there are some popular winter ski resorts. Garmisch-Partenkirchen is not far from Munich. There are also many ski resorts in the German-speaking section of Switzerland and in Austria.

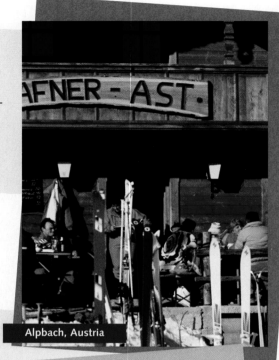
Alpbach, Austria

In the north of Germany, there are some lovely beaches that are popular in the summer. Since these beaches are on the North Sea, the water stays chilly and there is often a breeze. For this reason, people frequently sit in a *Strandkorb* to protect themselves from the wind.

There are some beautiful islands in the North Sea—Amrum, Sylt, and Spikeroog among them. Sylt, a popular vacation center, is connected to the mainland by a dam.

Northern coast, Germany

260 • *Welcome to German!*

10 Ich heiße... und ich komme aus...

Telling Who I Am and Where I'm From

FOCUS

Students will

- ask and respond to requests for one's name
- use the forms *ich heiße* and *heißt du?*, *ich komme* and *kommst du?*

TEACH

—**Wie heißt du?** What's your name?

—**Ich heiße Katerina Weiss. Und wie heißt du?** My name is Katerina White. And you?

—**Ich heiße Werner Hoffmann.** My name is Werner Hoffmann.

—**Woher kommst du, Werner?** Where do you come from Werner?

—**Ich komme aus Hannover. Und du, Katerina, woher kommst du?** I come from Hannover. And you, Katerina, where do you come from?

—**Ich komme aus Houston.** I come from Houston.

—**Ach so, du kommst aus den USA.** Oh, I see, you come from the USA.

—Wie heißt du?

  —Ich heiße Katerina Weiss. Und wie heißt du?

—Ich heiße Werner Hoffmann.

  —Woher kommst du, Werner?

—Ich komme aus Hannover. Und du, Katerina, woher kommst du?

  —Ich komme aus Houston.

—Ach so, du kommst aus den USA.

10 · Ich heiße... und ich komme aus... • 261

heißt du? What is your name?

ich heiße My name is

kommst du? Do you come?

Ich komme I come

Dialogue

1. Use the audio program to present the dialogue. Point to the speaker as each line is spoken. Or model the dialogue yourself, pointing to the appropriate speaker on the overhead transparency.

2. Have two students model the dialogue, using their real names. Prompt them if necessary.

Aktivitäten

A. If your furniture is movable, arrange it so that students can move about easily.

B. Alternate between the formal and the informal use of "you." *Wie heißt du?* vs. *Wie heißen Sie? Woher kommst du?* vs. *Woher kommen Sie?* If you don't have a beach ball, use another kind of ball or a beanbag.

When you hear a question with *–st* in German: *heißt du?, kommst du?,* you answer with *-e: ich heiße, ich komme. Du* is used to speak to a friend and *ich* is used to speak about yourself.

heißt du?	**ich heiße**
kommst du?	**ich komme**

Aktivitäten

A Walk around the classroom. Greet each of your classmates. Find out who each one is. Let each one know who you are.

B Get a beach ball. One person throws the ball as he or she asks, *Woher kommst du?* The one who catches the ball answers, *Ich komme aus...*

When speaking German, you must always be careful to choose between formal and informal speech. *Du* is used only when speaking to a friend or young people. It would be rude to use *du* with an adult whom you do not know. You must use the formal *Sie:*

Wie heißen Sie?

Woher kommen Sie, Herr Braun?

Aktivität

A Draw and cut out five stick figures. Give each one a name. Some will be stick figures of your friends and others will be of your teacher. Greet each of your stick figures in German. Ask their names and where they're from. Remember to use different terms with your friends and teachers!

Kultur

The German-Speaking World

Here are two friends from different areas of Europe. They both have something very important in common. They both speak German.

Wie geht's? Ich heiße Peter und ich komme aus Reutte in Österreich. Ich spreche Deutsch.

Wie geht's? Ich heiße Ingrid. Ich komme aus Gstaad in der Schweiz. Ich spreche auch Deutsch.

10 · Ich heiße... und ich komme aus... • 263

Aktivität

A. After students name and greet their stick figures, ask them to move about the room and greet other students' stick figures. Elicit that both the young and old in German-speaking countries may shake hands when meeting.

Kultur

Bring in maps of Austria and Switzerland and pictures of both countries to stimulate discussion.

ASSESS

Review the lesson and check student progress by using the following:

• Ask students to introduce themselves to each other using the name badges made in Lesson 2.

•   Activities Workbook, Lesson 10

CLOSE

Ask students to pretend that they are at the airport to meet a German-speaking cousin whom they have never seen. Have them prepare the dialogue that takes place.

Expansion

Ask students to think of the celebrity they would most like to meet. Then have them prepare an imaginary conversation with that celebrity. Use general interest, sports, and celebrity magazines to help students think of someone.

Welcome to
Japanese!

Mt. Fuji, Japan

Japanese is a fascinating language that is very different from many of the world's other languages. Japanese, unlike Spanish or German, does not belong to one of the major language families.

Japanese is the official language of Japan, a country of four main islands and 1042 smaller islands in the western Pacific. It is spoken by approximately 120 million people.

The Japanese make a great effort to be polite. They are almost apologetic in their speech. They do not want to offend. This desire has a great impact on the language. There are many polite and honorific forms in the Japanese language. A young person speaking to a friend will express the same idea in a different way when speaking to an older person. A woman would also express herself in a different way from a man.

For the Japanese, the group is more important than the individual. Japanese people always take into account the family or the company they work for before thinking of themselves.

Japan is a highly developed and industrialized country. It is a major economic and political force in the world today. A knowledge of its language and culture is a very valuable tool.

"Great Buddha," Kanakura, Japan

Tokyo, Japan

Rural village, Japan

Japanese to English

There are some Japanese words used in English. Do you know any of these words?

obi
ryokan
sushi

tatami
tempura
tsunami

Lesson 1

 Audio

 Transparencies

 Workbook

FOCUS

Students will

- learn how to introduce themselves
- change statements into questions
- learn the words for traditional Japanese clothing

TEACH

—**Sumimasen. Hanada-san desu ka[?]** Excuse me. Are you Ms. Hanada?

—**Hai, soo desu.** Yes, that's right.

—**Buraun desu. Hajimemashite. Doozo yoroshiku.** I'm Mr. Brown. How do you do? Nice to meet you.

—**Hanada desu. Hajimemashite. Doozo yoroshiku.** I'm Ms. Hanada. How do you do? Nice to meet you.

Dialogue

1. Use the audio program or the overhead transparency to present the dialogue.

2. Have two volunteers model the dialogue for the rest of the class. If the entire dialogue appears to be too much for your class, you may want to initially break it down into the first set of couplets.

3. Divide the class into pairs and have each pair practice the introductions a few times, or as long as it takes for them to feel comfortable. Then have the students go around the room introducing themselves randomly to each other.

266

Jiko shookai

Making Introductions

—Sumimasen. Hanada-san desu ka[?]

  —Hai, soo desu.

—Buraun desu. Hajimemashite. Doozo yoroshiku.

  —Hanada desu. Hajimemashite. Doozo yoroshiku.

Desu is similar to the verb "to be." Unlike English and the other languages you may have studied, *desu* is used for all forms: "am, is, are."

To form a question in Japanese, you put *ka* at the end of a statement. *Ka* is called a particle and it is like a question mark.

Statement: **Buraun desu.**

Question: **Hanada-san desu ka[?]**

Differences in Meaning

Japanese are extremely polite when they speak to each other. This is one of the reasons why the literal meaning of many Japanese expressions is often different from the informal meaning in English. For example, *Hajimemashite* is used to express "How do you do?" Literally, it means "It's the first time we meet." *Doozo yoroshiku* can express "It's nice to meet you" but it means "Please regard me favorably."

Sumimasen is an expression of apology, similar to "excuse me" or "I'm sorry." It is used to get someone's attention.

Names and Titles

When Japanese people introduce themselves, they often give their family name, not their first name. They give their family name with no title:

Hanada   **Okura**   **Yamaguchi**

When addressing others, however, they use the person's family name and a respectful title. There are many different honorific titles, but one of the most common is *san*. *San* is the equivalent of "Mr." or "Ms." in English. It is used for both males and females. Japanese never use *san* when talking about themselves.

Hanada-san   **Okura-san**   **Yamaguchi-san**

Activities

A **Let's practice saying all of the Japanese expressions we know.**

—Sumimasen.

  —Hajimemashite.

—Doozo yoroshiku.

  —Hanada-san desu ka[?]

—Hai, soo desu.

  —Buraun desu.

1 · Jiko shookai • **267**

Buraun desu. I'm (Mr./Mrs./Ms.) Brown.

Hanada-san desu ka[?] Are you (Mr./Mrs./Ms.) Hanada?

Differences in Meaning

These are very polite greetings and should be said standing up and with a slight bow to the listener. Although many westernized Japanese shake hands with foreigners when they are speaking English, bowing is preferred to shaking hands in most situations.

Names and Titles

Note that the suffix *-san* is never used with one's own name. Students should be reminded to use *-san* only to the listener. Except in very rare cases, *-san* should only be used with a person's family name.

Activities

A. Have students practice getting each other's attention by saying *Sumimasen.* (Excuse me.) Listeners can simply answer *hai* (yes?) with a questioning intonation. Have pairs of students bow to each other with one saying *Hajimemashite?* (How do you do?) and the other replying in kind. Then have the first speaker say *Doozo yoroshiku.* (Nice to meet you.) followed by the other saying the same phrase.

Have two students model the entire dialogue for the rest of the class, substituting their own names for *Buraun* and *Hanada.* Then have pairs of students practice the dialogue.

B   Work with a classmate and ask each other your names.

—Sumimasen. _____-san desu ka[?]

  —Hai, soo desu.

—_____ desu.

C   You are visiting Roppongi, a popular section of Tokyo. Reply to a Japanese person who says the following to you.

1. (Your name)-san desu ka[?]

2. Hajimemashite.

3. Doozo yoroshiku.

Roppongi District, Tokyo, Japan

D   Here's a photograph of Japanese teenagers who live in Kyoto. Describe their clothing. Is it like yours?

E Work with a classmate and have the following conversation in Japanese. Excuse yourselves. Ask one another "How do you do?" and introduce yourselves. Say that you are happy to meet.

Culture

Fashion in Japan

Modern Tokyo is probably one of the most fashionable cities in the world. The Japanese are very fashion-conscious. Look at these photographs of department store windows and people on the streets of Tokyo.

Shibuya District,
Tokyo, Japan

Ginza, Tokyo, Japan

Culture

Elicit students' opinions on the pros and cons of the fact that modern Japanese have largely given up traditional clothes for Western-style ones.

ASSESS

Review the lesson and check student progress by using the following:

- Activities Workbook, Lesson 1

CLOSE

Ask students to write a brief conversation between two students who meet on the street in Tokyo.

1 · Jiko shookai • 269

Have pairs of students practice the following:

Hanada-san desu ka[?]   Are you (Mr./Mrs./Ms.) Hanada?

Iie, chigaimasu.   No, I'm not.

<Listener's last name>-san desu ka[?]   Are you (Mr./Mrs./Ms. <last name>)?

Hai, soo desu.   Yes, that's right.

There is also a traditional Japanese dress—the *kimono*. Today it is worn only on formal occasions such as weddings.

A long undergarment called *nagajuban* is worn underneath the *kimono* and on top of the normal underclothes.

The *obiagé* supports the *obi*.

The *obi* is a sash for a *kimono*.

The *obijimé* holds the *obi* in position.

The baggy sleeves are called *tamoto*.

The material is silk, dyed in various patterns.

Furisodé is the formal *kimono* with long baggy sleeves worn by unmarried women. Married women wear the normal-sleeved *tomesodé*.

Tabi

Japanese Online

For more information about Japanese traditions, go to the Glencoe Web site: **glencoe.com**

The *montsuki* or *haori*: a half-coat emblazoned with the wearer's family crest.

Mon: crest

Sensu: folding fan

Hakama: a culotte-like garment worn over the *kimono*

Tabi should be worn with *montsuki*.

Formal wear

The *obi* is made either of stiff material (the *kaku-obi*) or of soft material (the *heko-obi*).

Less formal wear

270   •   *Welcome to Japanese!*

2 *Go-aisatsu*

Greeting People

—Konnichi wa.

　—Konnichi wa. O-genki desu ka[?]

—Hai, arigatoo gozaimasu. Yamaguchi-san wa[?]

　—Genki desu.

Kobe, Japan

2 · Go-aisatsu • 271

FOCUS

Students will

- use polite greetings
- use greetings related to the time of day
- use the tag particle *ne*

TEACH

—**Konnichi wa.** Hello.

—**Konnichi wa. O-genki desu ka[?]** Hello. How are you?

—**Hai, arigatoo gozaimasu. Yamaguchi-san wa[?]** Yes, thank you. And you, Mr. Yamaguchi?

—**Genki desu.** Fine.

Dialogue

1. Use the audio program or the overhead transparency to present the dialogue. Explain that *konnichi wa* (hello) is used from late morning to late afternoon (shortly before lunch to shortly before dinner).

2. Have two students model the dialogue for the rest of the class.

3. Divide the class into pairs and have each pair practice the introductions a few times, or as long as it takes for them to feel comfortable. Then have the students go around the room introducing themselves randomly to each other and substituting the listener's name for *Yamaguchi-san*.

4. Repeat the above steps, substituting first *ohayoo gozaimasu* (good morning) and then *konban wa* (good evening) for *konnichi wa* (hello).

Ohayoo gozaimasu. Good morning. (formal)

Konnichi wa. Good day.

Konban wa. Good evening.

The following are Japanese greetings to be said at various times of the day:

Ohayoo gozaimasu.
(morning)

Konnichi wa. *(day)*

Konban wa. *(evening)*

Culture

Formality and Politeness

When speaking Japanese, you must always consider the level of formality in your speech. The question, *O-genki desu ka[?]* literally means "How have you been lately?" so you do not say it to anyone you've seen recently. You use it only when you haven't seen a person in a while and you want to know about his or her health. There can be several answers to the question *O-genki desu ka[?]* From formal to informal, they are:

1. **Ee, genki desu.**
2. **Okagesama de, genki desu.**
3. **Ee okagesama de.**
4. **Hai, arigatoo gozaimasu.**

The expression "How are you?" in English is a way of saying "hello" rather than a question about your health. In Japan, a comment about the weather serves the same purpose. Someone may greet you and say:

Ii o-tenki desu ne[?] The weather's quite nice, no?

In response, you don't have to give an opinion or comment, just be polite and agree:

Soo desu ne.

Greeting Someone You've Seen Recently

—Okura-san, ohayoo gozaimasu.

—Aa, Kawamura-san, ohayoo.

—Ii o-tenki desu ne[?]

—Ee, soo desu ne.

2 · Go-aisatsu • 273

Activities

A. By using a prop clock with movable hands or drawing a clock on the chalkboard, indicate different times of the day. Have students practice the dialogue while choosing the greeting appropriate to the time of day you are indicating: *ohayoo gozaimasu* (good morning), *konnichi wa* (hello), or *konban wa* (good evening).

B. Possible answers: 1. Konnichi wa. 2. Ohayoo gozaimasu. 3. Ee, genki desu. / Okagesama de, genki desu. 4. (Ee) Soo desu ne.

C. Get students to practice Japanese-style bows while practicing dialogues with each other.

D. Review the material in Lesson 1 and combine it with the contents of this lesson into a lengthier dialogue.

The particle *ne* at the end of the sentence can serve many purposes. With a high intonation, *ne* is used to ask for someone's agreement:

Ii o-tenki desu ne[?]   Don't you think? That's right, isn't it?

When said with a falling intonation and extended to *nee*, the particle indicates that you agree with what the speaker is saying:

Soo desu nee.

Activities

A **Let's practice saying the Japanese expressions we know.**

—Ohayoo gozaimasu.

　Konnichi wa.

　Konban wa.

—O-genki desu ka[?]

　Ee, genki desu.

　Okagesama de, genki desu.

　Ee okagesama de.

　Hai, arigatoo gozaimasu.

—Ii o-tenki desu ne[?]

　Soo desu ne.

B **You are visiting Yokohama, located just outside of Tokyo. Speak to the person in Japanese who says the following to you.**

1. Konnichi wa.

2. Ohayoo gozaimasu.

3. O-genki desu ka[?]

4. Ii o-tenki desu ne[?]

Yokohama, Japan

C Get up from your desk and walk around the room. Greet several of your classmates in Japanese.

D Work with a classmate. Make up the following conversation in Japanese. Greet one another. You haven't seen each other in a while. You're both interested in knowing how the other is doing.

Businessmen, Osaka, Japan

*C*ulture
Ojigi

The traditional Japanese greeting is not a handshake but a bow from the waist. A bow is called *ojigi,* and is a way of showing both respect and affection.

This greeting can vary from a slight bow to a very low bow. It depends upon the relationship of the people and the amount of respect they wish to show.

Department store greeter, Tokyo, Japan

2 · Go-aisatsu • 275

Culture

Elicit students' opinions about the custom of bowing compared to that of shaking hands. Ask what they think is behind each custom. (Bowing indicates submission to "superior's" status by lowering one's [vulnerable] head, while the handshake shows a lack of hostility, since in ancient times the person's "sword hand" was occupied by the handshake.)

Explain to students that department store greeters (usually women) are often stationed at the entrances of stores in Japan to welcome customers.

ASSESS

Review the lesson and check student progress by using the following:

• Activities Workbook, Lesson 2

CLOSE

Ask students to expand the conversation they wrote in Close, Lesson 1, by asking about the other person's well-being.

Expansion

A. You may want to teach the additional greeting *doomo* often used when unexpectedly running into an acquaintance. *Doomo* is introduced later in its other use as a form of "thank you."

B. Have pairs of students practice the following:

Aa, Buraun-san! Doomo. Oh, (Mr./Mrs./Ms.) Brown, hello!

Hanada-san. Doomo. O-genki desu ka[?] (Mr./Mrs./Ms.) Hanada, hello! How have you been?

Lesson 3

- **Audio**

- **Transparencies**

- **Workbook**

FOCUS

Students will
- use expressions for "good-bye"

TEACH

—**Hayashi-san, shitsurei shimasu.**
Mr. Hayashi, you'll have to excuse me.

Sayoonara. Good-bye.

Dewa, mata. I'll see you later.

Ja, mata. So long.

---

3 *Wakareru toki ni...*

Saying "Good-bye"

—Hayashi-san, shitsurei shimasu.
Sayoonara.

Dewa, mata.

Ja, mata.

Shitsurei shimasu is a formal way to say "good-bye." It literally means "excuse me."

Sayoonara, the beautiful Japanese expression we hear used in English, is used to express a farewell to a person whom you do not plan to see again soon.

To say "see you later," you would use *dewa, mata* if you wish to be very formal. Less formal is *ja, mata.*

Activities

A Walk around the room. Say "good-bye" to some of your classmates in a formal way.

B Walk around the room and say "good-bye" to some of your classmates in a very informal way.

Reviewing All We Know

—Hanada-san, ohayoo gozaimasu.

　—Aa, Buraun-san, ohayoo.

—Ii o-tenki desu ne[?]

　—Ee, soo desu ne.

—Shitsurei shimasu.

　—Ja, mata.

3 · Wakareru toki ni... • 277

Dialogue

1. Use the audio program or the overhead transparency to present the dialogue.

2. Have two students model the dialogue for the rest of the class several times, each time choosing one of the three possible "good-byes": *dewa, mata; sayoonara;* or *ja, mata.*

3. Divide the class into pairs and have each pair practice the "good-byes" (with all variations) a few times, or as long as it takes for them to feel comfortable. Then have the students go around the room practicing with other students and substituting the listener's own name for *Hayashi-san.*

Activities

A. Have students practice saying "good-bye" to you using the formal patterns. You may wish to have them address you as *sensei* rather than (your name)-*san,* since this is the title by which all Japanese students actually address their teachers.

B. Have students say "good-bye" to each other using the casual *ja, mata.*

Reviewing All We Know

—**Hanada-san, ohayoo gozaimasu.** (Mr./Mrs./Ms.) Hanada, good morning.

—**Aa, Buraun-san, ohayoo.** Oh, (Mr./Mrs./Ms.) Brown, good morning.

—**Ii o-tenki desu ne[?]** Nice weather, isn't it?

—**Ee, so desu ne.** Yes, it is.

—**Shitsurei shimasu.** You'll have to excuse me.

—**Ja, mata.** So long.

1. Use the audio program to present the dialogue.

2. Have two students model the dialogue for the rest of the class.

Activities

A. Answers: 1. Hai, soo desu.
   2. Konnichi wa.   3. Soo desu ne.
   4. Ee, genki desu. / Okagesama
   de, genki desu.   5. Dewa, mata.

B. If your furniture is movable,
   arrange it so that students can
   move about easily.

Culture

Explain that *shitsurei shimasu* and
dewa, mata are very formal ways of
saying "good-bye." On the other
hand, *ja, mata* is quite casual and is
in a completely different register.

The famous *sayoonara* is only for
real partings such as trips or other
extended absences, almost never for
situations where the speakers expect
or are likely to meet again in the
near future.

Activities

A **You are in the large city of Osaka. Reply to the following.**

1. _____-san desu ka[?]   4. O-genki desu ka[?]
2. Konnichi wa.   5. Dewa, mata.
3. Ii o-tenki desu ne[?]

B **Work with a friend. Speak Japanese together. Have fun saying as much as you can to each other.**

Osaka, Japan

Culture

Written Japanese

Modern Japanese is written using three different writing systems. They are called *hiragana*, *katakana*, and *kanji*.

Hiragana and *katakana* have symbols that represent sounds much like the Roman alphabet. The *kanji* are Chinese characters. They are ideographs that represent sound and meaning. The *kanji* were taken to Japan in the fifth century. Before this time, Japan had no writing system. Since the *kanji* were designed for a completely different language, *hiragana* and *katakana* symbols were created. Each letter of *hiragana* and *katakana* represents one syllable. Each of these alphabets has 48 symbols. All sounds of the Japanese language can be represented in print using these two alphabets.

Katakana is used for foreign words used in Japanese other than Chinese or Korean. For example, *hottodoggu* and *hanbaagaa* are written in *katakana*.

Here is a Japanese food ad. Note the examples of the three writing systems.

katakana = "house" *kanji* = "foodstuffs" *hiragana*

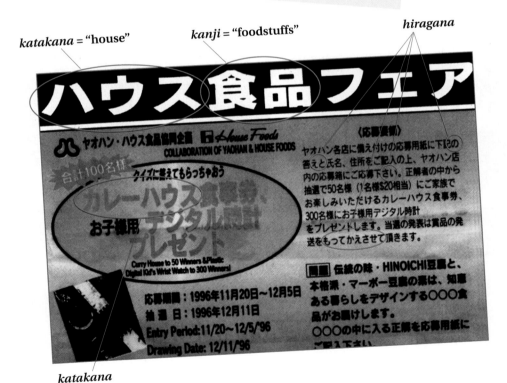

katakana

3 · Wakareru toki ni... • 279

Review the lesson and check student progress by using the following:

- Activities Workbook, Lesson 3

CLOSE

1. Ask students to conclude the conversation from Close, Lesson 2.
2. Elicit students' opinions about why Japanese make more of a ceremony of saying "good-bye" than many Westerners do. Ask students what they think about having two different expressions for "good-bye" (*sayoonara* and *dewa, mata*).

Expansion

As previously mentioned, Japanese students address their teachers with the honorific title *sensei.* When Japanese teachers address their students collectively, they use the term *minna-san,* or add the suffix *chan/kun* to a child's name: *Kelly-chan, George-kun.* You may wish to use one of these when addressing the class.

Lesson 4

 Audio

 Transparencies

Workbook

FOCUS

Students will

- learn classroom vocabulary
- learn how to ask the name of an object

TEACH

—Nan desu ka[?] What is it?

booru-pen ballpoint pen

enpitsu pencil

keshigomu eraser

hon book

nooto notebook

chooku chalk

kokuban-keshi board eraser

konpyuutaa computer

keisanki calculator

kaban bookbag

isu chair

tsukue desk

kami paper

paddo pad of paper

Vocabulary

1. Use the audio program to present the sentences and vocabulary. You may want to break to the list of vocabulary items and practice steps two and three with smaller lists of vocabulary, then go back and introduce a few more items, etc.

2. Using the overhead transparency or actual classroom objects, have students ask you the names of each. Then reverse the process and call on students by pointing to each item.

280

4 Kyooshitsu

Identifying Classroom Objects

To find out what something is, you ask:

—Nan desu ka[?]

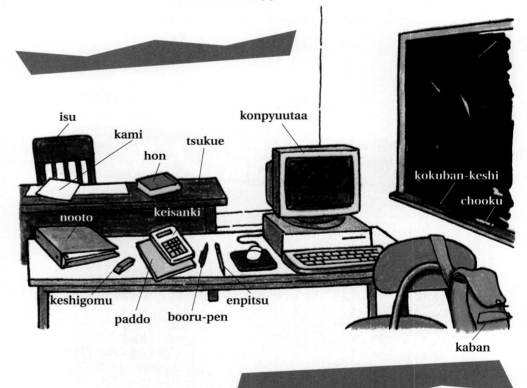

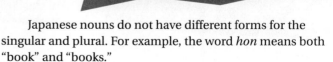

Japanese nouns do not have different forms for the singular and plural. For example, the word *hon* means both "book" and "books."

280 • *Welcome to Japanese!*

Activities

A Point to something in the classroom that you know how to say in Japanese. Ask a classmate what it is and have him or her respond.

B Look at each picture and say in Japanese what each person needs.

1.

2.

3.

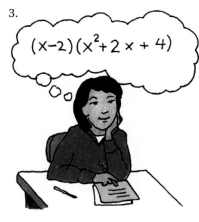

$$(x-2)(x^2 + 2x + 4)$$

4.

3. Have the entire class chorally repeat the name of each item you point to.

4. Have pairs of students practice asking the names of and identifying the various classroom objects covered in the lesson.

Activities

A. Answers: Nan desu ka[?] Hon desu. Enpitsu desu, etc.

B. Answers: 1. chooku 2. kaban
3. keisanki 4. isu

Culture

Bring in pictures of students in classrooms in Japan, studying for entrance exams, etc. typically wearing headbands *(hachi maki)* decorated with encouraging slogans.

ASSESS

Review the lesson and check student progress by using the following:

- Activities Workbook, Lesson 4

CLOSE

Elicit from students their opinion on the compulsory wearing of school uniforms in Japan. Explain that Japanese society values external conformity, and feels that the wearing of school uniforms prevents students from "standing out" from the group.

Expansion

Ask small groups of students to locate and cut out pictures of school supplies from old magazines. Have the groups prepare labels for them and attach them to the pictures. Mount the pictures on a poster or bulletin board for reference. With the computer, have them attach labels to the objects themselves. You may want to add these terms to the objects to be labeled:

hata flag
mado window
dooa door
yuka floor
tenjoo ceiling
chizu map

Culture
Schools in Japan

Schools in Japan are very strict and students must work very hard. They take competitive exams even to enter some elementary schools!

Japanese students attend six years of elementary school, three years of junior high school, and three years of high school. They start school at age seven. Uniforms are not worn in elementary school. Recently, however, yellow hats or helmets are often required for traffic safety.

Most junior high school students wear a uniform. It is still common to see boys of this age wearing a black, military-looking uniform called a *tsume-eri.* Girls wear a black or navy blue sailor suit called a *seeraa-fuku.*

Senior high students must study a great deal to prepare themselves for many difficult university entrance exams.

282 • *Welcome to Japanese!*

Lesson 5

5 · Suu-ji

Numbers

	0	rei, zero			
一	1	ichi	11	juu-ichi	21	ni-juu-ichi
二	2	ni	12	juu-ni	28	ni-juu-hachi
三	3	san	13	juu-san	30	san-juu
四	4	shi, yon	14	juu-shi, juu-yon	40	yon-juu
五	5	go	15	juu-go	50	go-juu
六	6	roku	16	juu-roku	60	roku-juu
七	7	shichi, nana	17	juu-shichi, juu-nana	70	nana-juu
八	8	hachi	18	juu-hachi	80	hachi-juu
九	9	ku, kyuu	19	juu-ku, juu-kyuu	90	kyu-juu
十	10	juu	20	ni-juu	100	hyaku

Activities

A Your teacher will write some numbers on the chalkboard. Then he or she will call out the number in Japanese and ask a student to circle the correct number.

B Count from 1 to 10 aloud.

C Work with a classmate. One of you will count from 20 to 30. The other will count from 40 to 50.

5 · *Suu-ji* • 283

FOCUS

Students will
- learn Japanese numbers from 0 to 100

TEACH

Vocabulary

1. Use the audio program or the overhead transparency to present the Japanese numbers to the class. You may want to break up the list and practice steps two and three with smaller groups of numbers, then go back and introduce a few more numbers.

2. Once all the numbers have been presented, have several students take turns going up to the chalkboard. There they should point to a number at random, then choose a student who will give the number in Japanese.

3. Have students call out a number in Japanese. Choose another student to come up and write out the number on the chalkboard, then have the entire class repeat it.

Activities

A. Have students count from 1 to 10 in groups.

B. Repeat this activity with the numbers 20–30, 40–50, 60–70, 80–90, and 90–100.

C. Depending on class size, divide the students into four or eight groups. Call out a number in Japanese that is a multiple of ten, starting with 20 (*ni-juu*). Have the members of each group in turn count off the numbers between that and the next multiple of ten. Then go on to the next multiple of ten with the next group.

D. Have students time each other with either a classroom clock or a wrist watch.

E. Bring a copy of Japanese numbers written in *kanji* to class.

ASSESS

Review the lesson and check student progress by using the following:

* Activities Workbook, Lesson 5

CLOSE

Elicit students opinions on the fact that there are virtually no plurals in Japanese. Ask them to imagine how it is possible to communicate without being able to distinguish between "house" and "houses," "child" and "children." You may also wish to discuss the lack of any articles: "a book," "books," "the book," "the books" are all the same word, *hon*.

D Have a contest with a friend. See who can count the fastest from 1 to 100 by tens.

E Work in groups of two. Take turns writing numbers from 1 to 100 on a piece of paper. Give the number your partner wrote on the paper in Japanese.

*C*ulture

Japanese Currency

The monetary unit in Japan is the *yen,* often pronounced "en." Presently, there are coins for 1, 5, 10, 50, 100, and 500 yen. There are also bills for 1,000; 5,000; and 10,000 yen.

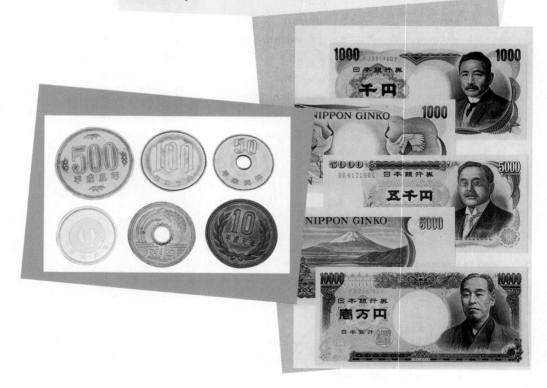

6 ◆ *Jikan*

Telling Time

To find out the time, you ask:

—**Sumimasen. Nan-ji desu ka[?]**

To answer, you say:

—**Ni-ji han desu. (2:30)**

ichi-ji

ni-ji

san-ji

yo-ji

go-ji

roku-ji

shichi-ji

hachi-ji

ku-ji

juu-ji

juu-ichi-ji

juu-ni-ji

shichi-ji-han

 Audio

 Transparencies

Workbook

FOCUS

Students will

• learn how to ask the time

• learn how to tell time

TEACH

Vocabulary

1. Use the audio program for pronunciation. With a prop clock with movable hands, or by referring to the overhead transparency, indicate the different times of day and have the class repeat chorally after each one. If there has been a time lapse since the previous lesson on numbers, review by pointing to the numeral indicating each hour and just have the students repeat *ichi, ni, san*, etc.

2. With the clock hands at the half hour, practice *ichi-ji han, ni-ji-han*, etc., calling on individual students.

3. Have students come up and point at random to any hour or the half hour, and call on other class members to give the time. Then have pairs of students practice the dialogue, letting the listener choose what time it is.

Activity

ASSESS

Review the lesson and check
student progress by using the
following:

•   Activities Workbook,
    Lesson 6

CLOSE

Using a weekly television guide
from a newspaper, have your
students make a TV-watching
schedule for the weekend. Limit
to a total of five to six hours. Have
them list the time in Japanese in
full and half hour increments, as
well as the programs.

Expansion

A. You may wish to introduce the
   word *ima,* meaning "now."

B. You may also wish to introduce
   the terms *gozen no... (ichi-ji),*
   etc. and *gogo no...* which mean
   "A.M." and "P.M." respectively.
   In all cases, be sure to observe
   the word order.

—**Ima nan-ji desu ka[?]**   What
   time is it now?

—**Gozen no san-ji desu.**   It is
   three P.M.

Activity

A   **Give the times on the clocks below.**

286   •   *Welcome to Japanese!*

286

7 **R**esutoran de...

FOCUS

Students will
- learn how to order food
- learn words for food
- learn how to ask the price of something

TEACH

—**Sumimasen. Piza wa arimasu ka[?]** Excuse me. Do you have pizza?

—**Hai, arimasu.** Yes, we do [have it].

—**Jaa. Piza o kudasai.** Ok. Please give me (some) pizza.

...arimasu ka[?] Do you have [. . .]?

Hai, arimasu. Yes, we do.

At a Restaurant

—Sumimasen. Piza wa arimasu ka[?]
—Hai, arimasu.
—Jaa. Piza o kudasai.

Ordering Food

If you want to ask if someone has something, you ask *arimasu* with the question particle *ka*.

If the answer is yes, you would say *hai*.

arimasu ka[?]   **hai, arimasu**

7 · *Resutoran de...* • 287

287

Dialogue

1. Use the audio program or the overhead transparency to practice the dialogue for ordering food with the class. Then go on to practicing the names of the various dishes below. Finally have pairs of students practice the dialogue, substituting other food vocabulary items for *piza*.

2. Use the audio program or the overhead transparency to practice the dialogue for asking the price of something: *Ikura[?]* How much? Practice the phrase in isolation first, then go on to the entire dialogue: *Ikura desu ka[?]* How much is it?

3. Repeat steps 1 and 2 with the Japanese dishes listed on page 290.

   sarada salad

   piza pizza

   juusu juice

   suupu soup

   supagetti spaghetti

Activity

A. Sample exchange:

—**Sumimasen. Piza wa arimasu ka[?]**

—**Hai, arimasu.**

—**Jaa. Piza o kudasai., etc.**

Arrange the classroom furniture so that the "customer" is seated at a restaurant "table."

Pronounce the following Japanese words for different foods. You should have little trouble guessing what they mean:

sarada	**suupu**
piza	**supagetti**
juusu	

When you order these foods, you would use the particle *o* followed by *kudasai* to be polite. *Kudasai* is similar to the English "please."

Piza o kudasai.

As you can see from this Japanese ad, pizza is popular in Japan.

Activity

 A **You are at a restaurant in Tokyo. Order the following foods. Ask a classmate to be your server. Then switch parts.**

1. piza
2. hanbaagaa
3. chiizu baagaa
4. chikin baagaa
5. supagetti

6. suupu
7. juusu
8. bifuteki
9. omuretsu
10. sarada

Ginza, Tokyo, Japan

Finding Out How Much Something Costs

—Sumimasen. Hanbaagaa wa arimasu ka[?]

—Hai, arimasu.

—Ikura desu ka[?]

—Ni-hyaku-ni-juu (220)-en desu.

—Jaa, hanbaagaa to furaido poteto o onegai-shimasu.

—Arigatoo gozaimasu. Yon-hyaku (400)-en desu.

Note that a polite way to ask a server for something is:

... o onegai-shimasu.

To find out how much something costs, you ask:

—**Ikura desu ka[?]**

—**Ni-hyaku (200)-en desu.**

The particle *to* means "and":

hanbaagaa *to* onion ringu

—**Sumimasen. Hanbaagaa wa arimasu ka [?]** Excuse me. Do you have hamburgers?

—**Hai, arimasu.** Yes, we do.

—**Ikura desu ka[?]** How much are they?

—**Ni-hyaku-ni-juu (220)-en desu.** They are 200 yen.

—**Jaa, hanbaagaa to furaido poteto o onegai-shimasu.** Ok, would you please give me a hamburger and French fries?

—**Arigatoo gozaimasu. Yon-hyaku (400)-en desu.** Thank you very much. That'll be four hundred yen.

1. Use the audio program and the overhead transparency to present the dialogue.

2. Have two students model the dialogue for the rest of the class. Then have them choose from the different Japanese and American foods listed on page 290.

...o onegai shimasu. Would you please . . .

—**Ikura desu ka[?]** How much is it?

—**Ni-hyaku (200)-en desu.** (That will be) two hundred yen.

hanbaagaa to onion ringu
hamburger and onion rings

You may wish to teach the following expressions used to express gratitude—"thank you." They are arranged from formal to informal:

Arigatoo gozaimasu.
Doomo arigatoo.
Arigatoo.
Doomo.

Activities

A. Have each pair practice the pronunciation a few times, or as long as it takes for them to feel comfortable.

B. Sample exchange:
—**Sumimasen. Omuretsu wa arimasu ka[?].**
—**Hai, arimasu.**
—**Jaa, omuretsu o onegai-shimasu, etc.**

Have one member of each pair be the customer and use pictures to ask the listener if a certain food is available. Encourage the "servers" to occasionally not have something by responding *Chotto...* with a trailing intonation. Its meaning is similar to "I'm sorry" and it is one of the ways to indicate a negative answer indirectly.

Practice first with Western food, then with Japanese food. Have students form new pairs and ask the "customers" to order at least two or more items, connecting each item with *to*: *Sushi to sashimi to tempura o onegai-shimasu.* (Please bring me some sushi, some sashimi, and some tempura.)

Culture

Japan is not the only country to use chopsticks for eating; this custom is shared with China and Korea also. However, the use of wooden chopsticks is unique to Japan. Chopsticks tell a great deal about what is a characteristic of Japanese cooking: that food is not intended to be cut after it has been served on the table. Chopstick etiquette dictates that chopsticks should be placed on a chopstick rest, not on the bowl, and you also should not pick up your bowl with your chopsticks in your hand.

Activities

A Read the conversation on page 289 with a classmate. Remember to use as much expression as possible!

B Order the following foods. Ask a classmate to be your server. Then switch parts. Don't forget to be polite and say *o onegai-shimasu.*

1. omuretsu
2. supagetti
3. fisshu baagaa
4. onion ringu
5. chikin suupu

Culture

Japanese Food

Although Japanese food is quite different from American-style food, Japanese restaurants are becoming popular here in the United States, especially in big cities. You may even know what the following dishes are:

Nihon ryoori
sushi
sashimi
tempura
sukiyaki
teriyaki
udon
soba
shabu shabu

Here is a typical take-out menu for a sushi restaurant.

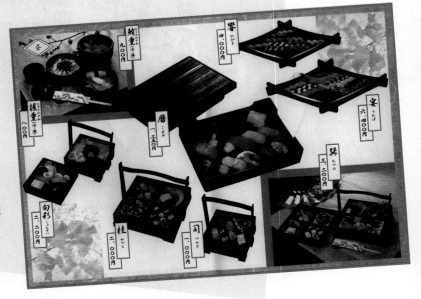

290 • *Welcome to Japanese!*

In Japanese restaurants you'll usually be given a pair of half-split wooden chopsticks, called *wari-bashi*, in a paper envelope. In Japanese homes, however, re-usable sticks of various materials are used.

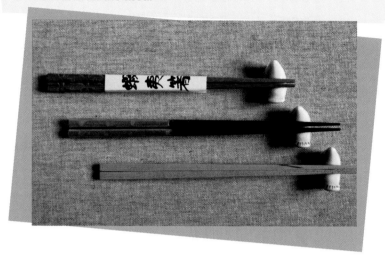

In restaurant windows there are true-to-life wax or plastic models of the dishes to be ordered. These are called *sampuru*.

Review the lesson and check student progress by using the following:

- Activities Workbook, Lesson 7

Discuss various Japanese foods with the students. Find out if anyone has eaten Japanese food and, if so, what dish it was. Elicit opinions on the idea of eating raw fish *(sushi)* or sliced beef cooked with soy sauce and sugar *(sukiyaki)*. You might also wish to explore the pros and cons of chopsticks compared to cutlery.

Expansion

If there is an ethnic market near you, plan a field trip to it. Ask students to make a "shopping list" of foods they went to see. Have them check off those that they found. When you return, have students draw and label the foods they saw.

Lesson 8

Audio

Transparencies

Workbook

FOCUS

Students will

- tell what languages they speak and understand

TEACH

—**Sumimasen. Nihongo o hanashimasu ka[?]** Excuse me, do you speak Japanese?

—**Hai, (nihongo o) hanashimasu.** Yes, I speak (Japanese).

—**Eigo o hanashimasu ka[?]** Do you speak English?

—**Hai, (eigo o) hanashimasu.** Yes, I speak (English).

Dialogue

1. Use the audio program to practice the dialogue in class, pointing to each speaker on the overhead transparency.

2. Divide the class into two groups. Have one group ask the dialogue questions chorally of the other group. Then have the other group respond. Finally, have the two groups reverse roles.

3. Have each pair of students ask the other if he or she speaks or understands a certain language, for example: *Eigo o hanashimasu ka[?]* Do you speak English? Have the listener answer with a positive and a negative, for example: *Hai, hanashimasu.* Yes, I speak (English); *Iie, hanashimasen.* No, I do not speak (English). Then have them reverse roles.

292

Nani-go o hanashimasu ka[?]

Telling What I Speak

—Sumimasen. Nihongo o hanashimasu ka[?]
  —Hai, (nihongo o) hanashimasu.
—Eigo o hanashimasu ka[?]
  —Hai, (eigo o) hanashimasu.

When you hear the question *hanashimasu ka[?]*, you answer *hanashimasu* if the the answer is "yes":

hanashimasu ka[?]   **hai, hanashimasu**

If the answer is "no", you answer with *hanashimasen*:

hanashimasu ka[?]   **iie, hanashimasen**

—Sumimasen. Nihongo o hanashimasu ka[?]
  —Iie, hanashimasen.
  (or)
  Hai, sukoshi hanashimasu.

292   •   *Welcome to Japanese!*

Let's do the same with "to understand."

wakarimasu ka[?]   hai, wakarimasu

wakarimasu ka[?]   iie, wakarimasen

—Sumimasen. Nihongo ga wakarimasu ka[?]

  —Iie, wakarimasen.

    (or)

    Hai, sukoshi wakarimasu.

Activities

A **Answer the following questions in Japanese with "yes."**

1. Nihongo o hanashimasu ka[?]
2. Eigo o hanashimasu ka[?]
3. Nihongo no hon ga arimasu ka[?]
4. Booru-pen ga arimasu ka[?]
5. Nihongo ga wakarimasu ka[?]
6. Eigo ga wakarimasu ka[?]

B **Answer the following questions in Japanese with "no."**

1. Nihongo o hanashimasu ka[?]
2. Nihongo no hon ga arimasu ka[?]
3. Nihongo ga wakarimasu ka[?]

Konnichi wa und moin moin!

Für einen modernen Wirtschaftsstandort wie Schleswig-Holstein ist ein vielseitiges Kultur- und Freizeitangebot genauso wichtig wie der aufgeschlossene Umgang miteinander. Ob Arbeitnehmer oder Unternehmer, ob in Husum, Kiel oder Tokio geboren – die Menschen leben und arbeiten hier einfach gern. Internationalität und Gastfreundschaft werden bei uns großgeschrieben – so groß, daß in Halstenbek eine japanische Schule errichtet wurde. Das zeigt, daß uns auch die „fernsten" Interessen ganz nah am Herzen liegen.

Schleswig-Holstein
Die Luft, die Zukunft atmet

Do you recognize the two languages in this ad?

... hanashimasu ka[?] Do you speak . . . ?

Hai, ... hanashimasu. Yes, I speak . . . .

... hanashimasu ka[?] Do you speak . . . ?

Iie, ... hanashimasen No, I don't speak . . . .

—**Sumimasen. Nihongo o hanashimasu ka[?]** Excuse me. Do you speak Japanese?

—**Iie, hanashimasen.** No, I don't (speak Japanese).

(or) **Hai, sukoshi hanashimasu.** Yes, I speak a little.

Wakarimasu ka[?] Do you understand?

Hai, wakarimasu. Yes, I understand.

(or) **Iie, wakarimasen.** No, I don't understand.

—**Sumimasen. Nihongo ga wakarimasu ka[?]** Excuse me. Do you understand Japanese?

—**Iie, wakarimasen.** No, I don't understand (Japanese).

(or) **Hai, sukoshi wakarimasu.** Yes, I understand a little.

Activities

A. Answers: 1. Hai, (Nihongo o) hanashimasu. 2. Hai, hanashimasu. 3. Hai, arimasu. 4. Hai, arimasu. 5. Hai, wakarimasu. 6. Hai, wakarimasu.

B. Answers: 1. Iie, hanashimasen. 2. Iie, arimasen. 3. Iie, wakarimasen.

ASSESS

Review the lesson and check student progress by using the following:

- Activities Workbook, Lesson 8

CLOSE

Ask students to sum up their impressions of the conventions of Japanese. Elicit detailed answers.

Lesson 9

Audio

Transparencies

Workbook

FOCUS

Students will

• learn the days of the week

• learn the months of the year

• learn how to ask when some-one's birthday is

TEACH

nichiyoobi Sunday

getsuyoobi Monday

kayoobi Tuesday

suiyoobi Wednesday

mokuyoobi Thursday

kin'yoobi Friday

doyoobi Saturday

—**Nan'yoobi desu ka[?]** What day of the week is it?

—**Getsuyoobi desu.** It's Monday.

9 Nan-nichi, nan-yoobi

Telling the Days of the Week

nichiyoobi

kayoobi

mokuyoobi

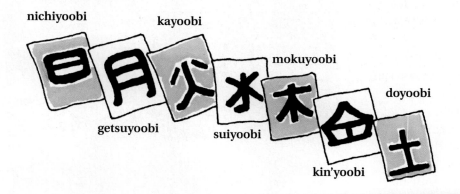

getsuyoobi

suiyoobi

doyoobi

kin'yoobi

To find out and give the day of the week, you say:

–Nan'yoobi desu ka[?]

–Getsuyoobi desu.

294 • *Welcome to Japanese!*

294

Telling the Months

ICHI-GATSU	NI-GATSU	SAN-GATSU	SHI-GATSU	GO-GATSU	ROKO-GATSU
1 2 3 4 5 6 7 8 9 10 11 12 13 14 15 16 17 18 19 20 21 22 23 24 25 26 27 28 29 30 31	1 2 3 4 5 6 7 8 9 10 11 12 13 14 15 16 17 18 19 20 21 22 23 24 25 26 27 28 29	1 2 3 4 5 6 7 8 9 10 11 12 13 14 15 16 17 18 19 20 21 22 23 24 25 26 27 28 29 30 31	1 2 3 4 5 6 7 8 9 10 11 12 13 14 15 16 17 18 19 20 21 22 23 24 25 26 27 28 29 30	1 2 3 4 5 6 7 8 9 10 11 12 13 14 15 16 17 18 19 20 21 22 23 24 25 26 27 28 29 30 31	1 2 3 4 5 6 7 8 9 10 11 12 13 14 15 16 17 18 19 20 21 22 23 24 25 26 27 28 29 30

SHICHI-GATSU	HACHI-GATSU	KU-GATSU	JUU-GATSU	JUU-ICHI-GATSU	JUU-NI-GATSU
1 2 3 4 5 6 7 8 9 10 11 12 13 14 15 16 17 18 19 20 21 22 23 24 25 26 27 28 29 30 31	1 2 3 4 5 6 7 8 9 10 11 12 13 14 15 16 17 18 19 20 21 22 23 24 25 26 27 28 29 30 31	1 2 3 4 5 6 7 8 9 10 11 12 13 14 15 16 17 18 19 20 21 22 23 24 25 26 27 28 29 30	1 2 3 4 5 6 7 8 9 10 11 12 13 14 15 16 17 18 19 20 21 22 23 24 25 26 27 28 29 30 31	1 2 3 4 5 6 7 8 9 10 11 12 13 14 15 16 17 18 19 20 21 22 23 24 25 26 27 28 29 30	1 2 3 4 5 6 7 8 9 10 11 12 13 14 15 16 17 18 19 20 21 22 23 24 25 26 27 28 29 30 31

To find out a person's birthday month, you ask:

—Yamaguchi-san no o-tanjoobi wa nan-gatsu desu ka[?]

—Tanjoobi wa roku-gatsu desu.

ichi-gatsu January
ni-gatsu February
san-gatsu March
shi-gatsu April
go-gatsu May
roku-gatsu June
shichi-gatsu July
hachi-gatsu August
ku-gatsu September
juu-gatsu October
juu-ichi-gatsu November
juu-ni-gatsu December

—**Yamaguchi-san no o-tanjoobi wa nan-gatsu desu ka[?]**
Ms. Yamaguchi, what month is (your) birthday?

—**Tanjoobi wa roku-gatsu desu.**
(My) birthday is (in) September.

Dialogue

1. Using the audio program for pronunciation and the overhead transparency for practice, present the days of the week. Point to each day of the week as you name it.

2. Use the same method to present the months, but pause before one as if you forgot it. Signal to the class to respond chorally. Repeat with other months.

3. Ask students what their birthday month is. Use the expression ____-san no o-tanjoobi wa nan-gatsu desu ka[?] What is the month of (name)'s birthday? Make sure the students drop the o- of o-tanjoobi when they answer.

9 · Nan-nichi, nan-yoobi • 295

Activities

A. Answers: school days—getsuy-oobi, kayoobi, suiyoobi, mokuy-oobi, kin'yoobi; school-free days—doyoobi, nichiyoobi

B. You may want to have students answer the questions orally in class and write the answers for homework for additional practice.

C., D. To make it easier to tally the birthdays, write the months on the chalkboard and have a student make a mark under each month for each birthday.

Culture

The Japanese calendar has many festivals *(matsuri)* unknown in the United States; most of these holidays are Shinto festivals. Shinto is the ancient Japanese religion based on nature; believing that rocks, trees, mountains, and winds have spirits, the ancient Japanese instituted ceremonies and rituals to pay homage to nature. The following *matsuri* have been converted to the western, non-lunar calendar.

O Sho Gatsu (January 1)—Families celebrate the New Year over three days.

Setsubun (February 2) Bean Throwing Day—To purify homes for the new year.

Hana Matsuri (March 3) Doll Festival/Girl's Day—Homes display collection of court dolls. (See photo on this page.)

Kodomo No Hi (May 5) Children's Day—Families fly wind socks *(koi nobori)* all over Japan. (See photo on this page.)

Tanabata (July 7) Star Festival—Children decorate bamboo branches with star shapes, hearts, and wish papers in honor of the Altair star and the Vega star.

Shichi Go San (November 15) Honorable 7-5-3. Every child turning seven, five, or three that year wears a fancy kimono, visits the shrine, and receives a package of treats.

296

Activities

A Give the days of the week you go to school in Japanese. Then give the days of the week you don't go to school.

B Answer the following questions.

1. Nan'yoobi desu ka[?]
2. O-tanjoobi wa nan-gatsu desu ka[?]

C Each of you will stand up and give your birthday month in Japanese. Listen and keep a record of how many of you were born in the same month.

Japanese festivals

D Based on the information from *Activity C,* tell in Japanese in which month most of the students in the class were born. Tell in which month the fewest were born.

Culture

Japanese Calendar

As you may have noticed, the months in Japanese are literally called the "first month," the "second month," the "third month," etc.

The calendar used in the Western world is the Gregorian calendar. The Japanese calendar does correspond with this calendar. However, a new era is proclaimed every time a new emperor ascends to the Japanese imperial throne. Years are counted according to the number of years in the reign of the emperor. When Emperor Akihito ascended to the throne in 1989, the Heisei era was proclaimed. Thus, 1998 is the 10th year of Heisei.

Emperor Akihito

Japanese Imperial Court

9 · *Nan-nichi, nan-yoobi* • 297

Discuss how students would like to celebrate *O Sho Gatsu*, *Setsubun*, *Hana Matsuri*, *Kodomo No Hi*, or *Tanabata*.

ASSESS

Review the lesson and check student progress by using the following:

•   Activities Workbook, Lesson 9

CLOSE

1. Have students research festivals and holidays in Japan. Good sources of information are the library, on-line resources, people who have lived in the country, and its embassy or consulate.

2. Have students list the holidays and compare the number to the number of holidays we celebrate in the United States.

Expansion

A. Celebrate the next Japanese holiday, based on the students' research efforts. Have students decorate the classroom. You may want to play Japanese music and even serve special food if it is feasible.

B. You may find some of the following words useful in adding scope to the vocabulary practice:

   kyoo   today

   kinoo   yesterday

   ashita   tomorrow

   kongetsu   this month

   sengetsu   last month

   raigetsu   next month

Note that in this case it is *-getsu*, but when counting months, it is *-gatsu*.

Photography

Cover: © Uniphoto

Agricola, Stephen/Stock Boston: 248-4; Amanita Pictures: 38-3 & 5, 104-3 & 5, 174-3 & 5, 238-3 & 5; Aurness, Craig/Westlight: 136T; Barton, Paul/The Stock Market: 83; Bartruff, Dave: 72T, 286-2, 296R; Berndt, Eric: 68T; Bishop, David/Envision: 183-5; Blake, Anthony/Tony Stone Worldwide: 97T; Bob Daemmrich Photos, Inc.: 2TL, 50, 78-2; Bock, Ed/The Stock Market: 47-3, 57B; Bognar, Tibor/The Stock Market: 136B; Brownell, David: 7-6; Buklarewicz: 268B; Chaplow, Michelle: 177; Cohen, Stuart/Comstock: 2BL, 139R, 171T; 245T; Comstock: 31B, 43, 63T, 78-1, 134, 200, 240C 252-3; Conklin, Paul/Monkmeyer Press: 7-1, 282T; Corbis/Bettman: 208, 210T; Daemmrich, Bob/The Image Works: 32T, 60B, 69T; David Ladd Nelson Photography: 284R; Davies, Grace/Omni-Photo Communications: 6M, 7-2, 7-3, 38-4, 104-4, 162-2, 162-5, 174-4, 238-4; Desmond/Monkmeyer Press: 242; Dixon, C.M.: 223M; Eccless, Paulina/Envision: 113-5; Ehlers, Chad/International Stock Photo: 271; Ehrad, Marcel/Liaison International: 113-2; Elk III, John: 139L; Envision: 47-1; Esbin-Anderson/Omni-Photo Communications: 38-6, 104-6, 174-6, 229L, 238-6; Ferry, Steven: 32B; Finnegan, Kristin/Tony Stone Images, Inc.: Fischer, Curt: 38-1 & 2, 104-1 & 2, 174-1 & 2, 238-1&2 78-4; Franga: 2ML, 262; Franken, Owen/Stock Boston: 12, 143L, 151; Frazier, David R./Photolibrary: 2BR, 20M, 20BL, 135, 168L, 172, 175, 201, 232L, 236R; Frerck, Robert/Odyssey/Chicago: 31T, 31M, 35M, 57T, 60T, 74, 76T, 78-5; Frerck, Robert/Tony Stone Worldwide .: 69B; Fried, Robert: 20T, 101T, 109, 117-3, 163B, 168R, 171B, 179, 180-3 & 4, 204B, 232R, 233T; Fujifotos/The Image Works: 283T, 265B, 268T, 286-3, 296R, 297; Furgason, Rod/Unicorn Stock Photos: 113-1; Galvin, Kevin/The Stock Market: 255B; Giordano, Luigi/The Stock Market: 184; Goldberg, Beryl: 35T; Granitsas/The Image Works: 240T; Greemberg, Jeff/Omni-Photo Communications: 205L; Griffith, P.J./Magnum Photos, Inc.: 288; Gscheidle, Gerard: 90; Gunnar, Keith/Bruce Coleman, Inc.: 263B; Gupton, Charles/Stock Boston: 72M; Gupton, Charles/Tony Stone Worldwide: 275T; Gupton, Charles/Uniphoto Picture Agency: 264R, 265T, 275B; Hamill, Larry: 44, 82, 108, 170, 179, 179, 180, 244, 245; Hanklin, Hazel: 32M; Heaton, Dallas & John/Westlight: 165, 197L; Heaton, Dallas & John/Uniphoto Picture Agency: 229R, 264L; Hile, Judy/Unicorn Stock Photos: 252-4; Hillstrom, D. E.: 233B, 248-5; Hoffman, B.W./Envision: 248-1, 252-1; Holbrooke, Andrew/The Stock Market: 25; Horsman, Bill/The Stock Market: 220; Kaiser, Henryk T./Envision: 248-2; Kozyra, James/Liaison International: 18TL, 183-4; Ladd Nelson, David/All-Japan Stock Photography: 2MR, 274, 284L; Lang, P./Photoworks: 63B; Latham, Tony/Tony Stone Images: 68B; Lauré, Jason: 9; Lee, Larry/Westlight: 165; Lefkowitz, Miriam/Envision: 69M; Lemass, James/The Picture Cube: 191B; Lewis, Philippa/Edifice-Corbis: 210B; Llewellyn/Uniphoto Picture Agency: 252-5; London, P./Envision: 248-3; Lovell, Craig/Corbis: 87; Lucas, R./The Image Works: 127T; Mariel, O./Figaro Magazine: 141; Magino, Larry/The Image Works: 159; Martson, Sven/Comstock: 78-3, 252-2; Menuez, Doug/PhotoDisc: 236R; Montaine/Monkmeyer: 135T; Muller, Werner H./Peter Arnold, Inc.: 255M; National Gallery of Art, Washington D.C.: 55B, 122; Needham, Steven/Envision: 18BR, 183-3; Nishio, Chie/Omni-Photo Communications: 282B; Northen, Carmen/Photobank: 65; North Wind Pictures: 217B; O'Rear, Charles/Westlight: 7-4; Perri, François/The Gamma Liaison Network: 72B; PhotoDisc: 240B, 260; Pizaro, Bob/Comstock: 162-1, 162-3, 162-4; Poplis, Paul/Envision: 18TR, 113-4; Powers, Guy/Envision: 47-2, 113BL; Purcell, Carl: 7-5, 117-4, 117-5; Ramey/Unicorn Stock Photos: 76B; Rogers/Monkmeyer: 18BL, 117-1, 186-3, 249; Rogge, Otto/The Stock Market: 7-7; Rowe, Wayne: 53, 94, 95, 98, 101B, 105, 114, 117-2, 119, 124, 127B, 130, 132, 138, 143R, 145, 150, 156, 161, 164, 188R, 204T, 228B; Sanguinetti/Monkmeyer Press: 48T; Sargent, Sam/Liaison International: 216; Scala/Art Resource, NY: 205R, 217T, 223T, 223B; Scribner/Macmillan: 71; Simmons, Ben/The Stock Market: 269R; Simson, David/Stock Boston: 163T; Siteman, Frank/The Picture Cube: 187-4; Snider, Lee/The Image Works: 186-1, 255T; Stott, R./The Image Works: 127M; Strange, Rick/The Picture Cube: 197R; Swarthout/ The Stock Market: 113-3; The Huntington-San Marino, California/Superstock: 27; Thevenart, Arthur/Corbis: 187-5; Thompson, R./Omni-Photo Communications: 228T; Tony Stone Worldwide: 269L; Tweedie, Penny/Tony Stone Images: 8; Uniphoto: 183-2; Varone, Steven/Omni-Photo Communications: 6L; Vohra, Aneal/Unicorn Stock Photos: 186-2; Wagner, Tom/Odyssey/Chicago: 278; Warren, Chris/International Stock: 188L; Warren, James William/ Westlight: 67; Wilson, Murray/Omni-Photo Communications: 6R; Wolf/Monkmeyer: 191T; Zanetti, Gerald/The Stock Market: 183-1, 248-6.

Illustration

Glencoe would like to acknowledge Len Shalansky who participated in illustrating this program.

Realia

Advertisement Courtesy of Ralston Purina Canada, Inc., 155; American Greetings: 81; Columbia House: 36; Megapress Images, 29; The Burger King print advertisement is reproduced with permission of Burger King Corporation, 1997, Miami, FL; Restaurant Viêt Nam: 115; Ristorante Rocco: 203; Japanese realia collected by Amy Titterington.